EXAMKRACKERS MCAT®

REASONING SKILLS:
VERBAL, RESEARCH & MATH

10TH EDITION

JONATHAN ORSAY

OSOTE
PUBLISHING

Major Contributors:
Joshua Albrecht, M.D., Ph.D.
Jennifer Birk-Goldschmidt, M.S.
Stephanie Blatch, M.A.
David Collins
Lauren Nadler

Contributors
Mark Alshak
Leena Asfour
Kaitlyn Barkley
Ari Cuperfain
Erik Davies, M.Ed.
Claudia Goodsett
Spenser Hayward
Ian Magruder
Laura Neubauer
Eileen Robinson
Christopher Stewart
Sara Streett, Ph.D.
Jennifer Van Etten
Eric Ward
Richmond Woodward

Art Director:
Erin Daniel

Designers:
Dana Kelley
Charles Yuen

Illustrators:
Stephen Halker
Kellie Holoski

ISBN 10: 1-893858-89-8 (Volume 6)
ISBN 13: 978-1-893858-89-3 (6 Volume Set)
10th Edition

To purchase additional copies of this book or the rest of the 6 volume set, call 1-888-572-2536 or fax orders to 1-859-305-6464.

Examkrackers.com
Osote.com

PHOTOCOPYING & DISTRIBUTION POLICY

The illustrations and all other content in this book are copyrighted material owned by Osote Publishing. Please do not reproduce any of the content, illustrations, charts, graphs, photos, etc., on email lists or websites.

Photocopying the pages so that the book can then be resold is a violation of copyright.

Schools and co-ops MAY NOT PHOTOCOPY any portion of this book. For more information, please contact Osote Publishing: email: support@examkrackers.com or phone 1.888.KRACKEM.

Acknowledgements

Although I am the author, the hard work and expertise of many individuals contributed to this book. The idea of writing in two voices, a science voice and an MCAT® voice, was the creative brainchild of my imaginative friend Jordan Zaretsky. I would like to thank David Orsay for his help with passages in this book. I wish to thank my wife, Silvia, for her support during the difficult times in the past and those that lie ahead.

Finally, I wish to thank my daughter Julianna Orsay for helping out whenever possible.

Introduction to the Reasoning Skills Manual

The Examkrackers manuals are designed to give you exactly the information you need to do well on the MCAT®. This manual provides six lectures that will prepare you to master the MCAT®. The first two lectures of the Reasoning Skills Manual will orient you to the MCAT® and will teach you the skills necessary for all sections of the test. The first lecture provides an in-depth introduction to the MCAT® and instruction on the math skills necessary to perform well on the exam. The second lecture addresses the research methods needed for success on 20% of questions on the science and psychology sections of the MCAT®, including instruction on how best to read a research-based passage and interpret the results. Research questions are the most difficult on the MCAT® and are the questions that help students beat the mean and get a high score. The next four lectures of this book focus on the Critical Analysis and Reasoning Skills section of the MCAT®. With step-by-step instructions, this manual will help you to strengthen your verbal and reasoning skills. This manual teaches the best techniques for reading MCAT® passages and identifying correct answers with speed and accuracy.

How to Use This Manual

The Examkrackers manuals include features to help you retain and integrate information for the MCAT®. Take advantage of these features to get the most out of your study time.

- **The 3 Keys** – The Three Keys unlock the material and the MCAT® by highlighting the most important things to remember from each chapter. The Three Keys are listed at the beginning and end of each lecture with reminders from Salty throughout the text. Examine the Three Keys before and after reading each lecture to make sure you have absorbed the most important messages. As you read, continue to develop your own key concepts that will guide your studying and performance.

- **The In-Class Exams** – These exams are designed to educate. They are similar to an MCAT® section, but are shortened and have most of the easy questions removed. We believe that you can answer most of the easy questions without too much help from us, so the best way to raise your score is to focus on the more difficult questions. The In-Class Exams are designed to help you prepare for test day, when you will be faced with an intensity that is difficult to simulate. These methods are some of the reasons for the rapid and celebrated success of the Examkrackers prep course and products. The questions that you get wrong or even guess correctly are most important. They represent your potential score increase. When you get a question wrong or have to guess, determine why and target these areas to improve your score.

Study diligently, trust this book to guide you, and you will reach your MCAT® goals.

I'm Salty the Kracker. Where you see purple text, that's me. I will help you develop your MCAT® intuition. My job is to make sure you 1. stay awake and 2. really understand and remember what you're reading. If you think I am funny, tell the boss. I could use a raise. If you get the munchies, reconsider... you'll want me around.

Table of Contents

LECTURE i — Introduction to the MCAT® and Math   1

i.1 Welcome to the Examkrackers MCAT® Manuals.....1
i.2 The Medical College Admission Test...............2
    Format..2
    Scoring...3
i.3 How the MCAT® Tests.........................4
i.4 How to Study for the MCAT®...................6
i.5 Preparing for MCAT® Day.......................8
    Physical Preparation..............................8
    Mental Preparation...............................9

i.6 MCAT® Math...................................9
i.7 Rounding......................................9
i.8 Scientific Notation............................13
    Multiplication and Division........................15
i.9 Logarithms...................................18
i.10 Equations and Proportionality..................19
i.11 Graphs......................................23
i.12 Units..27

LECTURE ii — Research and Reasoning Skills for the MCAT®   31

ii.1 Introduction.................................31
ii.2 The Scientific Method.........................32
ii.3 Methods and Measurements....................35
    Issues to Consider in Measurement.................35
    Experimental Methods............................37
ii.4 Statistics to Describe a Data Set................39
    Introduction to Statistics.........................39
    Measures of Central Tendency.....................41
    Measures of Dispersion..........................42
ii.5 Common Statistical Tests......................43
    Examining Relationships between Variables..........43
    Hypothesis Testing..............................45

ii.6 Results: Interpreting Data.....................48
    Test Statistics..................................48
    Interpreting p Values............................48
    Uncertainty and Error in Statistics.................49
ii.7 Results: Drawing Conclusions from the Data.......50
ii.8 Reading Research-Based
    MCAT® Passages and Interpreting Graphs.........52
    Read the Figure and Axis Titles....................57
    Determine What the Data Suggest..................57
    Look at the Range of Error........................58
ii.9 Ethics of Research............................58

LECTURE 1 — Introduction to CARS: Strategy and Tactics   61

1.1 Introduction.................................61
    Topic Areas Covered by CARS passages..............61
1.2 Studying for the CARS Section..................62
    Other CARS Strategies...........................62

    Take Our Advice................................62
    Expected Improvement...........................62
1.3 The Examkrackers Approach:
    Strategies for Success...........................63

Introduction to the MCAT® and Math

i.1 | Welcome to the Examkrackers MCAT® Manuals

These manuals will give you what you need to master the MCAT®. The best way to gain a high score on the MCAT® is to have a deep understanding of both its content and its testing methods. This lecture will begin with a general overview to acquaint you with the nuts and bolts of the exam. Then it will discuss how the MCAT® tests and why it tests this way.

Understanding how the MCAT® works will allow you to study efficiently. Knowing what to expect on test day will prepare you to get the most out of the Examkrackers manuals and out of your studying.

i.1 Welcome to the Examkrackers MCAT® Manuals

i.2 The Medical College Admission Test

i.3 How the MCAT® Tests

i.4 How to Study for the MCAT®

i.5 Preparing for MCAT® Day

i.6 MCAT® Math

i.7 Rounding

i.8 Scientific Notation

i.9 Logarithms

i.10 Equations and Proportionality

i.11 Graphs

i.12 Units

THE 3 KEYS

1. The MCAT® rewards flexibility and connections. Study concepts in order to simplify, understand, and organize content.

2. Remove the disguise of complexity from MCAT® passages and questions to reveal the simple science tested.

3. Keep MCAT® math simple: use proportionality, rounding, units, and scientific notation.

Hey there, fancy pants. Don't worry about the complex section names. The MCAT® tests the basic sciences. So let's stick with simple names:
1. Biological section
2. Physical section
3. Psychosocial section
4. CARS section

The new MCAT® has been made approximately 45% longer to make the scoring for each section more accurate. To prepare for the increased length, practice focus and stamina.

I will train, understand, practice and connect.

i.2 | The Medical College Admission Test

The MCAT® is one measure that medical schools use to judge a student's readiness for medical education. It is a test of your skills in applying what you know. Because it is standardized, the MCAT® tests a finite amount of material in a predictable way. This means that the ability to get a good score on the MCAT® is a skill that can be developed like any other. These manuals will first teach you what to expect from the MCAT® and will then describe the skills and information you need to succeed.

Format

The MCAT® consists of 4 distinct sections: Biological and Biochemical Foundations of Living Systems; Chemical and Physical Foundations of Biological Systems; Psychological, Social, and Biological Foundations of Behavior; and Critical Analysis and Reasoning Skills.

The MCAT® emphasizes biomolecular life processes, interpretation of scientific research, and connections between topics in the basic sciences. It tests psychology and sociology as they relate to human health and biology. Each section contains passages followed by questions. Passages are usually derived from published articles and essays, so with the exception of CARS passages, they will almost always include the methods and results of at least one experiment. The passages can vary in length and in the number of experiments discussed. There are also standalone questions between passages in all sections except the CARS section.

The Biological and Biochemical Foundations of Living Systems section contains 59 questions with a time limit of 95 minutes. The questions are spread over 10 passages, each with 4-5 questions, and around 15 standalone questions. This section covers the biological and biochemical mechanisms that underlie the processes of living organisms. Questions ask you to connect the levels of molecular, biochemical, cellular, organ, and system functions. Approximately 2/3 of the questions relate to biomolecular processes, while the other 1/3 test knowledge of biological systems. Developing your ability to move between levels of biological organization will allow you to succeed in this section.

The Chemical and Physical Foundations of Biological Systems section contains 59 questions with a time limit of 95 minutes. The questions are spread over 10 passages, each with 4-5 questions, and around 15 standalone questions. This section covers basic concepts in physics and chemistry, particularly related to medicine and processes in the human body. Approximately 3/4 of the questions test chemistry topics, while the other 1/4 test physics topics. This section will reward your comfort in making connections between the chemical, physical, and biological sciences.

The Psychological, Social, and Biological Foundations of Behavior section contains 59 questions with a time limit of 95 minutes. The questions are spread over 10 passages, each with 4-5 questions, and around 15 standalone questions. This section covers psychological, sociological, and biological factors relating to phenomena such as formation of identity, personal behavior, and group dynamics. Such topics will often be tested in the context of health, illness, and healthcare. Approximately 2/3 of the questions test psychology topics (including biological topics that are commonly taught in psychology classes), while the other 1/3 test sociology topics.

The questions in these three sections – the Biological, Physical, and Psychosocial sections – fall into two general categories. The first is made up of content or problem-solving questions that do not involve research skills. These questions make up a large proportion of the test. Standalone questions, which make up about 1/4 of the questions in each of these three sections, usually fall in this category. The second, more challenging category tests qualitative and quantitative understanding of research skills. This category represents 20% of questions in the Biological, Physical, and Psychosocial sections of the test. These questions, like those in the first category, also incorporate understanding of scientific concepts.

The Critical Analysis and Reasoning Skills (CARS) section contains 53 questions with a time limit of 90 minutes. There are 9 passages, each with 6-7 questions. The passages cover a variety of medically-related topics, including public health, medical ethics, and cultural studies, as well as other topics in the humanities and social sciences. Half of the passages cover humanities topics, and the other half focus on the social sciences. The CARS section tests narrative skills, such as analytic thinking and logic, rather than testing a specific base of knowledge.

This is an undeniably long test. The total seated time spent on the test is about 7.5 hours. Only 50 total minutes are allowed for breaks, and another 25 minutes are allotted for the exam tutorial. Overall, about 6.25 hours are spent on the passages and questions. Keep this in mind when developing a study schedule. As the test date approaches, build up endurance by taking full-length practice exams with the same timing as the actual test and by completing greater numbers of practice passages and questions in one sitting.

TABLE i.1 > **Structure of the MCAT®**

Section	Number of Passages and Questions	Time
Physical Sciences Section	10 passages, 59 questions (~ 15 stand alones)	95 minutes
Break		10 minutes
CARS Section	9 passages, 53 questions	90 minutes
Break		30 minutes
Biological Section	10 passages, 59 questions (~ 15 stand alones)	95 minutes
Break		10 minutes
Psychosocial Section	10 passages, 59 questions (~ 15 stand alones)	95 minutes

Scoring

Each section is scored on a scale of 15 points. The scale is then shifted by 117 such that the minimum score for each section is 118 (1 + 117) while the maximum is 132 (15 + 117). Among all MCAT® test-takers, the midpoint in the score distribution for each section is 125. You might be wondering why the Association of American Medical Colleges (AAMC) seemingly complicated scoring in this way. The AAMC developed this scale to be easily interpretable by medical schools. The midpoint for the combined score of all four sections is a round number: 500 (125 × 4 = 500). The median score is 500 with a maximum score of 528 and a minimum score of 472. Very few test takers will earn scores close to the maximum or minimum, so these numbers are less important. Most medical school applicants will earn scores that are near the median of 500 and can be compared easily to this round number. Of course, medical schools are looking for students who score well

A physician carries the most important underlying concepts in hand and is ready with a sense of how systems and physiology are connected. Details can be double checked or referenced as needed. MCAT® practice is medical practice.

Physicians must organize the narrative they receive from a patient to best understand the patient and the patient's needs. CARS practice is medical practice.

A physician is flexible in applying medical knowledge, as medicine rarely offers simple answers. Looking for the "best" answer among imperfect choices rather than the single "correct" one will help you do well on the MCAT®. MCAT® question practice is medical practice.

Recommended medical treatments constantly change as research progresses. Strong research and reasoning skills are critical for the best practice of evidence-based medicine. MCAT® research practice is medical practice.

above the median. Based on the information available, the average MCAT® score of applicants who are accepted to medical school will be about 512. Aim to score as far above 500 as possible. The Examkrackers manuals will help you do just that.

Converting the scores back into 15 points for each section may make it easier to quantify your goals and track progress toward them. Subtract 117 from each section score to produce the simpler 15 point scale. Suppose that on a practice test you scored 127 on the Physical section, 128 on the CARS section, 129 on the Biological section, and 130 on the Psychosocial section. These scores convert to 10 on the Physical section, 11 on the CARS section, 12 on the Biological section, and 13 on the Psychosocial section. Now consider your goal of scoring 512 points total, or 128 on each section, on the real MCAT®. Shifting the scale shows that this is the same as aiming for 11 on each section of the test.

> MCAT® passages will often deliberately include new information that is not itself being tested. Your job is to bring and apply the simple science you know to these new situations.

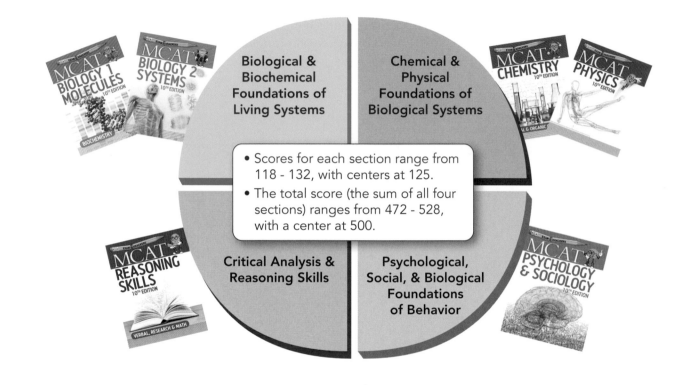

- Scores for each section range from 118 - 132, with centers at 125.
- The total score (the sum of all four sections) ranges from 472 - 528, with a center at 500.

Biological & Biochemical Foundations of Living Systems

Chemical & Physical Foundations of Biological Systems

Critical Analysis & Reasoning Skills

Psychological, Social, & Biological Foundations of Behavior

> MCAT® practice is medical practice. Be fully present, both mentally and physically, to each MCAT® passage and question you solve. Attend fully to the MCAT® just as you will attend wholly to each patient you encounter.

When setting your score goals and studying with Examkrackers materials, it is important to remember that the Examkrackers practice tests include a disproportionate number of "medium" and "difficult" questions. You are likely already capable of answering the "easy" questions, which make up about a third of the test, but need more practice with the trickier ones. Mastery of the challenging questions will result in a high score. For that reason, the estimated scaled scores presented with the in-class exams are not intended to be strictly predictive of actual MCAT® scores. Your goal with Examkrackers materials should be to see your scores on practice tests improve over time.

i.3 | How the MCAT® Tests

Knowing how the MCAT® tests will allow you to study accordingly. The MCAT® is a test of how well you understand and apply the basics of what you know, not how many facts you can memorize. Although some amount of rote memorization is necessary for the MCAT®, it is not sufficient to do well. The MCAT® invites you to bring an understanding of the simple science and to apply what you have learned in one discipline to problems in another discipline. Each section of the MCAT® integrates aspects across the biological, physical, and social sciences in its passages and questions. Even the titles of the sections are integrated – such as the *Chemical* and *Physical* Foundations of *Biological Systems* – reflecting the integrated nature of the test itself. The MCAT® asks you to make connections between topics and to apply what you know in new circumstances. The MCAT® can be challenging even for excellent pre-medical students. Exams in introductory science courses reward memorization and the "click" of one correct answer to every question. The MCAT® rewards a deeper understanding of why the simple science makes sense, as well as the ability to solve problems when the answer is not clear-cut. Thinking flexibly, using underlying concepts rather than relying on memorization, and integrating what you have learned across disciplines are key MCAT® skills. Most questions require you to integrate information from multiple places: basic science concepts across the disciplines, passage information, and interpretation of figures.

The MCAT® requires you to organize, simplify, and remain composed in the face of unfamiliar material or seemingly complex terminology. In fact, the AAMC deliberately makes both passages and questions seem more complex than what is tested. They use terminology and topics in passages and questions that are not commonly taught in introductory courses. By including unfamiliar and complex details that are not actually tested, MCAT® passages create an "intimidation factor." This is particularly the case in passages that include multiple experiments and figures. You can overcome this intimidation by focusing on applying the basic science that is necessary to find the best answer. When facing seemingly incomprehensible questions, learn to see past the complexity of the terminology and root out the underlying science.

The best way to tackle a complex research-based passage is to mentally organize the information in terms of the parts of a scientific article, such as the introduction, methods, and results. Many passages are organized similarly to the articles from which they are derived. Identifying parts of the passage with the parts of a scientific paper makes it easier to access information that is necessary for the questions. If a question asks about experimental methods, for instance, you can quickly recall or reference the part of the passage that discussed the methods.

The fear of the unknown...oh, wait, no unknowns here. The more you know about the MCAT®, the better you can use our materials to KRACK the MCAT®!

Understand Key 1: MCAT® passages and questions test a deep understanding of simple science and the connections between concepts. As you study, create a simple and organized mental map of important concepts. When faced with what you don't know, apply what you do know.

Some passages in the CARS section will seem to be disorganized and written poorly or in a disjointed way. CARS passages may be missing introductory or transitional sentences that normally would be orienting. The passage may jump back and forth between two points of view. This disorganized writing is intentional. It tests how you organize the information you receive and whether you can follow the author's argument while reading for the author's opinion.

The MCAT® rewards flexibility in thinking about the material and applying what you know. It differs from other tests in the type of answer choices provided. Frequently you will find more than one answer that seem to work; sometimes no answer choice seems quite right. Identifying the answer to an MCAT® question means choosing the best answer rather than one that "clicks" but does not answer the question as well. The MCAT® rewards students who develop a tolerance for uncertainty and the ability to discern nuance.

The new MCAT® emphasizes research skills, both in its passages and in 20% of the questions asked across three sections of the test. The MCAT® asks you to interpret articles and studies, follow experiments, understand research techniques, critique methods, and interpret findings.

The Examkrackers method will help you develop the habits and skills that you need to succeed on test day.

Ah yes, the MCAT® muscle is located right next to the Criticalus Thinkae and Problemas Solveras.

i.4 | How to Study for the MCAT®

The Examkrackers method was developed by individuals who achieved very high MCAT® scores through study and practice. Significant experience and thorough research inform every page of the manuals. The Examkrackers manuals are carefully organized to best prepare you for success on the MCAT®. They teach content conceptually, encourage the skills necessary for MCAT® success, and are designed to help you develop mental connections.

The Examkrackers manuals are structured to give you a deep understanding of the concepts while making the science simple. Supplementing with unnecessary detail may make you feel more comfortable, but it will not lead to success on practice tests or on the real MCAT®. No matter how much you memorize, the AAMC will always come up with complex, unfamiliar details intended to shake the test-taker's confidence in his or her science knowledge. While you will find it helpful to take notes on relationships between topics or particularly difficult content as you review the manuals, do not try to write out a full outline of the details. The key to success on the MCAT® is to develop an in-depth understanding of the concepts. Using the concepts to build a mental model will allow you to stay focused and confident in order to apply the science to new information.

As you review the basic science, practice completing MCAT® passages and questions. Many students make the mistake of focusing on details of the tested scientific topics without simultaneously building the problem-solving skills that the MCAT® primarily tests. Your preparation of the material should go hand in hand with the unique ways that the MCAT® will ask you to apply that material. Stay in touch with the style of the MCAT® by taking regular practice tests as you review.

See the Examkrackers website for the "Examkrackers Home Study Schedule" if you would like a more detailed study plan.

On the day before the MCAT®, take some time off and relax! Trust that you have studied hard and are ready. Go into the MCAT® refreshed and confident.

Keep your friends close and the MCAT® closer.

Concepts on the MCAT® are like my trusted wrench. If I know how to use it, it doesn't matter how complicated the problem is, I can fix it!

The Examkrackers method is a four part approach designed to strengthen your MCAT® skills:

1. Refresh: Preparation & Exposure
2. Remember: Concept Building
3. Relate: Practice, Practice, and More Practice
4. Repeat: Repetition for Success

Refresh is the first part of the Examkrackers method. Re-exposure to basic scientific topics is accomplished by a thorough review of the material and terminology tested on the MCAT®. Examkrackers manuals cover all of the topics necessary for your success on the MCAT®. It does not make sense to waste time studying material that the MCAT® does not test unless that material helps you understand the material that IS tested. The Examkrackers manuals let you know what to study by putting tested topics in bold.

Remember is the concept-building step of the Examkrackers method. Most important to your review of content is how you organize the information, both in your notes and mentally. Make your knowledge base easily accessible on MCAT® day – that is, organized, conceptual, connected, and portable – so that your mind is uncluttered and fully available to attend to the passage or question at hand.

This step will move you beyond the habit of memorization. The Examkrackers manuals emphasize connected, conceptual thinking. The Three Keys, Signposts, and Salty will offer help in the form of portable concepts, connections, mnemonics and occasionally some comic relief. Preparing concepts rather than content will allow you to apply your knowledge to any MCAT® question that you encounter. Each lecture contains 24 practice questions to reinforce your understanding as you read.

Relate is the practice piece of the Examkrackers approach. It is arguably the most valuable in raising your MCAT® score. Ample practice is the best way to learn how to improve your performance and relate your knowledge base to the MCAT® itself. Getting accustomed to the MCAT®'s style is essential to success. Our manuals include In-Class Exams, each with 3 passages and 23 questions, which allow you to apply what you've learned to a simulated MCAT®.

Take full length practice exams regularly. This will give you a baseline score from which to improve as well as regular, specific clues to changing your score. Every question you get wrong represents a potential score increase. Examine the questions that you get wrong to determine how you were led astray and what habits you will change on your next practice test. Use the questions you guess on or get wrong as a guide to subject areas that require extra review.

Repeat is the reinforcement step of the Examkrackers approach. Repetition allows you to strengthen skills and topic areas that need attention. Once you identify a skill that you need to improve to get MCAT® questions right the first time, practice, practice, practice! Repeat it each time you take practice questions. Be careful here, because repeating a bad habit can reinforce it. When you review practice tests, be aware of what kind of thinking brings you to the best answer and what habits lead you astray. Only repeat what works!

As you prepare for MCAT® success, make friends with the test. Think of it as a game or a puzzle to solve. It is not a mountain in your way, it is a mountain that will be fun to climb. Be confident in your preparation, in your MCAT® knowledge, and in yourself. You are more likely to see improvement if you have a great MCAT® attitude!

Use Key 2: MCAT® passages and questions are "dressed up" in detail that is not needed to answer the questions. The AAMC deliberately uses unfamiliar vocabulary. Ask yourself what simple concept is really being tested. Remember to narrate the passage using what you know to cut through the complexity and stay oriented. Memorization does not increase MCAT® scores, and is risky. The MCAT® tests your understanding of basic science, not your memory for detail. As you study, ask yourself why things make sense.

Preparing for MCAT® Day

Three months is the ideal time frame for MCAT® preparation. Stretching out intensive studying makes it more difficult to retain all of the information. As time goes by, material from the first weeks is forgotten, and spreading out the content makes it harder to connect the topics into larger concepts.

Many students make the mistake of first reviewing the material for many weeks before beginning practice questions and exams. Reviewing science by itself does not increase MCAT® scores. Taking MCAT®-style exams is the best way to boost your score. Plan to take one regular, full-length MCAT® exam per week. It is critically important to spend time evaluating the questions you got wrong to learn what to do differently. When you miss a question, review the science, and then work on your own to solve the question before looking at the answer explanation, which denies you the opportunity to learn to solve the question yourself. This process builds reliable MCAT® logic, skills, and confidence. Once you have solved the question, read the answer explanation to supplement your approach.

Complete the majority of your review at least thirty days before your MCAT® date. Then switch to a schedule of less review and far more practice. Your comfort with MCAT®-style passages and questions will increase dramatically in these weeks of intense practice and repetition.

One week before the MCAT®, significantly decrease the intensity of your study schedule. The last week before taking the MCAT® should consist of very light studying and revisiting remaining areas that need reinforcement. The decreased workload will help you avoid burnout before MCAT® day and will mentally refresh you for your real MCAT®. During this time, don't overdo it. Trust in what you know and the studying you have completed.

Below are tips for the last week before the MCAT®. Follow our advice in order to be at your best on MCAT® day.

Physical Preparation

Familiarity – Visit your test center, traveling by the same route and method that you will use on test day. Investigate parking, places to get food, and, if you can, the seating situation in the room.

Sleeping patterns – Leading up to the MCAT®, plan the timing of your peak activity to coincide with the time of your MCAT®. If you have scheduled an 8 am test, make sure you are actively studying and taking practice tests at 8 am in the weeks leading up to the MCAT®. Go to sleep and wake up at the same time that you will on the day of the exam. Sleep at least 8 hours every night the week before the MCAT®. Leave plenty of time to wake up before the start of the test. Have an MCAT® friend call you to make sure your alarm worked.

Exercise – Exercise moderately this week. Do not exercise too strenuously in the day or two leading up to the exam.

Food – Eat healthily to keep your energy levels high. Healthy eating will also help you sleep better. Think ahead about what you will eat and drink during breaks on test day.

Mental Preparation

Studying – You cannot review everything on the MCAT® in one week. Instead, choose your weakest remaining subject and become an expert at it. Then move on to your next weakest subject. Study less each day until the day before the exam, and take that day off. Do not study the night before the MCAT®, no matter what.

Visualization – Visualize MCAT® day. There will be distractions everywhere, but you will be unaffected, remaining focused on the test.

Confidence – Approach the MCAT® with confidence. Do not second guess yourself.

The day before the MCAT®, do not study. Rest and do something fun! A positive mood and a refill of energy and motivation will help you succeed on test day.

On the day of the MCAT®, it is normal to have a highly stimulated sympathetic nervous system. For many students, this results in greater awareness of distractions. People seem more intense, and lights may seem brighter or sounds louder. Practice the skill of focus leading up to the MCAT® so that you can choose not to be misled by distractions, whether internal or external. Instead trust that your adrenaline and sharpened senses are powerful tools that will help you do well on the MCAT®. Attuned senses and a stimulated nervous system will increase your performance abilities. Trust in your studying, your skills, and the time you have invested. Enter the MCAT® with confidence, knowing that you are ready.

Practice doing MCAT® math quickly in your head.

i.6 | MCAT® Math

The MCAT® will not test your math skills beyond the contents of this book. The MCAT® does require knowledge of the following, up to a second year high school algebra level: ratios, proportions, square roots, exponents and logarithms, scientific notation, quadratic and simultaneous equations, and graphs. In addition, the MCAT® tests vector addition and subtraction, basic trigonometry, and very basic probabilities (seen in the context of genetics problems). The MCAT® does not test dot product, cross product or calculus.

Calculators are not allowed on the MCAT®, nor would they be helpful. From this moment until MCAT® day, do all math problems in your head whenever possible. Do not use a calculator, and use your pencil as seldom as possible when you do any math.

If you find yourself doing a lot of calculations on the MCAT®, it is a good indication that you are doing something wrong. Most problems can be solved using simple reasoning about proportions or elimination of unreasonable answers rather than lengthy calculations. As a rule of thumb, **spend no more than 3 minutes on any MCAT® physics question**. Once you have spent 3 minutes on a question without being able to resolve it, stop what you're doing and read the question again for a simple answer. If you do not see a simple answer, make your best guess and move to the next question.

i.7 | Rounding

Exact numbers are rarely useful on the MCAT®. In order to save time and avoid errors when making calculations on the test, use round numbers. Rounding appropriately is an essential part of reducing the complexity of MCAT® problems. For instance, the gravitational constant g should be rounded up to 10 m/s² for the purpose of calculations, even when instructed by the MCAT® to do otherwise.

This is me after I hurt myself with complicated calculations on my first practice test.

Learn Key 3: The MCAT® does not allow calculators, but you don't need one. Simplifying calculations with proportionality (direct/indirect), units, scientific notation, and rounding will keep MCAT® math easy. Remember to draw an up or down arrow beside rounded numbers as a reminder.

Calculations like 23.4×9.8 should be thought of as "something less than 23.4×10, which equals something less than 234 or less than 2.34×10^2." Therefore, if you see a question requiring the calculation of 23.4×9.8 followed by these answer choices:

A. 1.24×10^2
B. 1.81×10^2
C. 2.29×10^2
D. 2.35×10^2

Wrong way

Answer is something less than $23.4 \times 10 = 234$.

Right way

then answer choice C is the closest answer under 2.34×10^2, and C should be chosen quickly without resorting to complicated calculations. Rarely will there be two possible answer choices close enough to prevent a correct selection after rounding. If two answer choices on the MCAT® are so close that you find you have to write down the math, it is probably because you've made a mistake. If you find yourself in that situation, look again at the question for a simple solution. If you do not see it, guess and go on.

Remain aware of the direction in which you have rounded. In the example just given, since answer choice D is closer to 234 than answer choice C, you may have been tempted to choose it. However, a quick check on the direction of rounding would confirm that 9.8 was rounded upward, so the answer should be less than 234. Again, assuming the calculations were necessary to arrive at the answer, an answer choice which would prevent the use of rounding, such as 2.32×10^2, simply would not appear as an answer choice on a real MCAT®. It would not appear for the very reason that such an answer choice would force the test taker to spend time making complicated calculations, and those are not the skills that the MCAT® is designed to test.

If rounding is used in each calculation in a series of calculations, the rounding errors can be compounded and the resulting answer can be useless. For instance, we may be required to take the above example and further divide "23.4×9.8" by 4.4. We might round 4.4 down to 4 and divide 240 by 4 to get 60, but each of our roundings would have increased our result, compounding the error. Instead, it is better to round 4.4 up to 5, dividing 235 by 5 to get 47. This is closer to the exact answer of 52.1182. To increase the accuracy of multiple estimations, **try to compensate for upward rounding with downward rounding.**

Notice, in the example above, that when we increase the denominator, we decrease the quotient (overall term). For instance:

$$\frac{625}{24} = 26.042 \qquad \frac{625}{25} = 25$$

Rounding the denominator of 24 up to 25 results in a decrease in the quotient.

When rounding squares, remember that you are really rounding twice. $(2.2)^2$ is really 2.2×2.2, so when we say that the answer is something greater than 4 we need to keep in mind that it is significantly greater because we have rounded down twice. One way to increase your accuracy is to round just one of the factors, leaving you with something greater than 4.4. This is much closer to the exact answer of 4.84.

Another strategy for rounding an exponential term is to remember that difficult-to-solve exponential terms must lie between two easy-to-solve exponential terms. For instance, 2.2^2 is between 2^2 and 3^2, closer to 2^2. This strategy is especially helpful for square roots. The square root of 21 must be between the square root of 16 and the square root of 25. The MCAT® square root of 21 must be between 4 and 5, or about 4.6.

$$\sqrt{25} = 5$$
$$\sqrt{21} = ?$$
$$\sqrt{16} = 4$$

For more complicated roots, recall that any root is simply a fractional exponent. For instance, the square root of 9 is the same as $9^{1/2}$. This means that the fourth root of 4 is $4^{1/4}$. This is the same as $(4^{1/2})^{1/2}$ or $\sqrt{2}$. We can combine these techniques to solve even more complicated roots.

It is worth your time to memorize:

$$\sqrt[3]{27} = 3$$
$$4^{\frac{2}{3}} = \sqrt[3]{4^2} = \sqrt[3]{16} = ? \approx 2.5$$
$$\sqrt[3]{8} = 2$$
$$\sqrt{2} \approx 1.4 \ and \ \sqrt{3} \approx 1.7$$

You are most likely to see these roots in the context of trigonometric functions. The MCAT® will probably give you any values that you need for trigonometric functions; however, since the MCAT® typically uses common angles, it is a good idea to be familiar with trigonometric values for common angles. Use the paradigm below to remember the values of common angles. Notice that the sine values are the reverse of the cosine values. Also notice that the numbers under the radical are 0, 1, 2, 3 and 4 from top to bottom for the sine function and bottom to top for the cosine function, and all are divided by 2.

Rounding is an effective tool for solving MCAT® math. Practice it. Remember, there will not be a calculator available to you on the MCAT®.

TABLE i.2 > Sines and Cosines of Common Angles

θ	Sine	Cosine
0°	$\frac{\sqrt{0}}{2}$	$\frac{\sqrt{4}}{2}$
30°	$\frac{\sqrt{1}}{2}$	$\frac{\sqrt{3}}{2}$
45°	$\frac{\sqrt{2}}{2}$	$\frac{\sqrt{2}}{2}$
60°	$\frac{\sqrt{3}}{2}$	$\frac{\sqrt{1}}{2}$
90°	$\frac{\sqrt{4}}{2}$	$\frac{\sqrt{0}}{2}$

> Motion and Force
> PHYSICS

Physics problems involving force and the movement of objects often require knowing the sines and cosines listed here.

Less practiced test takers may perceive a rounding strategy as risky. On the contrary, the test makers actually design their answers with a rounding strategy in mind. Complicated numbers can be intimidating to anyone not comfortable with a rounding strategy.

Practice Problems

Solve the following problems by rounding. Do not use a pencil or a calculator.

1. $\dfrac{5.4 \times 7.1 \times 3.2}{4.6^2}$

    A.   2.2
    B.   3.8
    C.   5.8
    D.   7.9

2. $\dfrac{\sqrt{360 \times 9.8}}{6.2}$

    A.   9.6
    B.   13.2
    C.   17.3
    D.   20.2

3. $\dfrac{\sqrt{2} \times 23}{50}$

    A.   0.12
    B.   0.49
    C.   0.65
    D.   1.1

4. $\dfrac{(2 \times 45)^2}{9.8 \times 21}$

    A.   11
    B.   39
    C.   86
    D.   450

5. $\sqrt{\dfrac{2 \times 9.8^2}{49}}$

    A.   0.3
    B.   0.8
    C.   1.2
    D.   2

Answers

1. C is the best answer. Remember that when we round squares, we are really rounding twice. To get a more accurate estimate, multiply 4.6×5 in the denominator to get 23. Rounding down to 7 and 3 in the numerator, we can rewrite the equation as $\frac{5.4 \times 21}{23} \cdot \frac{21}{23}$ is about 1, so the answer is close to 5.4. The closest answer given is 5.8, making choice C the best answer.

2. A is the best answer. First notice that 360 is equal to 36×10, and we can easily take the square root of 36. We can rewrite the equation as $\frac{\sqrt{36 \times 10 \times 9.8}}{6.2}$. Rounding 9.8 up to 10 gives us $\frac{\sqrt{36 \times 10^2}}{6.2} = \frac{6 \times 10}{6.2}$. Since we rounded up in the numerator, the answer is a little less than $\frac{60}{6.2}$, and choice A is the best answer.

3. C is the best answer. Recall that $\sqrt{2}$ is about 1.4. Without doing any calculations, we can tell that 1.4×23 is less than 50, so choice D can be eliminated. We can also tell that 1.4×23 is more than 25, so the answer should be greater than 0.5. This means that choices A and B can be eliminated, and choice C is the best answer.

4. B is the best answer. Squaring 2 in the numerator and rounding 9.8 up to 10 in the denominator allows us to rewrite the equation as $\frac{4 \times 45^2}{10 \times 21}$, which simplifies to $\frac{2 \times 45^2}{5 \times 21}$. Rounding 21 down to 20 in the denominator gives us $\frac{2 \times 45^2}{100}$, which simplifies to $\frac{45^2}{50}$ or $\frac{45 \times 45}{50}$. We can divide 45 by 50 to find that the answer is something a little less than 45, and choice B is the best answer.

5. D is the best answer. Taking the square root of each number separately gives us $\frac{1.4 \times 9.8}{7}$. Rounding 9.8 to 10 then gives us $\frac{14}{7}$, so choice D is the best answer.

i.8 | Scientific Notation

One important math skill tested rigorously by the MCAT® is your ability to use scientific notation. Scientific notation is used to express values that are either very large or very small. Think of the mass of the Earth relative to a one kilogram bag of flour. Now think of the mass of a single atom relative to the same one kilogram bag of flour. The mass of the Earth in kilograms is approximately 6 with 24 zeroes at the end of it. Written out:

Mass of Earth = 6,000,000,000,000,000,000,000,000 kg.

On the opposite end of the spectrum, the mass of a carbon atom in kilograms is: 0.0000000000000000000000000199 kg. That is 26 zeroes after the decimal place and before the one.

Scientific notation allows us compress these values so that they are easier to visualize and compare with other values at a glance. In scientific notation, all values are written as the product of exactly two terms. The first term consists of one non-zero digit followed by a decimal place, and then by any number of digits after the decimal place. The second term is an exponential term and will always be of base 10 with the exponent taking on any possible value. This manual will define the terms in scientific notation as follows:

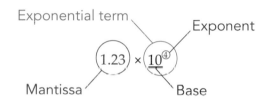

Writing values in this way can make analyzing data much simpler. For instance, if we wanted to know how much heavier the Earth is compared to a single carbon atom, we would have a tough time setting up our calculation and counting all of the zeroes. But with scientific notation, it is easy. Let's illustrate how to construct a value in scientific notation with the following example.

One mile is equal to 1609 meters. Let's think of this as 1609.0 instead. In order to get 1609.0 to the form in the caption above, we must move the decimal point over three spaces to the left, as in 1.6090. Mathematically, moving three spaces to the left corresponds to dividing by 10^3. To keep the equality, we must multiply our result by 10^3. So taking these two operations together, we end up with:

$$1609.0 = 1.6090 \times 10^3.$$

Here's another way of thinking about it: 1609.0 is equivalent to writing 1609.0 multiplied by 1000 and divided by 1000 becaue $\dfrac{1000}{1000}=1$. In other words,

$$1609.0 = 1609.0 \times \frac{1000}{1000} = \frac{1609}{1000} \times 1000$$

The term on the left becomes 1.609, and the second term, 1000, can be rewritten as 10^3. So we get our scientific notation value, 1.609×10^3.

Don't use a calculator here! Get used to doing MCAT® math.

We can go the other way as well to work with smaller numbers. One inch is equal to 0.0254 meters. To get 0.0254 in the form we need – namely 2.54 – we must move the decimal to the right two times. This is equivalent to multiplying by 10^2. Once again, to keep everything equal, we must divide our result by 10^2. Dividing by 10^2 is the same as multiplying by 10^{-2}. So,

$$0.0254 = 2.54 \times 10^{-2}.$$

In order to maximize your MCAT® score, familiarize yourself with the techniques and shortcuts of scientific notation. Although it may not seem so, scientific notation was designed to make math easier, and it does. Practice the following techniques until you come to view scientific notation as a valuable ally.

MAGNITUDE: It is important that you gain a feel for the exponential aspect of scientific notation. 10^{-8} is much greater than 10^{-12}. It is 10,000 times greater! For instance, when comparing one solution whose concentration of particles is 3.2×10^{-11} mol/L with a second solution whose concentration of particles is 4.1×10^{-9} mol/L, visualize the second solution as hundreds of times more concentrated than the first.

Pay special attention to magnitudes when adding. Try solving:

$$3.74 \times 10^{-15}$$
$$+ \ 6.43 \times 10^{-3}$$

On the MCAT®, the answer is simply 6.43×10^{-3}. This is true because 6.43×10^{-3} is so much greater than 3.74×10^{-15} that 3.74×10^{-15} is negligible. For this reason, you can round off the answer to 6.43×10^{-3}. After all, the exact answer is 0.00643000000000374.

Try solving:

$$5.32 \times 10^{-4}$$
$$\times \ 1.12 \times 10^{-13}$$

Paying attention to the difference in magnitudes when adding is particularly important in the context of acid-base chemistry, as you will see in the *Chemistry* manual.

The MCAT® answer is something greater than 5.3×10^{-17}. We cannot ignore the smaller number in this case because we are multiplying. **In addition or subtraction, a number at least 100 times smaller can be considered negligible. This is not true in multiplication or division.**

The fastest way to add or subtract numbers in scientific notation is to make the exponents match. For instance:

$$2.76 \times 10^4$$
$$+ \ 6.91 \times 10^5$$

The MCAT® answer is something less than 7.2×10^5. To get this answer quickly we match the exponents and rewrite the equation as follows:

$$2.76 \times 10^4$$
$$+ \ 69.10 \times 10^4$$

This is similar to the algebraic equation:

$$2.76y$$
$$+ \ 69.10y$$

where $y = 10^4$. We simply add the coefficients of y. Rounding, we have $3y + 69y = 72y$. Therefore, 72×10^4, or 7.2×10^5, is the answer.

When rearranging 6.91×10^5 to 69.1×10^4, we simply multiply by 10/10 (a form of 1). In other words, we multiply 6.91 by 10 and divide 10^5 by 10.

$$6.91 \times 10^5 = 69.1 \times 10^4$$
$\times 10$
$\div 10$

A useful mnemonic for remembering which way to move the decimal point when we add or subtract from the exponent is to use the acronym LARS:

Left Add, Right Subtract

In the example above, we subtracted from the exponent to convert 10^5 into 10^4. According to LARS, when you subtract from the exponent, you move the decimal in the mantissa to the right, so we moved the decimal in 6.91 to the right to get 69.1.

Another way to keep track of the decimal point is to remember that the mantissa and the exponent always go in opposite directions. If the exponent gets smaller, the mantissa gets bigger by moving the decimal to the right. If the exponent gets larger, the mantissa gets smaller by moving the decimal to the left.

Multiplication and Division

When multiplying numbers in scientific notation that have the same base, add the exponents; when dividing, subtract the exponents. $10^4 \times 10^5 = 10^9$. $10^4/10^{-6} = 10^{10}$.

To understand the rule of multiplication intuitively, consider the example of $10^5 \times 10^3$. This can be rewritten as $(10 \times 10 \times 10 \times 10 \times 10) \times (10 \times 10 \times 10)$. Since 10 is being multiplied by itself 8 times, this is the same as 10^8. The new exponent is equal to the sum of the original two exponents.

As for division, consider the example of $\frac{10^5}{10^3}$. This can be rewritten as $\frac{10 \times 10 \times 10 \times 10 \times 10}{10 \times 10 \times 10}$. As usual, terms that are multiplied in both the numerator and denominator can be cancelled out, leaving only 10×10 or 10^2. The new exponent is equal to the original exponent in the numerator minus the original exponent in the denominator.

When multiplying or dividing with scientific notation, we deal with the exponential terms and mantissa separately, *regardless of the number of terms*. For instance:

$$\frac{\left(3.2 \times 10^4\right) \times \left(4.9 \times 10^{-8}\right)}{\left(2.8 \times 10^{-7}\right)}$$

should be rearranged to:

$$\frac{3 \times 5}{3} \times \frac{10^4 \times 10^{-8}}{10^{-7}}$$

giving us an MCAT® answer of something greater than 5×10^3. (The exact answer, 5.6×10^3, is greater than our estimate because we decreased one term in the numerator by more than we increased the other, which results in a low estimate; and because we increased the term in the denominator, which also results in a low estimate.)

When taking a term written in scientific notation to some power (such as squaring or cubing it), we also deal with the decimal and exponent separately. The mantissa is raised to the exponent outside the parentheses, while the original exponent is multiplied by the exponent outside the parentheses. The MCAT® answer to:

$$(3.1 \times 10^7)^2$$

is something greater than 9×10^{14}. Recall that when taking an exponential term to a power, we multiply the exponents. The first step in taking the square root of a term in scientific notation is to make the exponent even. Then we take the square root of the mantissa and exponential term separately.

$$\sqrt{8.1 \times 10^5}$$

Make the exponent even.

$$\sqrt{81 \times 10^4}$$

Take the square root of the mantissa and exponential term separately.

Notice how much more efficient this method is. What is the square root of 49,000? Most students start thinking about 700, or 70, or something with a 7 in it. By using the scientific notation method, we quickly see that there is no 7 involved at all.

$$\sqrt{49{,}000} = \sqrt{4.9 \times 10^4} \approx 2.2 \times 10^2$$

Try finding the square root of 300 and the square root of 200.

TABLE i.3 > Exponent Rules

Operation	Rule
Addition	$x^a + y^a = (x + y)^a$ (exponents must be the same)
Subtraction	$x^a - y^a = (x - y)^a$ (exponents must be the same)
Multiplication	$y^a \times y^b = y^{a+b}$ (bases must be the same)
Division	$y^a / y^b = y^{a-b}$ (bases must be the same)
Raising to a power	$(y^a)^b = y^{a \times b}$

Remember – the rules for adding, subtracting, multiplying, and dividing numbers in scientific notation only work when the two numbers have the same base!

Practice Problems

Solve the following problems without a calculator. Try not to use a pencil.

1. $\dfrac{2.3 \times 10^7 \times 5.2 \times 10^{-5}}{4.3 \times 10^2}$

   A. 1.2×10^{-1}
   B. 2.8
   C. 3.1×10
   D. 5.6×10^2

2. $(2.5 \times 10^{-7} \times 3.7 \times 10^{-6}) + 4.2 \times 10^2$

   A. 1.3×10^{-11}
   B. 5.1×10^{-10}
   C. 4.2×10^2
   D. 1.3×10^{15}

3. $[(1.1 \times 10^{-4}) + (8.9 \times 10^{-5})]^{\frac{1}{2}}$

   A. 1.1×10^{-2}
   B. 1.4×10^{-2}
   C. 1.8×10^{-2}
   D. 2.0×10^{-2}

4. $\frac{1}{2}(3.4 \times 10^2)(2.9 \times 10^8)^2$

   A. 1.5×10^{18}
   B. 3.1×10^{18}
   C. 1.4×10^{19}
   D. 3.1×10^{19}

5. $\dfrac{1.6 \times 10^{-19} \times 15}{36^2}$

   A. 1.9×10^{-21}
   B. 2.3×10^{-17}
   C. 1.2×10^{-9}
   D. 3.2×10^{-9}

Answers

1. B is the best answer. First multiply the bases in the numerator by adding the exponents. $10^7 \times 10^{-5} = 10^{(7-5)} = 10^2$. Dividing both the numerator and denominator by 10^2 gives us $\frac{2.3 \times 5.2}{4.3}$. Rounding each number in the numerator to the nearest whole number, the answer is something more than 10 divided by 4.3, or something more than 2.

2. C is the best answer. The terms in parentheses are both many orders of magnitude smaller than 4.2×10^2. Remember that in addition or subtraction, a number at least 100 times smaller can be considered negligible. This means that choice C is the best answer.

3. B is the best answer. Notice that all of the answer choices have the same exponent, so the problem cannot be solved just by finding the right order of magnitude. First add the numbers within the bracket by making the exponents the same. 8.9×10^{-5} can be rearranged to 0.89×10^{-4}. Now the numbers can be added: $(1.1 \times 10^{-4}) + (0.89 \times 10^{-4})$ is about 2×10^{-4}. Taking the square root of both the mantissa and the exponent is about 1.4×10^{-2}.

4. C the best answer. Squaring (2.9×10^8) is a little less than 9×10^{16}. $3.4 \times 1/2$ is something more than 1.5. Multiplying (1.5×10^2) by (9×10^{16}) gives us something more than 13.5×10^{18}. Since the mantissa is greater than 10, the correct answer will have the exponent 10^{19}. Choices A and B can be eliminated. Choice D is what we would get if we forgot to multiply by $\frac{1}{2}$, and choice C is the best answer.

5. A is the best answer. The key to this question is that the exponents in the answer choices are very different from each other. This means that the rounding can be rough. First, rewrite the equation as $\frac{1.6 \times 15}{36^2} \times 10^{-19}$. 1.6×15 must be less than 36×36, so the numerator is smaller than the denominator, and the mantissa is equal to something less than 1. Since the number being multiplied by 10^{-19} is smaller than 1, the exponent in the answer must be smaller than -19, and choice A is the best answer.

Logarithms

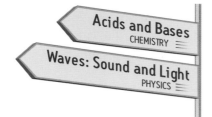

Logarithms are particularly relevant to medical practice through the pH scale. As discussed in the *Biology 2: Systems* manual, certain metabolic and disease states lead to changes in the acidity of the blood, measured in pH. An MCAT® question on either the Biological or Physical section could ask you to carry out logarithmic calculations in the context of alkalosis (decreased acidity of the blood/increased pH) or acidosis (increased acidity of the blood/decreased pH).

This will be helpful on the MCAT® if you need to solve an equation with log fractions, such as or Nernst (electrochemistry).

It is important to be able to handle problems involving logarithms, especially in the natural sciences. Logarithms are typically used when a certain physical property can have any value ranging across multiple orders of magnitude. These include the concentrations of dilute solutes in solution (the pH scale) and the intensity of sound waves (as in the decibel scale).

The logarithmic scale is used to compress very large or very small numbers into more manageable values. In this respect, it is similar to scientific notation. Questions involving logarithms will be written as follows:

$$\log_b x = y$$

The subscript b is called the base. This equation can be read as saying that "b raised to the y power is equal to x." Mathematically, this is expressed as

$$b^y = x$$

Logarithms can be tricky since the base is not always the same. However, for the MCAT® the base will usually be ten. So suppose we wanted to find the log of 1000. We would set up the problem as follows:

$$\log_{10} 1000 = y \rightarrow 10^y = 1000$$

We can see that we need to multiply 10 by itself three times to reach 1000 ($10 \times 10 \times 10 = 1000$). This means that the base 10 log of 1000 is 3. Similarly, since

$$10^{-y} = \frac{1}{10^y}$$

we have $\log_{10} 0.001 = y \rightarrow 10^y = 0.001$, and the base 10 log of 0.001 is -3.

It is also important to be able to round with logarithms. Consider the following example:

$$\log 88 = ?$$

We know that $\log 10 = 1$ and $\log 100 = 2$. We can predict that $\log 88$ will fall somewhere between 1 and 2, and indeed, $\log 88 = 1.94$. In general, we can round by first writing the equation in scientific notation and then using the method that follows. Suppose we needed to find the logarithm of 67,000. We would first write this as:

$$\log (6.7 \times 10^4)$$

We can rewrite this equation by splitting up the two terms and adding them together:

$$\log (6.7 \times 10^4) = \log (6.7) + \log (10^4)$$

The second term is equal to exactly 4, and the first term will be somewhere between 0 and 1. This means that we would expect our answer to be greater than 4 but less than 5. Actually, $\log(67,000) = 4.83$. For the logarithm of a number smaller than 1, such as 0.054, we would again convert to scientific notation and use the same process:

$$\log(0.054) = \log(5.4 \times 10^{-2}) = \log (5.4) + \log(10^{-2}) = \log(5.4) + (-2)$$

We can then predict that the solution will be between -1 and -2. The actual value of $\log(0.054)$ is -1.27.

The method we used on the previous page is based on a rule that all logarithms follow. Recall from the previous section that we added exponents when multiplying numbers in scientific notation and subtracted the exponents when dividing. Logarithms follow similar rules for multiplication and division. If the product of two terms is contained within a logarithm, the solution will be equal to the sum of the individual logarithms. In other words,

$$\log(A \times B) = \log(A) + \log(B)$$

Similarly,

$$\log\left(\frac{A}{B}\right) = \log(A) - \log(B)$$

Remember to take the sign of the exponent into account when multiplying and dividing exponents. A common mistake is to add a logarithm that should be subtracted or vice versa in a problem involving numbers with negative exponents. In the example of log (0.054), you would get the wrong answer if you added 2 at the end instead of subtracting it. This can be extended to any exponent, so a general formula is,

$$\log A^2 = \log(A \times A) = \log(A) + \log(A) = 2\log(A)$$

Let's take this one step further. Consider the logarithm of a number squared: $\log(A^2)$, for example. This can be rewritten by expanding A^2 to $A \times A$.

This can be extended to any exponent, so a general formula is,

$$\log(A^n) = n\log(A)$$

For MCAT® day, remember that $10^0 = 1$, so log 1 = 0. This is one example of a general shortcut: for numbers like 10, 100, 1000, etc., the base 10 logarithm is equal to the number of zeros. Since 100 has two zeros, log 100 = 2. This is just a simple way of saying that the base 10 logarithm of 10 raised to an exponent is equal to that exponent.

Most of the logarithms you encounter on the MCAT® will be base 10 logarithms of the form we have seen above. However, you may also come across logarithms using base e. Logarithms of base e are referred to as 'natural logs' and are written as ln(x). The mathematical constant e has a value of approximately 2.72, but for the MCAT®, we will approximate it as 3. Whereas for base 10, the log of 100 (10 × 10) is 2, for base e, the ln of 9 (3 × 3) is around 2. Natural logs appear in a handful of thermodynamics equations, but it is unlikely that you will be required to compute complicated base e logarithms.

i.10 | Equations and Proportionality

Much of the natural science content on the MCAT® involves relating properties to one another. Questions will commonly ask you to predict how a change in one property affects another property, particularly in physics and chemistry questions. Some of these relationships are more straightforward than others, but every relationship on the MCAT® can be expressed in the form of an equation, where the combination of terms on the left side is equal to the combination of terms on the right side. There are many different ways to visualize equations, but we will focus on two: algebraically and graphically. This section will consider algebraic equations, and the following section will demonstrate how equations can be represented by graphs.

Algebraic equations are numerical descriptions of natural processes. On the MCAT®, proportional relationships between variables as given in an equation can often be used to circumvent lengthy calculations. In some cases, the MCAT® question simply asks the test taker to identify the relationship directly. **When the**

Here's a more intuitive way to think of proportionality. When two things are directly proportional, they increase or decrease together. Consider the example of grocery shopping: the more food you buy, the more money you spend. Food bought and money spent are directly proportional. When two things are inversely proportional, one decreases as the other increases. Going back to grocery shopping, the more food you buy, the less money you have left. Food bought and money left in your wallet are inversely proportional.

MCAT® asks for the change in one variable due to the change in another, it is making the assumption that all other variables remain constant.

In the equation $F = ma$, we see that if we double F while holding m constant, a doubles. If we triple F, a triples. The same relationship holds for m and F. This type of relationship is called a direct proportion.

$$\overset{\times 2}{F} = m\overset{\times 2}{a}$$

F and a are directly proportional.

If we change the equation to $F = ma + b$, the directly proportional relationships are destroyed. Now if we double F while holding all variables besides a constant, a increases, but does not double. **In order for variables to be directly proportional to one another, they must both be in the numerator or denominator when they are on opposite sides of the equation, or one must be in the numerator while the other is in the denominator when they are on the same side of the equation. In addition, all sums or differences in the equation must be contained in parentheses and multiplied by the rest of the equation. No variables within the sums or differences will be directly proportional to any other variable.**

If we examine the relationship between m and a, in $F = ma$, we see that when F is held constant and m is doubled, a is reduced by a factor of 2. This type of relationship is called an **inverse proportion**. Again the relationship is destroyed if we add b to one side of the equation. **In order for variables to be inversely proportional to each other, they must both be in the numerator or denominator when they are on the same side of the equation, or one must be in the numerator while the other is in the denominator when they are on opposite sides of the equation. In addition, all sums or differences in the equation must be contained in parentheses and multiplied by the rest of the equation. No variables within the sums or differences will be directly proportional to any other variable.**

$$F = \underset{\div 2}{m}\overset{\times 2}{a}$$

m and a are inversely proportional.

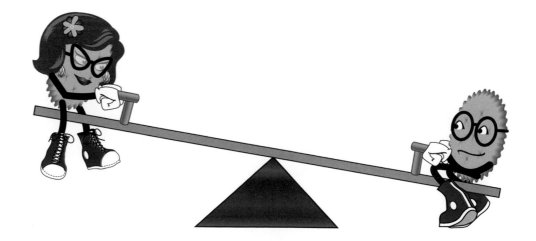

Equations can be used to better understand the scientific processes that they describe. On the flip side, considering the processes being described can make the equation easier to understand and recall. Suppose we are given the following equation:

$$Q = \frac{\Delta P \pi r^4}{8 \eta L}$$

This is Poiseuille's Law, which describes the flow rate of a real fluid through a horizontal pipe (Q). The volume flow rate Q of a real fluid through a horizontal pipe is equal to the product of the change in pressure ΔP, π, and the radius of the pipe to the fourth power r^4, divided by 8 times the viscosity and the length L of the pipe.

Poiseuille's Law will be covered in the context of the circulatory system. Despite the complicated appearance of the equation, it can be understood intuitively by considering the characteristics represented by each variable. Recall that the variables in the numerator of the right side of the equation must be directly proportional to Q. (π is a constant rather than a variable, so it does not have a proportional relationship with Q.) ΔP is the difference in pressure between the ends of the pipe; r is the radius of the pipe. Think about the effect that each of these has on water running through a hose. If you turn up the pressure, water comes out more quickly. What if you made the hose larger by increasing the radius? This also increases the rate of flow of the water. Simple intuition demonstrates the direct proportionality that is shown by the equation. If you were trying to remember Poiseuille's Law, this type of thinking would allow you to recall that ΔP and r belong in the numerator. Notice that the term in the equation is actually r^4. The exponent shows that even small changes in the radius of a pipe can have a dramatic effect on the velocity of the fluid flowing through it.

Now consider the variables in the denominator, which are there because they must be inversely proportional to Q. η is the viscosity of the fluid, meaning its thickness or resistance to flow; L is the length of the pipe. An increase in a fluid's resistance to flow will cause flow rate to decrease. (Which do you think will flow more quickly through a pipe—molasses or water? Water, which is less viscous than molasses.) Increasing the length will decrease flow rate because energy from the fluid is lost through friction against the walls of the pipe. (Imagine molasses running through an extremely long hose. You would expect the molasses to slow down or even stop before coming out the end of the hose.) As in the case of the variables in the numerator, reasoning about the variables in the denominator shows that their placement makes sense. An increase in these variables must lead to a decrease in flow rate; the variables are indirectly proportional to Q.

Narrating equations in this way makes both equations and the phenomena that they represent easier to understand and recall. Use this method to make sense of new equations and the relationships between variables.

With rare exception, DON'T MEMORIZE. Instead, describe relationships and make connections. When you memorize, there is a high risk that you do not understand what you are committing to memory. If you understand it, you won't need to memorize it. The MCAT® rewards understanding over memory.

An equation is a shorthand for a story. If you tell the story and understand why it makes sense, you can use that understanding to rebuild the equation when you need it. Tell yourself the story: talk through the relationships between variables and notice why they are logical. "When pressure increases, it makes sense that flow rate would increase..." This approach is more reliable than your memory on MCAT® day!

MCAT® THINK

Water ($\eta = 1.80 \times 10^{-3}$ Pa s) flows through a pipe with a 14.0 cm radius at 2.00 L/s. An engineer wishes to increase the length of the pipe from 10.0 m to 40.0 m without changing the flow rate or the pressure difference. What radius must the pipe have?

$$Q = \frac{\Delta P \pi r^4}{8 \eta L}$$

    A.   12.1 cm
    B.   14.0 cm
    C.   19.8 cm
    D.   28.0 cm

See answer on page 30.

Practice Questions:

1. The coefficient of surface tension is given by the equation $\gamma = (F - mg)/(2L)$, where F is the net force necessary to pull a submerged wire of weight mg and length L through the surface of the fluid in question. The force required to remove a submerged wire from water was measured and recorded. If an equal force is required to remove a separate submerged wire with the same mass but twice the length from fluid x, what is the coefficient of surface tension for fluid x? ($\gamma_{water} = 0.073$ mN/m)

   A. 0.018 mN/m
   B. 0.037 mN/m
   C. 0.073 mN/m
   D. 0.146 mN/m

2. A solid sphere rotating about a central axis has a moment of inertia

$$I = \frac{2}{3}MR^2$$

   where R is the radius of the sphere and M is its mass. Although Callisto, a moon of Jupiter, is approximately the same size as the planet Mercury, Mercury is 3 times as dense. How do their moments of inertia compare?

   A. The moment of inertia for Mercury is 9 times greater than for Callisto.
   B. The moment of inertia for Mercury is 3 times greater than for Callisto.
   C. The moment of inertia for Mercury is equal to the moment of inertia for Callisto.
   D. The moment of inertia for Callisto is 3 times greater than for Mercury.

3. The force of gravity on an any object due to earth is given by the equation $F = G(m_o M/r^2)$ where G is the gravitational constant, M is the mass of the earth, m_o is the mass of the object and r is the distance between the center of mass of the earth and the center of mass of the object. If a rocket weighs 3.6×10^6 N at the surface of the earth what is the force on the rocket due to gravity when the rocket has reached an altitude of 1.2×10^4 km? ($G = 6.67 \times 10^{-11}$ Nm^2/kg^2, radius of the earth = 6370 km, mass of the earth = 5.98×10^{24} kg)

   A. 1.2×10^5 N
   B. 4.3×10^5 N
   C. 4.8×10^6 N
   D. 9.6×10^6 N

4. The kinetic energy E of an object is given by $E = \frac{1}{2}mv^2$ where m is the object's mass and v is the velocity of the object. If the velocity of an object decreases by a factor of 2 what will happen its kinetic energy?

   A. Kinetic energy will increase by a factor of 2.
   B. Kinetic energy will increase by a factor of 4.
   C. Kinetic energy will decrease by a factor of 2.
   D. Kinetic energy will decrease by a factor of 4.

5. Elastic potential energy in a spring is directly proportional to the square of the displacement of one end of the spring from its rest position while the other end remains fixed. If the elastic potential energy in the spring is 100 J when it is compressed to half its rest length, what is its energy when it is compressed to one fourth its rest length?

   A. 50 J
   B. 150 J
   C. 200 J
   D. 225 J

Answers

1. **B is the best answer.** γ and L are inversely proportional.

2. **B is the best answer.** Since the bodies are the same size and Mercury is 3 times denser, Mercury is 3 times more massive. Mass is directly proportional to moment of inertia.

3. **B is the best answer.** The radius of the Earth can be rewritten as 6,370 × 10³ km, or about 6 × 10³ km. The new altitude of the rocket, 1.2 × 10⁴ km (which is the same as 12 × 10³ km), is about twice the radius of the Earth. Since the rocket was originally on the surface of the Earth, one radius away from the center of the Earth, the new r is three times the original r. The square of r is inversely proportional to F, so F must be divided by 9.

4. **D is the best answer.** E is directly proportional to v^2.

5. **D is the best answer.** The spring is compressed, not stretched, so the displacement increases as the length of the spring decreases. Imagine a spring 100 cm long at rest. (Any length can be used, but 100 is an easy number to work with.) The initial displacement is 50 cm, and the final displacement is 75 cm. The displacement is increased by a factor of 1.5. Since energy is proportional to the square of displacement, the energy is increased by a factor of 1.5^2. 1.5^2 is greater than 1.4^2 and greater than 2. It follows that the energy is greater than 2 × 100 or 200. Choice D is the only answer choice greater than 200.

i.11 Graphs

A graph visually demonstrates the change in one variable that occurs due to changes in another variable. The MCAT® requires that you recognize the graphical relationship between two variables in certain types of equations. The four graphs below are the most commonly used. Memorize them. The first is a directly proportional relationship, the second is an exponential relationship, the third is an inversely proportional relationship, and the fourth is a logarithmic relationship.

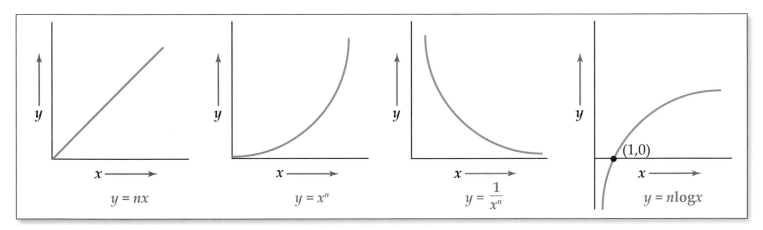

$$y = nx \qquad y = x^n \qquad y = \frac{1}{x^n} \qquad y = n\log x$$

Let's look at the second graph and assume that n = 2.

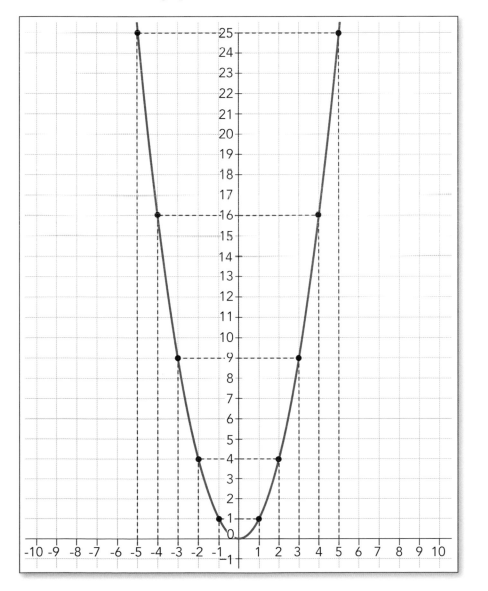

Note: n is greater than zero for the graph of $y = nx$. If n were equal to zero, the graph would simply be a straight line at $y = 0$. Also note that n is greater than one for the other three graphs. This is because x^1 is simply equal to x.

Don't worry if you don't remember the equation above. Just try and follow the math and how it corresponds to the graph.

When x is 2, y is $(2)^2$, which is 4. When x is 5, y is $(5)^2$, which is 25. As the graph shows, as n grows, y increases faster and faster. In other words, y experiences exponential growth. Consider the equation for an object moving with constant acceleration: $d = v_0 t + \frac{1}{2}at^2$, where d is the distance travelled, v_0 is the initial speed of the object, a is the acceleration and t is the time elapsed. If we assume an object initially at rest ($v_0 = 0$) with constant acceleration of $2m/s^2$, the above relationship becomes, $d = t^2$. This relationship would be identical to the graph above with distance travelled as the y-axis and time as the x-axis.

As long as the value of n is within the given parameters, the general shape of the graph will not change.

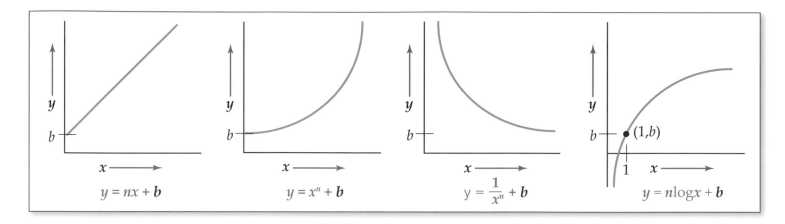

$$y = nx + b$$

$$y = x^n + b$$

$$y = \frac{1}{x^n} + b$$

$$y = n\log x + b$$

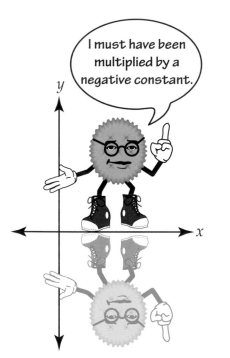

I must have been multiplied by a negative constant.

When graphs are unitless, multiplying the right side of an equation by a positive constant will not change the shape of the graph. If one side of the equation is negative, or multiplied by a negative constant, the graph "flips" across the x axis. The value of y for any given value of x now has the same magnitude as before but has the opposite sign.

Whenever the MCAT® asks you to identify the graphical relationship between two variables, assume that all other variables in the equation are constants unless told otherwise. Next, manipulate the equation into one of the above forms (with or without the added constant b) and choose the corresponding graph.

If you are unsure of a graphical relationship, plug in 1 for all variables except the variables in the question and then plug in 0, 1, and 2 for x and solve for y. Plot your results and look for the general corresponding shape.

Work through the following Practice Questions to see more examples of how equations can be represented graphically.

Practice Questions

1. The height of an object dropped from a building in the absence of air resistance is given by the equation $h = h_o + v_o t + \frac{1}{2}gt^2$, where h_o and v_o are the initial height and velocity respectively and g is -10 m/s^2. If v_o is zero which graph best represents the relationship between h and t?

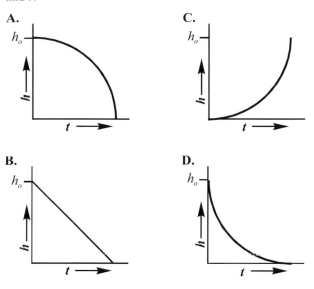

2. Which of the following graphs best describes the magnitude of the force (F) on a spring obeying Hooke's law $(F = -k\Delta x)$ as it is compressed to Δx_{max}?

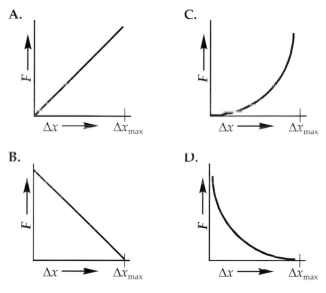

3. Which of the following graphs shows the relationship between frequency and wavelength of electromagnetic radiation through a vacuum? $(c = v\lambda)$

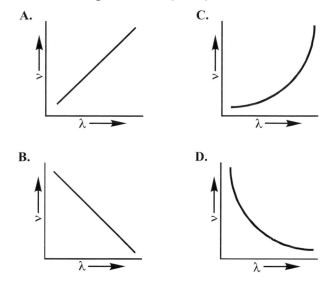

4. Which of the following graphs best describes the magnitude of the electrostatic force $F = k(qq)/r^2$ created by an object with negative charge on an object with a positive charge as the distance r between them changes?

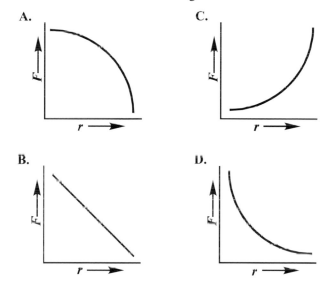

5. Which of the following graphs demonstrates the relationship between power P and work W done by a machine? ($P = W/t$)

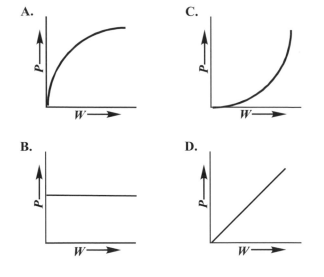

A.

B.

C.

D.

Often on the MCAT®, you must be able to quickly and confidently convert between one unit and another. Suppose we wanted to convert 34 centimeters to meters. First we must know the conversion rate between meters and centimeters, namely that 1 meter = 100 centimeters. We can rewrite this equality as:

$$\frac{1 \text{ meter}}{100 \text{ centimeters}} = \frac{100 \text{ centimeters}}{1 \text{ meter}} = 1$$

Of course, if we multiply any number by 1, the number is unchanged. 34 centimeters × 1 equals 34 centimeters. Likewise, $\frac{1 \text{ meter}}{100 \text{ centimeters}}$ is the same thing as 1. If we cancel the centimeter units and divide by 100, we arrive at 0.34 meters:

$$34 \text{ centimeters} \times \frac{1 \text{ meter}}{100 \text{ centimeters}} = 0.34 \text{ meters}$$

If it helps, you can visualize this equation in two steps as follows:

$$34 \cancel{\text{ centimeters}} \times \frac{1 \text{ meters}}{100 \cancel{\text{ centimeters}}} = \frac{34 \cancel{\text{ centimeters}}}{100 \cancel{\text{ centimeters}}} \times 1 \text{ meter} = 0.34 \text{ meters}$$

But just as $4 \times \frac{6}{2}$ and $\frac{4}{2} \times 6$ both equal 12, it makes no difference how the equation is written in terms of the final answer.

Although converting from centimeters to meters is relatively straightforward, it is still helpful to know how to use the method above for two reasons. First, it is easy to mix up the direction of the conversion and arrive at 34 centimeters = 3400 meters (wrong) instead of 34 centimeters = 0.34 meters (correct). If you write out the equation, the numerator and denominator will only cancel if you have arranged the conversion factor correctly:

Problem: Convert 34 centimeters to meters. There are 100 centimeters per meter.

Wrong way: 34 × 100/1 = 3400 meters

Right way: 34 centimeters × (1 meter)/(100 centimeters) = 0.34 meters

---

Second, more complicated conversions can be carried out more easily using this method. Suppose we wanted to find out how many seconds are in 10 years. We would write the following equation:

$$10 \text{ years} \times \frac{365.25 \text{ days}}{1 \text{ year}} \times \frac{24 \text{ hours}}{1 \text{ day}} \times \frac{60 \text{ minutes}}{1 \text{ hour}} \times \frac{60 \text{ seconds}}{1 \text{ min}}$$
$$= 3.16 \times 10^8 \text{ seconds}$$

Physics and chemistry questions commonly require conversions where two units are involved: one in the numerator and one in the denominator. The same method can be used for these problems. Suppose the solution to a problem involving velocity is 10 m/s, but all of the answer choices are written in units of km/hr. Use dimensional analysis to convert the units from the solution:

$$\frac{10 \text{ } m}{s} \times \frac{1 \text{ } km}{1000 \text{ } m} \times \frac{60 \text{ } s}{1 \text{ } min} \times \frac{60 \text{ } min}{1 \text{ } hr} = 36 \text{ } km/hr$$

SI units will be covered in more detail in the *Physics* manual, so don't worry if the equations seem foreign to you at this point. Just focus on the units.

Another important aspect of unit manipulation is in understanding equations themselves. Knowing the units for a given physical property can be helpful in terms of understanding the equation, or even constructing a forgotten equation from scratch. For example, if you know that the SI units for speed are meters per second (m/s), it follows that since meters are a measurement of distance and seconds are a measurement of time, speed can be expressed as distance divided by time. More complex equations can also be constructed in a similar manner.

Let's turn to energy as an example. The SI unit for energy is the Joule, but let's suppose we wanted to express energy in terms of simpler units like meters, kilograms and seconds. In the example of gravitational potential energy, energy can be described as mass times acceleration due to gravity (g) times height, *Energy = Mass × g × Height*. The units for mass are kilograms (kg), the units for height are meters (m), and since g is an acceleration, its units are meters divided by seconds squared $\frac{m}{s^2}$. If we write out our equation in terms of units,

$$Energy = Mass \times Acceleration\ due\ to\ gravity \times Height$$

$$Joules = (\text{kg}) \times \left(\frac{m}{s^2}\right) \times (m) = \frac{\text{kg}\,m^2}{s^2}$$

We've now arrived at a way of expressing energy in terms of the most fundamental units. The important thing to realize is that energy must have these same units in any equation. Let's consider another equation involving energy (as work), where energy is equal to force times distance, Energy = Force × Distance. The units for distance are meters (m), and the units for force are Newtons (N). If we write out the equation in terms of units,

$$Energy = Force \times Distance$$

$$Joules = N \times m = N\,m$$

The equations above show that Joules can be accurately expressed in two different ways: $\frac{\text{kg}\,m^2}{s^2}$ and $N\,m$. Since there can be multiple correct ways to express an equation in terms of its units, it is important to be able to convert between units quickly. Whenever you come across a new equation on the MCAT®, break it down into its individual units. You may then be able to eliminate wrong answers, or even arrive at the best answer, simply by looking at the units. For instance, if an unfamiliar equation appears in a MCAT® passage and a question asks you to express energy with respect to new terms, it is possible that only one of the four answer choices will have a combination that leads to $Joules = \frac{\text{kg}\,m^2}{s^2}$. This answer is automatically correct.

The MCAT® may try to trick you by having different units in the passage, questions, and answer choices. A wrong answer choice may have the right number but the wrong units. You can avoid falling for these answer choices by attending to the units before selecting an answer.

$$\sqrt[3]{27} = 3$$
$$4^{\frac{2}{3}} = \sqrt[3]{4^2} = \sqrt[3]{16} = ? \approx 2.5$$
$$\sqrt[3]{8} = 2$$
$$\sqrt{2} \approx 1.4 \ and \ \sqrt{3} \approx 1.7$$

$$\log 1 = 0$$

Sines and Cosines of Common Angles

θ	Sine	Cosine
0°	$\dfrac{\sqrt{0}}{2}$	$\dfrac{\sqrt{4}}{2}$
30°	$\dfrac{\sqrt{1}}{2}$	$\dfrac{\sqrt{3}}{2}$
45°	$\dfrac{\sqrt{2}}{2}$	$\dfrac{\sqrt{2}}{2}$
60°	$\dfrac{\sqrt{3}}{2}$	$\dfrac{\sqrt{1}}{2}$
90°	$\dfrac{\sqrt{4}}{2}$	$\dfrac{\sqrt{0}}{2}$

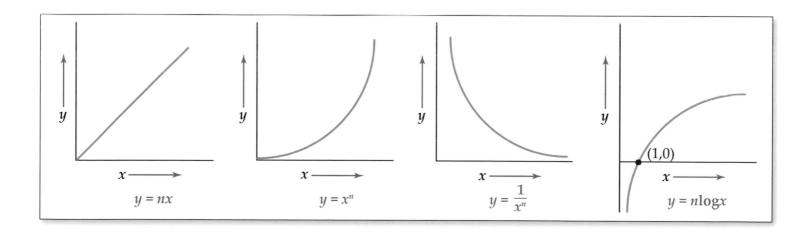

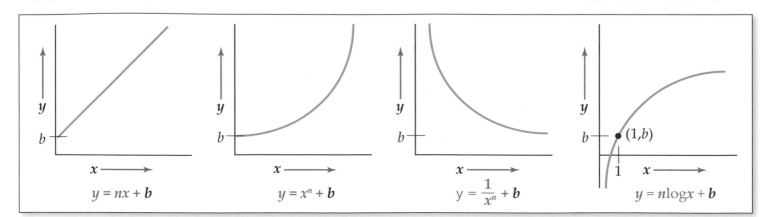

$$y = nx + b \qquad y = x^n + b \qquad y = \frac{1}{x^n} + b \qquad y = n\log x + b$$

MCAT® THINK ANSWER

Pg. 21: The only way to answer this question is with proportions. Most of the information is given to distract you. Notice that the difference in pressure between the ends of the pipe is not even given and the flow rate would have to be converted to m³/s. To answer this question using proportions, multiply L by 4 and r by x. Now pull out the 4 and the x. We know by definition, $Q = \Delta P\pi r^4/8\eta L$; therefore, $x^4/4$ must equal 1. Solve for x, and this is the change in the radius. The radius must be increased by a factor of about 1.4.

$14 \times 1.4 = 19.6$. The new radius is approximately 19.6 cm. The closest answer is C.

$$Q = \frac{\Delta P\pi r^4}{8\eta L}$$

$$Q = \frac{\Delta P\pi (xr)^4}{8\eta (4L)}$$

$$Q = \frac{\Delta P\pi r^4}{8\eta L} \times \frac{x^4}{4}$$

$$4 = x^4$$

$$x = \sqrt{2}$$

DON'T FORGET YOUR KEYS

1. The MCAT® rewards flexibility and connections. Study concepts in order to simplify, understand, and organize content.

2. Remove the disguise of complexity from MCAT® passages and questions to reveal the simple science tested.

3. Keep MCAT® math simple: use proportionality, rounding, units, and scientific notation.

Research and Reasoning Skills for the MCAT®

ii.1 Introduction

ii.2 The Scientific Method

ii.3 Methods and Measurements

ii.4 Statistics to Describe a Data Set

ii.5 Common Statistical Tests

ii.6 Results: Interpreting Data

ii.7 Results: Drawing Conclusions from Data

ii.8 Reading Research-Based MCAT® Passages and Interpreting Graphs

ii.9 Ethics of Research

ii.1 | Introduction

About 20% of questions in the Biological, Physical, and Psychosocial sections of the MCAT® will test research skills. These questions require analytical thinking and reasoning skills. Critical thinking about research is emphasized on the MCAT® because the ability to analyze research is crucial to practice as a physician. The field of medicine constantly adapts in response to new findings relevant to the causes, effects, and treatments of disease. Evidence-based medicine is centered on the principle that physicians should draw upon the results of current, high-quality studies when making clinical decisions about individual patients. In other words, although physicians' expertise and patients' wishes are still critical, physicians should also examine the latest research, or evidence, when determining a treatment plan.

The ability to interpret studies and their results is necessary to do well in all sections of the MCAT®. Passages that are explicitly based on particular studies are most common in the context of biology, biochemistry, sociology, and psychology. Passages about general chemistry, organic chemistry, and physics may simply describe reactions or other phenomena rather than presenting a hypothesis and study. However, each section will include questions that test research skills. This means that you must be comfortable with research questions in a variety of contexts.

This lecture will make it simple. Although various types of research methodology will appear on the MCAT®, the fundamental ideas are the same. You do NOT need years of lab experience or an advanced statistics class to gain the level of understanding of research required for the MCAT®. The research skills it will test are an extension of the critical and logical thinking that will help you gain success on the test as a whole. Many of the skills described in this lecture, particularly determining the key ideas of a passage and evaluating flaws, are closely related to the type of analytic thinking required to excel in the CARS section.

This lecture will first provide an overview of how the scientific method guides the practice of research, followed by a framework for understanding the components of the scientific method based on the structure of a research paper. Next, it will cover issues of methodology and measurement. The lecture will then cover the basic skills of quantitative analysis that are required for the MCAT®, including common statistical analyses. The following section will discuss how researchers draw conclusions by analyzing and interpreting data, with an emphasis on the features of study design that are necessary for conclusions of causality. The lecture will then provide an example of a passage that could be seen on the MCAT®, along with a demonstration of the analysis required to interpret research-based passages. The reading of the sample passage will also include the skill of interpreting graphical data, which is often key to understanding both the passage as a whole and any statistical analyses. The lecture concludes with a discussion of research ethics.

The major skills that you need to answer questions involving research methods are: identifying research questions and variables, considering strengths and weaknesses of measurements and methodologies, interpreting quantitative analysis of data, and evaluating the conclusions drawn from data analysis.

THE 3 KEYS

1. In an experimental setup, the independent variable is manipulated and the dependent variable is measured and/or observed.

2. Correlated factors do not necessarily indicate a causal relationship.

3. Narrate research-based passages and questions: identify the hypothesis, variables, methods, and results. Interpret the data as it relates to the hypothesis.

Although you must understand how researchers think and how scientific research is conducted, you will obviously not carry out actual experiments as part of the MCAT®! Instead the emphasis will be on your ability to interpret the work carried out by others. Throughout the lecture there will be tips on how to translate your understanding of research to answering questions correctly on the MCAT®.

ii.2 | The Scientific Method

The scientific method represents the process by which researchers develop research questions, hypotheses, and studies. The standardized guidelines of the scientific method allow researchers to easily share their work and interpret the findings of others. The purpose of research is to create shared scientific knowledge. Therefore, the shared "language" of the scientific method is a crucial tool. Furthermore, the scientific method sets out the fundamental principles of research: the creation and evaluation of scientific questions.

Most students of the sciences have encountered the scientific method before. However, an abstract knowledge of the scientific method does not automatically translate to the ability to recognize and reason about each step in the context of an actual study. This section will review the scientific method in the context of the research-based skills required for the MCAT®.

The steps of the scientific method are presented in Figure ii.1 and are described further below. In broad terms, the scientific method involves asking a question, proposing a possible answer to that question, designing a study that will produce data that can support or undermine that possible answer, collecting the data, and then analyzing the data to determine the implications for the original question. Research articles tend to have a standard organization, with sections that correspond to one or more steps of the scientific method. An introduction section lays out the motivation for a research question and provides a hypothesis to be tested. A methods section lays out the experimental approach that the authors used to approach the question, and the results section presents the data that was obtained. The discussion section concludes the article, interpreting the data and suggesting future investigations based on the findings. This framework can be used to remember the steps of the scientific method and how the elements of a research study work together to answer questions.

FIGURE ii.1 | The Scientific Method

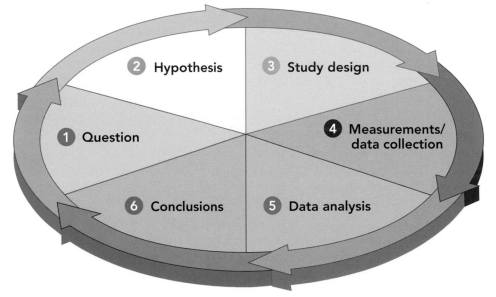

1) Question: The purpose of a study is to find an answer to a specific question. A wide variety of possible questions can motivate the development of a study. However, a successful study is based on a testable research question. A testable research question is one that can be accurately modeled and evaluated through the methods used in scientific research.

A research question is often inspired by observation. In other words, the researcher observes some real-world phenomenon and develops a question about it. However, research is a collaborative enterprise; no one tries to reinvent the wheel. Instead, when researchers are developing their questions of interest, they are influenced by past findings. The process of background research, meaning the examination of the work of other researchers who have studied related questions, allows a researcher to learn from the mistakes and discoveries of other researchers. It also helps them to ask questions that have not been answered before and that will further the understanding of the field.

Theory also influences the development of research questions. A theory is a proposed explanation of the causes and mechanisms of a natural phenomenon. A theory is broader than a hypothesis, and is not testable in a single experiment. Instead, it is supported by the results of multiple studies that test smaller facets of the overall theory. Like the scientific method itself, the relationship between theory and research can be understood as a cycle. Theoretical claims inspire the development of research questions, and studies that answer those questions lead to modification of theory, which then leads to questions for future studies, and so on. Theory is discussed further in the first lecture of the *Psychology and Sociology* manual.

Different types of research involve different types of research questions. One important distinction is the one between basic and applied research. **Applied research** attempts to find practical solutions to problems, while **basic research** tries to explain the fundamental principles of how the world works. Basic research can be thought of as the production of scientific knowledge for its own sake, rather than for application to a particular situation. This is not to say that basic research is somehow less useful than applied research. Basic research provides the necessary base for applied research. Applied research would not be possible without the fundamental understanding that basic research provides.

Applied and basic research can be carried out in the context of many different fields, each of which ask questions about specific types of phenomena. Perhaps the most fundamental distinction is between natural and social science. **Natural science** is the study of processes in the natural world, such as the laws of physics or the life processes of biological organisms. In contrast, **social science**, as the name implies, examines phenomena in the social world, often focusing on behavior and interactions. The MCAT® will include studies from both the natural and social sciences. All research follows the principles laid out in the scientific method, but the goals of social and natural science research are often different. Natural science asks questions about laws of nature that will allow extremely reliable predictions. However, the issue of whether such laws even exist in the realm of the social world is debatable. Rather than attempting to find rigid laws such as those described by the natural sciences, social science research seeks to discover patterns of behavior and explain relationships between different social and psychological phenomena.

2) Hypothesis: The hypothesis is the researcher's prediction of the answer to the research question. Like the research question, a hypothesis is informed by past findings and scientific theories, so it is an educated prediction rather than a blind guess. Hypotheses must be testable, like research questions. In other words, a claim that cannot be tested scientifically cannot be used to develop a study and is not a scientific hypothesis. So what does it mean for a hypothesis to be testable? A testable hypothesis is a prediction that a study can either support or refute. Usually this prediction concerns the relationship between two variables.

Applied and basic research may cover similar topics, but have different goals. For example, basic research on the human genome could attempt to sequence a specific gene for a large sample of people to assess human variation and identify forms of the gene that may be linked with causing disease. Applied research might develop gene therapies that target and silence disease-causing forms of the gene.

The natural and social sciences often differ in their limitations on study design and, by consequence, conclusions that can be drawn from the results. This will be discussed later in the lecture.

TABLE ii.1> Layout of Primary Research Papers

Scientific method step	Paper section
1. Question 2. Hypothesis	Introduction
3. Study design	Materials and Methods
4. Measurements/data collection 5. Data analysis	Results
6. Conclusions	Discussion

Use the layout of primary research papers to understand research design. Research-based passages on the MCAT® are usually structured similarly. Recognizing the components will give you an organizational framework for understanding these passages.

Understand Key 1: Experiments attempt to demonstrate that one phenomenon causes another. The only way to establish a causal relationship between two phenomena is to change one (the independent variable) and see if the other (dependent variable) changes. Consider a flashlight that won't turn on. To see if the cause is a dead battery, you would change the battery and try to switch on the flashlight. The independent variable is the cause that the experimenter changes, and the dependent variable is the measurement or effect the experimenter records.

Variables are aspects of the study that can have different values and be measured or categorized. Suppose that the research question for a study was "Does daily consumption of aspirin reduce the incidence of myocardial infarction?" A research hypothesis associated with this question could be "Consumption of 81 mg of aspirin every day for twelve months leads to a decreased incidence of myocardial infarction during a two-year follow-up period." This hypothesis involves the components of a testable hypothesis: a prediction, a relationship, and variables.

The research hypothesis usually predicts that one variable causes a change in another variable. The variable that is predicted to have a causal effect is the **independent variable**. In an experimental setting, the independent variable is the one that researchers control and manipulate. The **dependent variable** is hypothesized to "depend" on the independent variable, and it is what the researchers measure. The hypothesis given above predicts that aspirin consumption (the independent variable) decreases the incidence of myocardial infarction (the dependent variable).

Although the two concepts are closely related, it is important to understand the difference between a research question and a hypothesis. Remember, a hypothesis is a proposed answer to the question that the study is designed to explore. For example, consider the following statements:

"The authors were interested in the relationship between aspirin consumption and incidence of myocardial infarction."

"The authors proposed that daily consumption of 81 mg of aspirin leads to decreased incidence of myocardial infarction."

The first describes a question, while the second refers to a hypothesis. Sometimes a passage will actually use the word "question" or "hypothesis." However, you must be able to identify the question and hypothesis when they are described but not explicitly named, as in the example above.

3) **Study design**: Once the question and hypothesis have been developed, a study is designed to produce results that have the potential to support or refute the hypothesis. In the example above, researchers might give aspirin to one study group but not the other, and then determine whether the group that receives aspirin has a lower incidence of myocardial infarction. Different types of research methods and how they affect the conclusions that can be drawn from the results will be discussed later in this lecture.

4) **Measurement/data collection**: To answer a hypothesis, it is necessary to come up with an appropriate method of measurement to collect data. This process includes *operationalization*, or approximating the true variables of interest with one that can be measured or tabulated. Consider a psychological study that is interested in the effect of stress on memory formation. The hypothesis might be that stress results in poorer memory formation. The independent variable is stress, and the dependent variable is quality of memory formation. But "stress" and "memory formation" are not items that can actually be measured in a lab. Operationalization of these variables is what makes the collection of data possible, and could occur in a variety of ways depending on the resources and preferences of the researchers. "Stress" could be operationalized as the presence of a particular event in the lab that is thought to cause stress, such as study participants witnessing a theft. "Memory formation" could be operationalized as a subject's score on a specific test of memory, such as recalling a list of items.

5) **Analysis**: Once data has been collected, statistical analyses provide methods of describing and interpreting the measured data. Statistical analysis can show whether the data support or undermine the hypothesis in mathematical terms. The goal of statistical analysis is to determine whether differences in the dependent variable can be attributed to changes in the independent variable, or whether they

were due to chance. The basic knowledge of statistical analysis that is required for the MCAT® will be covered later in this lecture.

6) **Conclusions:** Statistical analysis generally returns numerical results that must be interpreted by the researcher. Statistics are a necessary step in evaluating whether the results support or undermine the hypothesis, but the researcher must take the final step of interpreting the statistical analysis and determining the implications of the study. Often the interpretation of the data will have to do with whether or not the independent variable caused a change in the dependent variable. The implications of the study involve the conclusions that can be drawn about the "real world" based on the group of subjects involved in the study. The features of study design that allow particular conclusions to be drawn will be examined later in this lecture.

Of course, for the MCAT®, you will not have to use the scientific method to design studies. Instead the scientific method is your key to understanding the passages that present the work of other researchers. You will notice that these passages, like the primary research articles from which they were adapted, are often roughly organized according to the steps of the scientific method. A typical research-based passage starts by considering past findings that influence the research question and then narrows in on the specific study by presenting the question and/or hypothesis, as well as the methods used (the study design). Then the passage presents the data graphically and/or verbally. The passage may then discuss data analysis and conclusions, or the test-taker may be asked to answer questions about these steps.

For extra practice, try reading every section of a research article except the discussion. Then write a brief interpretation of the data and compare it with the authors' interpretation.

ii.3 | Methods and Measurements

As discussed above, developing research questions and hypotheses are crucial to the scientific process. However, good research questions without appropriate research methods are useless for drawing conclusions. In order for research to be useful and successful, scientists must carefully choose measurement techniques and research methods that allow for the appropriate collection of data and interpretation of results that address the research questions.

Issues to Consider in Measurement

Recall that a variable is an aspect of the system under study that can vary, or have different values. This means that part of carrying out a study involves measuring or categorizing the variables of interest. The data collected fall into one of the following measurement scales: nominal, ordinal, interval, or ratio. The type of measurement scale employed in data collection is important because it is a factor in determining both the kind of statistical analysis that can be applied to the data and what conclusions can be drawn about the study.

In a *nominal scale,* data are classified into non-ordered categories. For example, eye color might be recorded as blue, grey, green, hazel, brown, or amber. Notice that there is no intrinsic ordering to these categories (i.e., there is no particular reason that blue should come before grey).

By contrast, an *ordinal scale* allows for classification into ordered categories. Pain, for instance, might be described as mild, moderate, or severe. However, it is difficult to compare values within an ordinal system. There is no way of knowing if the increase in pain from mild to moderate is equivalent to the increase from moderate to severe. In other words, ordinal scales do not convey relative degree of difference. Interval or ratio scales must be used to collect data that involve meaningful degrees of difference.

In an *interval scale*, the intervals between values on the scale are meaningful. For example, when measuring temperature in degrees Celsius, the difference in temperature between 40°C and 50°C is the same as the difference between 70°C and 80°C. However, a limitation of the interval scale is that the ratios between

Not accurate
Not precise

Accurate
Not precise

Not accurate
Precise

Accurate
Precise

Accuracy and precision are often confused. Accuracy is how well measurements reflect the true value of something, while precision refers to how well multiple measured values agree with each other.

values in the scale are not meaningful. For example, water at 80°C is not twice as hot as water at 40°C. In order to make meaningful ratios between values, a ratio scale must be used. Unlike an interval scale, which has an arbitrary zero point, a *ratio scale* has an absolute zero. As a result, ratios between values are meaningful. For example, because the Kelvin scale of temperature measurement has a point of absolute zero, unlike the Celsius scale, it is accurate to say that 80 K is twice as hot as 40 K. Variables such as age, height, and weight are typically measured using ratio scales.

No matter what kind of measurement scale is used, variability is an inherent part of the data collection process. Any single measured value is unlikely to exactly represent the true value of the thing being measured. Deviation between observed measurements and the true value is referred to as *error*. Error can generally be broken down into two main categories: random error and systematic error.

Random error is present in all types of measurement and shifts measurements in unpredictable ways. Human error and lack of instrument sensitivity contribute to random error. Imagine a chemist is trying to determine the boiling point of an unknown liquid. He measures the boiling point ten times and records his results. When the mercury is between degree marks on the thermometer, the chemist may sometimes round up and sometimes round down, resulting in random error in his measurements. Random error decreases **precision**, which is a measure of how closely individual measurements of the same value agree with each other.

By contrast, **systematic error** shifts all measurements in a standardized way. Systematic error can arise from a variety of causes. For example, if the chemist's thermometer consistently reports temperatures at two degrees greater than what they really are, the chemist will incorrectly estimate the boiling point of his unknown liquid by two degrees. Systematic error decreases the accuracy of the measurements obtained, which is how well the measured values reflect the true value. In this way, systematic error can result in *bias*, a systematic difference between the results obtained and the true value. Biases in measurement are commonly introduced by the observer, instrument, or subject. *Observer bias* occurs when an observer intentionally or unintentionally records a distorted measurement, whereas *instrument bias* results from systematic malfunctioning of a mechanical instrument. Finally, *subject bias* is introduced when a study participant intentionally or unintentionally reports a distorted measurement. For example, suppose that researchers surveyed people to ask how many cigarettes they had smoked per day over the past twenty years. Respondents with cancer might, on average, overestimate their cigarette smoking compared to respondents without cancer because the experience of having cancer biases people to recall more smoking. This recall bias decreases the accuracy of the survey as an instrument to measure the true rate of smoking.

FIGURE ii.2 Random vs. Systematic Error

Any imprecision in the measurement process will cause a certain amount of random error for each measurement of a value. When several measurements of the same value are taken, their average is believed to represent the true value. However, if systematic error is present, all measurements may be shifted away from the actual true value in a standardized way.

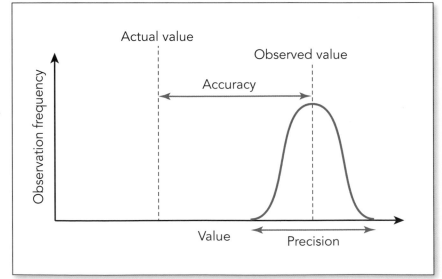

The precision of a measurement is affected by the number of significant figures (also called significant digits) in that measurement. Significant figures, and thus precision, depend on the measuring tools available.

There are special rules for determining significance when zero is a digit in the measurement. Zero digits that come at the end of a number are significant if followed by a decimal point (as in 400.) or preceded by a decimal point (as in the last zero of 0.040). Zeros that come at the beginning of a number (as in the first two zeros of 0.040) are not significant.

Try the following example of a question you could see on the MCAT® that indirectly tests understanding of precision.

Electrocardiography (EKG) is a technique that uses electrodes on the skin of the thorax to monitor electrical impulses as they travel through the heart. In the atrioventricular (AV) node, impulses are usually conducted with a velocity of 0.5 m/s. If a standard EKG setup uses electrodes with receptive fields just under 50 mm across, what is the minimum sampling rate needed to guarantee detection of electrical activity from the AV node electrode?

    A.   1 Hz
    B.   10 Hz
    C.   100 Hz
    D.   1000 Hz

See answer on page 60.

Experimental Methods

As scientists develop a research question, they must choose a research method in order to refine their question into one that can be used to test a specific hypothesis. Research methods can be broadly classified as experimental or non-experimental. Each method allows researchers to refine the research question differently.

In experimental studies, scientists manipulate one or more variables in order to observe the outcome. To experimentally study the relationship between coffee and pancreatic cancer, scientists could manipulate the variable of coffee consumption by feeding different amounts of coffee to laboratory animals, such as mice. The research question, "Does drinking coffee cause pancreatic cancer?" would then be refined to something like, "Does consumption of four ounces of brewed coffee every day for six months by laboratory mice lead to an increased incidence of pancreatic cancer as determined by computed tomography scans during a one-year follow-up period?"

Sometimes, the proposed research question is difficult to approach with an experimental method for reasons related to feasibility, affordability, or ethics. For example, it would not be feasible to manipulate the amount of coffee consumed by a group of human research subjects for a long period of time. If our researchers wanted to study the relationship between coffee and pancreatic cancer in humans, they might choose a non-experimental research method. In non-experimental or **observational studies**, scientists merely observe variables without manipulating them. Researchers could choose to observe the amount of coffee consumed by a group of people and then measure the incidence of pancreatic cancer in the group. The research question would be refined to, "Do people with pancreatic cancer report having drunk more coffee during the past twenty years than do people without pancreatic cancer?" There are several different types of observational studies commonly used in medical research, described in the table on the following page.

TABLE ii.2 > Types of Observational Study Design

Observational study design	Description	Time frame considered	Example
Cross-sectional study	Studies a sample of the population at one point in time	Present	A researcher measures current coffee intake and the current rate of pancreatic cancer.
Cohort study	Studies a sample of the population over time	Future	A researcher measures baseline coffee intake and, later, the rate of pancreatic cancer.
Case-control study	Studies two sample populations, one with and one without an outcome	Past	A researcher asks people with and without pancreatic cancer about past coffee intake.

Remember Key 2: Just because two sets of data are correlated does not mean that one causes the other. Use of acetaminophen by breastfeeding mothers is correlated with asthma in their children, but this does not mean that acetaminophen use caused the children to develop asthma. The asthma may instead have been triggered by the pathogen that caused the illness for which the mom took acetaminophen, rather than by the acetaminophen itself.

When an experimental method is used, scientists often perform control experiments (see figure below). These are particularly common in laboratory experiments in the biological sciences. Control experiments help scientists determine whether the whole experiment truly shows what it is intended to show. **Positive controls** are groups in which an effect is expected because scientists manipulate them in a way that is already known to produce the effect. By contrast, **negative controls** are groups in which no effect is expected.

In the study involving coffee and pancreatic cancer, scientists could perform a positive control experiment by manipulating a gene that is known to cause pancreatic cancer. Demonstrating the ability to detect cancer in the group with this gene helps validate the use of computed tomography (CT) scans as a measurement tool.

The scientists could perform a negative control experiment by keeping a group of mice in the exact same conditions as the experimental group, but giving them water instead of coffee. Any change in the incidence of pancreatic cancer in this group will be due to a factor other than coffee. Thus, in this example, the negative control experiment strengthens the argument that any change in the incidence of cancer in the coffee group is due to the coffee and not to other factors.

In summary, the choice of specific methods influences the conclusions that can be drawn from study results and allows scientists to refine their experimental question. Remember that the study design constrains the research question and that the results of the study will only answer a very specific question. The scientists in the given example will not get an answer to the general question, "Does drinking coffee cause pancreatic cancer?" from their experiment, no matter what the results are.

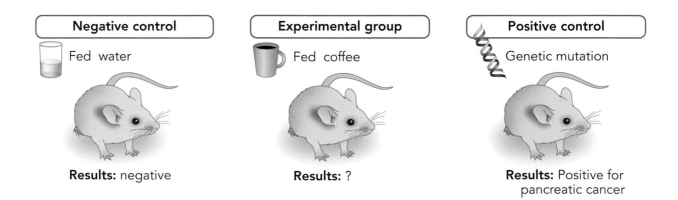

Negative control	Experimental group	Positive control
Fed water	Fed coffee	Genetic mutation
Results: negative	**Results:** ?	**Results:** Positive for pancreatic cancer

ii.4 | Statistics to Describe a Data Set

Research-based passages adapted from specific studies in both the natural and social sciences are likely to appear throughout the MCAT®. A basic understanding of statistics is necessary for understanding research methodology and interpreting data and results. This section will explain how statistics can be used to describe a data set, examine relationships between variables, and test specific hypotheses. It will cover some of the most commonly used statistical tools and will review how to draw conclusions about the meanings of data through statistical analysis. It is important to realize that the MCAT® does NOT require knowledge of advanced statistics! Questions about statistics on the MCAT® will likely appear in the context of specific information given in the passage, rather than requiring the selection of a specific test or complex reasoning about the features of different statistical tests.

Statistics are used to analyze data sets. A data set is a list of values for a certain variable or collection of variables. The values in a data set can be numerical or categorical. *Numerical data* (also called *quantitative data*) represent variables that can be measured and recorded as a number (either interval or ratio), such as height. *Categorical data* (also called *qualitative data*) represent variables that can be observed and recorded as a category. Categorical data can sometimes consist of numbers (such as a rating of 1 through 10 on a pain scale), but unlike quantitative data, the numbers are not a measurement of a value but rather represent a specific category (a little pain, moderate pain, etc.).

A closely related distinction is between *continuous* and discrete data. Continuous data are obtained through measurement and usually have values that fall somewhere on a continuous number line. For instance, the length of your arm may be 22 inches, 22.4 inches, or 22.43 inches depending on the level of specificity in the measurement. In comparison, *discrete* data are counted, not measured, and are restricted to certain values or categories. Discrete data include both nominal and ordinal systems of measurement, but may also apply to data that are numerical, usually consisting of values restricted to whole numbers. A researcher recording the number of relapses a patient experiences after treatment for cancer may record two relapses, but not 2.63 relapses.

Introduction to Statistics

Statistics are a way to increase the objectivity involved in analyzing data. Without mathematical guidelines, researchers might bring personal bias to data analysis and interpret results that are not actually supported by the data. Statistics also help organize and summarize data sets. Once data are collected, they can seem like a meaningless list of numbers. One way to make sense of the contents of the data set is through *descriptive statistics*, which are just what they sound like. Descriptive statistics describe the scope and content of the data set to show researchers the patterns present in their data. For the MCAT®, it is important to be familiar with commonly used descriptive statistics for both the central tendency (which estimates the center of a data set) and the dispersion (which shows how spread out the values are) of the data.

Even the best-crafted research methodology results in data that appear to be just a pile of numbers, and can be difficult to interpret without organization and analysis. The point of statistics is to take a set of numbers (however unwieldy) and turn it into an intelligible story. Statistics allow the researcher to answer research questions and draw conclusions that are supported by the research results.

For a quick check to know if a data set is continuous or discrete, think about how the data were obtained. If values were counted (as in the example of cancer relapses), the data are discrete. If the values were measured (as in the example of arm length), chances are the data are continuous.

Many of the most commonly used descriptive statistics may already be familiar to you. Use this section to refresh and solidify your knowledge so that these basic techniques are second nature. That way, when you encounter data interpretation on the MCAT®, you will have more time to spend on more difficult problems.

When dealing with biological data, the distribution of a data set can provide biologically meaningful clues about a variable within a population. Biological data often naturally follow a normal distribution, in which the data are clustered around a central value and the left and right sides of the distribution are symmetrical. Uneven data distribution, or skew, could indicate outside forces such as natural selection at work. For example, if measurements of feather length in a population of birds are strongly skewed toward longer feathers, this may indicate that short feathers are at a selective disadvantage. For the MCAT®, assume that all data are normally distributed unless stated otherwise.

Consider the simple data set in Table ii.3. A class of 15 students was given a pop quiz consisting of five multiple choice questions. Table ii.3 contains the scores of each student on the quiz. As a mere collection of numbers, it is difficult to visualize the spread of the data even within this small data set. One technique that can be used to visualize the data is a *frequency distribution*, which displays the frequency of occurrence for each score and can be represented as either a table or a chart. Frequency distributions can be used with both quantitative and qualitative variables. They provide both a way to visualize the data at a glance and the ability to draw some quick inferences. Further insight into the nature of the data set can then be obtained through the use of descriptive statistics such as measures of central tendency and dispersion.

FIGURE ii.3 | Examples of Normal and Skewed Distributions

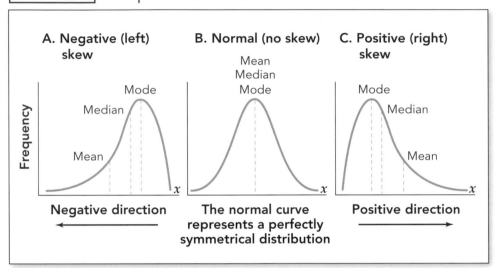

FIGURE ii.4 | Construction of Frequency Distributions

A. Unorganized data

B. Data organized on a number line

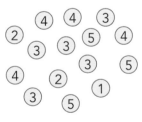
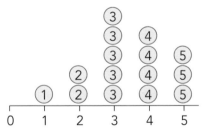

TABLE ii.3 > Data Frequency

4	4	3	5	3
3	2	5	1	2
3	3	4	5	4

Consider the given data set before delving into its descriptive statistics. Is it continuous or discrete? Is it skewed toward one side or fairly symmetrical, and how might this affect measures of central tendency? Are the values clumped together or spread out? When given a chart or a table on the MCAT®, these are the kinds of questions that will give you a quick, intuitive feel for the data at a glance.

C. The above organization is the foundation of a frequency chart.

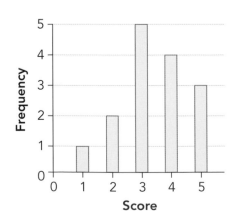

D. A frequency table serves the same purpose.

Scores	Tally	Frequency
0		0
1	I	1
2	II	2
3	ⷭHⷮT	5
4	IIII	4
5	III	3

Measures of Central Tendency

Measures of **central tendency** include various methods of representing the "middle" of the data set. They provide a quick summary by identifying the central position of values within the data set. The most common measures of central tendency include mean, median, and mode. The mean, also called the *average*, generally refers to the arithmetic mean, which is calculated by dividing the sum of all values in the data set by the number of values within the data set. The advantage of the mean as a representation of central tendency is that it minimizes error in predicting any one value in the data set by taking all values into account. However, because of this, the mean is particularly sensitive to the influence of outliers. An *outlier* is a data point that is far away (either higher or lower) from the other values observed or measured. Even just one outlying data point can dramatically skew the mean, making it a less accurate representation of the central position of the majority of data points in the data set.

The mean cannot be used as a measure of central tendency in all data sets. In order for the mean to be a useful representation of central tendency, the difference between values for a variable must also be meaningful (i.e. data must be either interval or ratio).

The **median** of a data set is the middle value once all values have been organized by magnitude. For data sets with an odd number of values, the median is simply the middle value. When a data set contains an even number of values for a particular variable, the median is the average of the two middle values. The median divides the data set in half so that for a particular variable, there are as many values above the median as below it. Unlike the mean, the use of median as a measure of central tendency is appropriate for ordinal data.

The **mode** is the value that occurs most often for a variable in a data set. In other words, it is the most common outcome recorded for that variable. The mode is readily identifiable as the longest bar on a frequency chart or the highest incidence on a frequency table. Mode is the only measure of central tendency that is appropriate to use with nominal data.

Do a self-test to check your understanding of mean, median and mode. Quickly calculate each of the three measures of central tendency for the data set given in Table ii.3. Check your answers on page 60.

TABLE ii.4 > **Measurements of Central Tendency and Appropriate Applications**

Measurement Scale	Definition	Mode	Median	Mean
Nominal	Unordered categories	X	–	–
Ordinal	Ordered categories	X	X	–
Interval	Meaningful intervals between values	X	X	X
Ratio	Meaningful ratios between values	X	X	X

To understand the difference between median and mean, think about how both are affected by outliers. When an outlier value (red dot) is added to the dataset represented by black dots, the median is relatively unchanged. The mean is affected much more strongly.

FIGURE ii.5 | Mean and Median

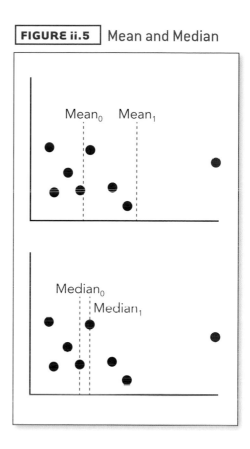

Suppose you have a data set consisting of three numbers: 1, 101, and 102. 101 is the median because it is the middle value of the rank ordered data set, even though it is very far from the mean of the data. In this case, assuming that you believe the outlier value is a meaningful data point, the mean is a better measure of central tendency.

Although the central tendency of any data set resulting from interval or ratio measurement scales can be appropriately explored through mean, median, and mode, the preferred method for non-skewed data is the mean. For interval or ratio data that are skewed or contain outliers, the median is the best measurement. Only median and mode are appropriate for ordinal data, and the central tendency of nominal data can only be represented by mode.

Measures of Dispersion

Measures of dispersion describe how closely clumped together or widely spread apart the values are within a data set. Three of the most commonly used measures of dispersion are range, interquartile range, and standard deviation. The **range** of a data set is calculated by subtracting the value of smallest magnitude from the value of greatest magnitude. To use the example data set of the pop quiz scores, the highest score recorded was a 5 while the lowest score was a 1. The range of the data is therefore $5 - 1 = 4$. If one or more students had scored a zero on the pop quiz, the range of the data would equal 5. A larger range indicates a greater amount of dispersion amongst the data points, while a small range suggests data that are clumped toward a central value.

The interquartile range also uses subtraction to gauge dispersion. To calculate interquartile range, the values in a data set must be organized by magnitude and quartiles must be determined. Just as the median divides a frequency distribution in half, quartiles divide a distribution into four equal parts. The distribution is divided into quartiles at the 25%, 50%, and 75% points. These are known as the first, second, and third quartiles, respectively. Note that the second quartile is the middle value, so it is equal to the median. The **interquartile range** is calculated by subtracting the value of the first quartile from that of the third quartile. Interquartile range provides a summary of the amount of dispersion present in the middle half of the data. Trimming the upper 25% and lower 25% of the data from analysis eliminates the influence of any outliers.

Calculating standard deviation is more mathematically rigorous than the calculations for range and interquartile range, but the underlying principles are the same. Like range and interquartile range, **standard deviation** is a measure of the dispersion of values in a data set, and is expressed in the same units as the values themselves. Unlike these statistics, the calculation for standard deviation takes each value into account and assesses how far, on average, values are from the mean value. The difference between each value in the data set and the mean is calculated and then squared. The standard deviation is then obtained by calculating the mean of these squared values and, finally, taking the square root of the result. A large standard deviation indicates widely dispersed data, while a small standard deviation indicates more tightly grouped values around a central point.

Measures of central tendency establish approximately where the values of a data set exist along a number line, but they provide no information about how tightly those values are grouped together. In descriptive statistics, a measure of central tendency is most often used together with a measure of dispersion to provide a more complete picture of the data set. By summarizing how clumped or spread out the data are, the measure of dispersion indicates how well the measure of central tendency approximates individual values in the data set. A single, representative central value, such as a mean or a median, will more accurately reflect individual values in a data set that is crowded toward that middle value than it will if the data are widely dispersed over a large range.

FIGURE ii.6 | Range and Interquartile Range

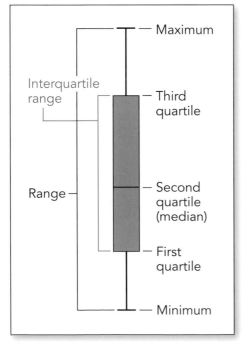

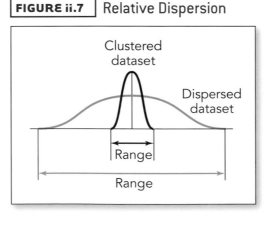

FIGURE ii.7 | Relative Dispersion

The MCAT® will NOT require you to calculate a standard deviation. You only need to be generally familiar with where this value comes from and what it represents. Remember, a greater standard deviation means data are more dispersed.

Common Statistical Tests

Examining Relationships between Variables

In scientific inquiry, statistics are used to determine whether the data collected support or refute the hypothesis of the experiment. Statistical tests generally address the question of how likely (or unlikely!) is it that any differences between the observed data and hypothesized outcomes have occurred by chance alone. When statistical tests indicate that any differences observed are very unlikely to have occurred by simple chance, the general assumption is that variables within the experiment must have some effect on each other. This section will briefly cover some of the most commonly used statistical tests and the conditions under which they can be applied.

Experimenters often set out to explore the relationship between an independent variable and one or more dependent variables in a study. Statistical tests can address the question of whether the values for one variable display a reliable pattern with corresponding values for the other variable. For instance, if the independent variable is increased, does the dependent variable reliably increase? Decrease? Or does it have no effect? The tests of this kind that are most likely to appear on the MCAT® are linear regression and correlation. Regression and correlation can be used when the all of the variables examined are continuous rather than categorical. Both of these tests are a way of getting an unbiased, mathematical view of the data. If researchers simply examined the data set on a scatter plot and attempted to spot a relationship between the variables, they might think that they observe the hypothesized relationship between variables, even if it is not truly present in the data set. Regression and correlation provide an accurate view of the existence and strength of a relationship between variables.

Simple *linear regression* describes the degree of dependence between one variable and another and is often used as a predictive tool. In linear regression, data are usually displayed in a scatter plot, such as the one in Figure ii.8, with the independent (explanatory) variable on the x-axis and the dependent (responsive) variable on the y-axis. For an example of when linear regression might be used, consider that a researcher records observations of 100 lizards, measuring both ambient temperature and how many centimeters each lizard moved in a one hour period. Linear regression addresses the question of whether differences in ambient temperature will influence how far a lizard has moved in an hour by fitting a straight line (the line of best fit) to the data. Once an equation for the line of best fit is determined, the linear regression model can be used to estimate values for the dependent variable based on known values of the independent variable. Based on this model, a researcher might be able to predict that a lizard placed in a room at 40°C will move approximately 17 cm in an hour.

The MCAT® will not ask you to perform any of these statistical tests! You may be asked to interpret the meaning of such tests if their results are presented in a passage, or to identify which tests are appropriate given a collection of data, questions, and hypotheses.

It is important to note that while linear regression makes an assumption about a one-way influence of one variable on another, it does not provide any information on causality. Even if a linear regression shows that lizards tend to move more in warmer temperatures, it does not say why that is the case. One researcher might argue that cold-blooded animals have more energy to move when they are warmer, while another might speculate that at high temperatures the floor becomes uncomfortable on the lizard's feet if it stays still too long. The point is that linear regression describes a mathematical relationship between two variables, but does not provide insight about why that relationship exists.

Correlation is similar to regression in that it also examines relationships between variables. However, unlike regression, correlation makes no assumptions about which variable is exerting influence on the other. Correlation estimates the degree of association between two variables with an outcome called a *correlation coefficient*. A correlation coefficient is a measure of linear association between two variables. The value of a correlation coefficient can vary between –1 and 1. If all values on a scatter plot fit perfectly on a line with positive slope, the correlation coefficient is equal to 1. Similarly, a correlation coefficient of –1 indicates a perfect linear relationship with negative slope between two variables. A correlation coefficient of 0 indicates no relationship between two variables whatsoever. Correlation only provides information on the degree of association between two variables without providing insight on causality.

FIGURE ii.8 | Correlation Coefficient

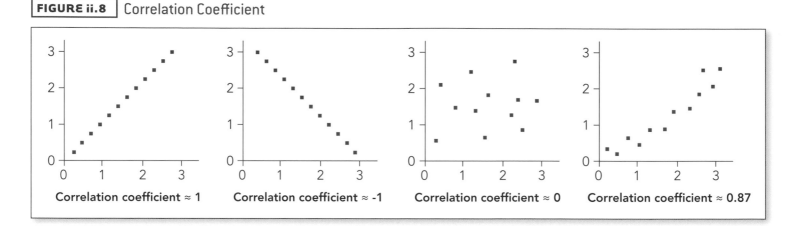

Correlation coefficient ≈ 1   Correlation coefficient ≈ -1   Correlation coefficient ≈ 0   Correlation coefficient ≈ 0.87

Regression and correlation are similar and sometimes confused with each other. Regression assumes that one variable influences another, while correlation simply describes the relationship between two variables without assuming the direction of influence or even the existence of influences at all. Let's consider two data sets to illustrate the difference between regression and correlation. One data set seems to indicate a relationship between leg length and arm length in adult men. However, it does not make sense to assume that longer arms cause legs to be longer. Nor does it make sense to assume that longer legs cause arms to be longer. We do not know which (if either) of these variables influences the other. It is possible that neither of these variables affects the other and both are controlled by outside influences. In this example, correlation would be an appropriate test to show that arm length and leg length tend to be correlated in men. For the second data set, consider the data recording inches of rainfall and maximum height of wheat grown during each of 50 consecutive years. We can make the assumption that rainfall may have some effect on wheat growth and test this hypothesis with a regression analysis. Correlation would not be appropriate in this case because no matter how high the wheat grows, it is not likely to make it rain more.

FIGURE ii.9 | Regression and Correlation

The variables leg length and arm length can be analyzed using correlation because neither causes the other. The lack of a clear independent and dependent variable means that a graph examining these two variables can assign either variable to either axis. By comparison, a change in rainfall may cause a change in wheat height, but a change in wheat height is not likely to cause a change in rainfall. By convention, the independent variable, rainfall, is placed on the x-axis while the dependent variable, wheat height, is on the y-axis. A regression should be used to explore a possible causal relationship between rainfall and wheat height.

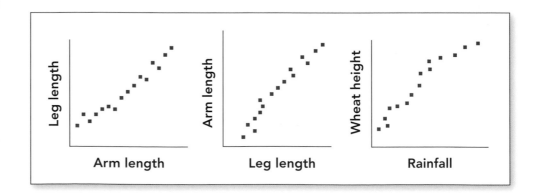

Hypothesis Testing

As discussed earlier in this section, statistical tests are often used to either support or refute specific hypotheses of the experiment. For these statistical tests, the default assumption or *null hypothesis* is that there is no difference between the observed results and those expected if the independent variable has no effect. Statistical tests are used to assess the likelihood that any differences found are attributable to chance. When the tests indicate that the observed results are likely to be the result of chance (within the realm of likely variation), the null hypothesis is accepted. When tests indicate that the results diverge from the expected in a way that is very unlikely to be due to chance alone, the null hypothesis is rejected and the *alternative hypothesis* is adopted. The following section examines the three most common statistical tools for hypothesis testing: the chi-square analysis, t-test, and analysis of variance.

The *chi-square test* (χ^2) can only be used when all variables in question are categorical. It shows whether two distributions of categorical data differ from each other. The chi-square test is often employed to determine whether the observed distribution of a categorical variable differs from the expected distribution for that variable. As an example, a researcher recreating Mendel's experiments with pea plants might expect that plants resulting from the self-pollination of heterozygotes would exhibit a 3:1 ratio of purple to white phenotypes. If the researcher produces 400 second generation offspring, the expected results would be 300 plants with purple flowers and 100 plants with white flowers. When the researcher tallies the actual incidence of purple vs. white flowers, she finds 228 with purple flowers and 172 with white flowers. The results are different than what was expected, but are they different enough to indicate that other forces are influencing flower color, or could this variation from the expected have occurred by chance? This kind of question, because it deals with tallies of categorical responses, can be addressed with a chi-square test. In this case, the null hypothesis and alternative hypothesis would be as follows:

Null hypothesis (H_0): The tally of purple and white flowers do not differ significantly from the expected ratio of 3:1.

Biological Molecules and Enzymes
≡ BIOLOGY 1

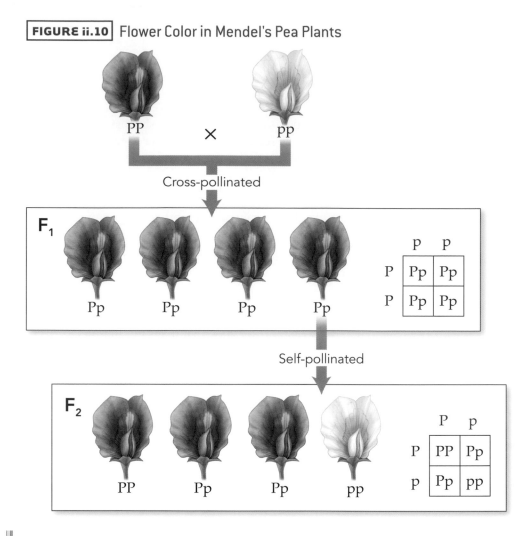

FIGURE ii.10 Flower Color in Mendel's Pea Plants

Alternative hypothesis (H_1): The tally of purple and white flowers do differ significantly from the expected ratio of 3:1.

If the alternative hypothesis is accepted, it suggests to the researcher that outside variables were most likely involved in influencing the flower color results.

The *t-test* compares the mean values of a continuous variable (the dependent variable) between two categories or groups (where group membership is the independent variable). Suppose that a researcher records the body temperatures of 100 people at rest. A t-test could be used to determine whether the average body temperature of those sampled differed significantly from the usual human body temperature of 98.6°F. The null hypothesis would be that the average temperature does not differ significantly from 98.6°F. The alternative hypothesis would state that the average temperature does differ significantly from 98.6°F.

In addition to comparing the mean of a group to a specific value, a t-test can also compare the means of two groups. For example, a t-test could be used to evaluate whether the average body temperature of males differed significantly from the average body temperature of females. In this case the categorical groups would be male and female, while the continuous variable would be body temperature.

A t-test is called one-tailed or two-tailed depending on the nature of the questions asked. A *two-tailed t-test* is used to explore the possibility of a relationship in both directions. Using the above example, if a researcher had no reason to believe that either women have a higher body temperature than men or that men have a higher body temperature than women, she would use a two-tailed test to allow for both options. However, suppose the researcher had seen previous research suggesting that men have a higher body temperature than women and wanted to see

Genetics
BIOLOGY 1

if her data support that claim. She would use a one-tailed t-test because she is only interested in whether the body temperature of men is higher than that of women, and is not interested in whether it might be lower. Compare the null and alternative hypotheses for such tests:

ONE TAILED:

H_0: The body temperatures of men and women are equal.

H_1: The body temperatures of men are higher than the body temperatures of women.

TWO TAILED:

H_0: The body temperatures of men and women are equal.

H_1: The body temperatures of men and women are not equal.

The advantage of a two-tailed test is that it explores the possibility for difference in both directions. The advantage of a one-tailed test is that it has greater *statistical power* and is therefore more sensitive and able to recognize differences between groups.

The t-tests described above are more specifically known as *unpaired* or *independent sample* t-tests. In contrast, a *paired t-test* compares the distributions of two groups when each value within a group has a natural partner in the other group. A paired t-test can be used in many experimental setups, but it is commonly used for before-and-after studies. For instance, if a study is trying to determine whether a new medication is effective at lowering blood pressure, the researchers may record "before" and "after" values of each participant's blood pressure. The blood pressures of the participants before medication will probably vary considerably. With so much variation within groups, it can be difficult to detect differences between the groups without a very large sample size. A paired t-test can be used to evaluate whether there is a significant difference in blood pressure between groups (before vs. after treatment) by taking into account that the individual values within the groups are paired, in that they come from the same participant.

As described above, t-tests are useful for a wide variety of experimental setups and can address many types of research questions by comparing the means of two groups. However, in some cases researchers need to compare data from more than two groups simultaneously. For instance, suppose a team of researchers designs a study to explore how diet effects cholesterol levels in rats. They randomly assign the rats into four groups, each of which is fed a different diet. At the end of six weeks, the researchers want to compare the mean cholesterol levels between the four groups of rats. This requires an *analysis of variance*, more commonly known as an *ANOVA*. An ANOVA is very similar to a t-test. It is used to compare the distributions of a continuous variable (cholesterol level) between the groups of a categorical variable (diet type). Like a t-test, ANOVAs begin with the null hypothesis that there is no difference between test groups. The distinction between an ANOVA and a t-test is that a t-test can only be used to analyze differences between two groups, while an ANOVA can be used when three or more groups are present.

Remember that t-tests and ANOVAs are used to answer the same kinds of questions, but when you are looking for differences between two groups or one group and a specific value, use a t-test. When you are looking for differences between three or more groups, use an ANOVA.

Much of the information about statistical tests is background knowledge that will not be directly tested on the MCAT®. This table has everything you need to know if asked to choose a statistical test for a data set described in a passage.

TABLE ii.5 > Common Statistical Tests

Test	Test statistic	Variables	Used to...	Example research question
Regression	N/A	All continuous	Determine whether an independent variable influences a dependent variable	Do hot chocolate sales vary with temperature?
Correlation	N/A	All continuous	Determine whether change in one variable is reliably associated with change in another variable	Does the number of books read by a person correlate to his/her reading speed?
Chi-square	χ^2	All categorical	Determine whether two distributions of categorical variables differ from each other (often comparing expected and actual results)	Does political affiliation differ by state?
t-test	t	1 continuous (DV); 1 categorical (IV, with 2 groups)	Determine whether two groups differ in their distributions of a single variable	Do men and women differ in IQ?
ANOVA	F	1 continuous (DV); 1 categorical (IV, with 3 or more groups)	Determine whether three or more groups differ in their distributions of a single variable	Do students learn best in low light, medium light, or bright light?

ii.6 | Results: Interpreting Data

Test Statistics

Hypothesis-testing statistics use mathematical calculations to compare the observed results to the expected results. The calculations involved in these statistical techniques are beyond the scope of the MCAT®. However, the numbers produced by the calculations indicate to researchers whether the null hypotheses of their experiments should be accepted or rejected. The end of these calculations produces a number known as a test statistic. The symbols representing the relevant test statistic for the chi-square, t-test, and ANOVA are χ^2, t, and F, respectively.

The calculated test statistic can be compared with a known likelihood distribution for that test statistic, such as the one shown of the student's t distribution in Figure ii.11. Each distribution represents the relative probability of all possible values for a given test statistic. The distributions follow a normal (bell) curve, where the center of the distribution represents the most likely outcome for the test statistic while the tails represent significantly less likely outcomes. Because all possible outcomes are represented, the area under the curve is equal to 1 (or 100 percent of outcomes). The area under the curve to the right of any specific value of t represents the likelihood of obtaining that value of t by chance and is represented by the symbol p.

Interpreting p Values

A *p value* is usually presented in any results summarizing statistical hypothesis testing. Interpreting the p value of a statistical test is how scientists decide if their data support or refute the hypotheses of their experiments. To see how p values are interpreted, examine the second part of Figure ii.11. In this graph, the likelihood of obtaining the given value of t is p = 0.3, or 30%. Whether any particular p value indicates a significant difference between the groups studied is open to interpretation. Most people would consider a 30% probability of any differences between groups occurring purely by chance to be a large probability, so they would likely not reject the null hypothesis. In other words, they would conclude that there were no differences between the groups studied. By contrast, Figure ii.11 also displays an example where p = 0.04. A 4% chance of differences between groups occurring by chance would be a low enough likelihood to convince many people that there are actual differences between the groups. Research studies generally set a "cut-off" point for p values they will consider statistically significant before beginning statistical analysis so the researchers' ideas about significance will not be biased by the results. The most common cut-off is p < 0.05, or a 5% probability of results occurring by chance, although many studies also use a value of p < 0.01 for a more conservative approach. When a test returns a p value below the established cut-off point, the test is said to have reached **statistical significance** and the null hypothesis is rejected.

> When used in everyday language, the word significant simply means that something is important or meaningful. When used in the context of statistics, significance has a very specific meaning: the p value returned from a statistical test indicates that there are differences between groups tested that are unlikely to be due to chance.
>
> The information in this section about how a p value is determined provides a useful background, but on the MCAT® you will likely just be asked to interpret a given p value. Remember, when a p value is SMALL, the difference between groups is SIGNIFICANT.

FIGURE ii.11 The Student's t Distribution and p Values

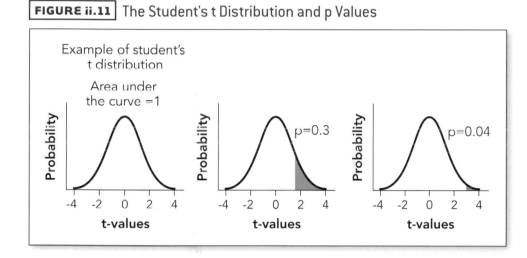

Uncertainty and Error in Statistics

Because all measurements are subject to error, error exists in any collection of data. One measure of error is standard deviation. Recall that standard deviation is a measure of how far values in a sample tend to fall from the mean of the sample. A small standard deviation indicates greater precision in data collection. Similar to standard deviation is *standard error*. The mean of one sample is unlikely to equal the population mean, but the distribution of means from many samples provide an estimate of the population mean. The standard deviation of a distribution of sample means is known as standard error and provides an estimate of the accuracy with which a sample represents a population.

Because of error, estimated values may not accurately reflect true values. Therefore, researchers often describe the **uncertainty** of their findings by including a range of values within which the true value is likely to fall. **Confidence intervals** use a normal distribution to provide an estimated range of values that is likely to include the true value. Similar to hypothesis testing, establishing the correct distributions for estimating uncertainty is dependent on sample size of the study. Most commonly, researchers employ a 95% confidence interval, meaning that there is a 95% chance that the true value lies between the upper and lower limits of the interval. However, other *confidence levels,* including 90% and 99%, are also common.

ii.7 | Results: Drawing Conclusions from Data

As described above, statistical methods are useful tools to organize data, recognize patterns, and identify relationships between variables. However, to obtain results from the data, the researcher must interpret the outcomes of the statistical tests. It is through this interpretation that scientists are able to answer research questions and draw conclusions from the results of their studies. Validity describes the degree to which conclusions based on the study's data are warranted. Studies have different levels of internal and external validity based on aspects of study design.

Internal validity is the degree to which a causal relationship between the independent and dependent variables is demonstrated. When asked to interpret data on the MCAT®, it is important to critically consider what elements of causality can reasonably be inferred as a result of the experimental setup and data analysis. A relationship between variables does not mean that some form of causality can automatically be assumed. This idea is often described by saying that "correlation is not causation." A correlation between variables must be present for the possibility of causality to even be considered, but correlation does not automatically mean that there is a causal relationship.

Confounding variables are a common threat to internal validity. A *confounding variable* (or "confounder") is a variable that is correlated with the independent variable and has a causal effect on the dependent variable. Suppose that a researcher wanted to see if exposure to sunlight effects running speed in white rats. If she placed all of the largest rats into one grouping for level of sun exposure, and size is correlated with running speed, size would be a confounding variable.

The best way to minimize the effects of both known and unknown confounders is to use **random assignment** to divide participants into different treatment groups. This means that differences between the research subjects that are not being measured or manipulated by the researchers, and thus could act as confounding variables, are evened out across the groups. In practice, the requirement of random assignment means that experimental methods can lead to inferences of causality but non-experimental methods cannot. In other words, if the researchers observe the effect of the independent variable after the fact rather than actually controlling the independent variable, correlation is the most that can be concluded.

MCAT® THINK

The issue of inferring causality often arises in social science research, which tends to be interested in variables that cannot be controlled by researchers for ethical or practical reasons. For example, suppose a social science researcher is interested in the effect of the quality of environmental stimulation on neurological development in youth. An experimental study design could take young children and randomly assign them to enriched or deprived environments and then measure neurological development. Obviously, such a study cannot actually be carried out, and the researcher will choose an observational method that can at least establish a correlation between the variables of research. (In fact, in the actual study on which this example is based, the researchers chose to use an animal model so that random assignment could be used. As a result, inferences of causality were possible.)

Random assignment makes it unlikely that an unknown third variable is responsible for any relationship that is found between the dependent and independent variable. However, the question of which variable has a causal influence on the other still needs to be resolved. To conclude that the independent variable has a causal influence on the dependent variable, the condition of temporality must be met. **Temporality** means that the cause comes before the effect. In other words, variable A can only cause a change in variable B if it happens before the observed change.

Temporality is a very simple concept, but understanding how the need for temporality to establish causation influences the progress of research is not as intuitive. Consider the following hypothetical example: a researcher in the lab observes that at the end of embryological development, chick embryos producing high levels of protein X also have particularly large beaks. In other words, a correlation has been observed. The researcher can use statistical analysis to describe the data and confirm that there is a correlation, but there is no way to know whether a rise in the level of protein X during development actually caused an increase in beak size. Another possible explanation is that a larger amount of beak tissue causes an increase in the production of protein X. To address the question of which change might cause the other, the researcher must determine which came first: an increase in the level of the protein or the development of unusually large beaks. The researcher might observe a new batch of chicks, recording both protein X level and beak volume every day throughout development. The researcher finds that when embryos experience a rise in protein X, beak size dramatically increases a few days later. Because beak size increases AFTER protein X increases, increased beak size cannot cause increased protein levels. According to the condition of temporality, it is still possible that higher protein levels can cause greater beak size. Simply observing that something happens first is insufficient to establish that it causes what happens later, though. In order to explore causality, the researcher would need to design an experiment in which he would randomly divide a new set of developing embryos into two groups. After taking initial measurements of beak size, the chicks in one group would receive an injection of the protein. If the chicks in this group then developed significantly larger beaks than those of the other group while all other variables were held constant, the researcher could then conclude that protein X causes an increase in beak size.

In summary, prior to inferring that an association represents a causal relationship, a researcher must consider four rival explanations: chance, bias, effect-cause and confounding variables. The first and second explanations suggest that the association was false. False associations due to chance follow from random error resulting in poor precision, whereas those due to bias follow from systematic error resulting in poor accuracy.

The third and fourth explanations, by contrast, maintain that a real association exists but is not a cause-effect relationship. Instead, the relationship may be effect-cause. In other words, the causal relationship may be opposite of the one that was hypothesized. For example, if the hypothesis was that increased coffee consumption leads to hypothyroidism, it may in fact be the case that hypothyroidism leads to increased coffee consumption. Appropriate temporality, where the cause comes before the effect, is required to eliminate the possibility of an effect-cause relationship. Alternatively, the relationship may be confounding, meaning that some third variable associated with coffee consumption leads to hypothyroidism. Random assignment protects against confounding. See Table ii.6 for a summary of the potential explanations for an observed association between variables.

TABLE ii.6 > Explanations for an Observed Association Between Variables X and Y

Explanation	Type of association	Conclusion
Chance (random error)	False	X is not associated with Y
Bias (systematic error)	False	X is not associated with Y
Effect-cause	Real	Y is a cause of X
Confounding	Real	Z is associated with X and is a cause of Y
Cause-effect	Real	X is a cause of Y

The issues with inferring causality all have to do with the internal validity of a study. **External validity**, or generalizability, is the degree to which the results of a study can be generalized to other situations. Remember that scientists select a sample of subjects to study from a larger population. If the sample differs from the larger population in a way that affects the variables of the study, the external validity of the study is reduced. For example, many studies use college students as test subjects, but the results of research performed on a group composed entirely of young, healthy participants may not accurately extrapolate to the population at large. Additionally, external validity diminishes if the conditions of the study cause the subjects to behave differently from the larger population in a way that affects the variables of interest.

Appropriately analyzing data is essential to identifying pertinent results and drawing relevant conclusions. As discussed in the previous section, data analysis can reveal relationships between variables. An ANOVA may indicate that diet affects blood cholesterol level; a correlation analysis could demonstrate that when there is more rain, wheat tends to grow taller. Data analysis can even be used to make predictions that are beyond the scope of the data. For example, through extrapolations of their regression analysis, scientists could speculate that lizards in the hottest climates in the world would tend to be the most active. A well-constructed experimental method combined with careful and appropriate data analysis allows scientists to answer a variety of research questions and to draw conclusions from their data. However, it is also important to recognize that there are limits to the conclusions that can reasonably be drawn from data. These limits are affected by the methods and analysis techniques the researcher chooses, as well as factors beyond their control. Critical thinking about these limits is likely to be tested on the MCAT®.

ii.8 | Reading Research–Based MCAT® Passages and Interpreting Graphs

As you practice reading research-based passages in all of the sciences, you will gain a better understanding of how the knowledge and logic described throughout this lecture will be tested in the context of an actual passage. This section presents a sample passage to demonstrate the process of understanding a research-based passage, including the interpretation of complex graphs. As you read the passage, try to identify the research question, hypothesis, and independent and dependent variables.

Sample Passage I

Insulin resistance is a condition in which cells exhibit a diminished response to insulin, a hormone that promotes glycogen synthesis. In order to overcome this resistance and maintain glucose homeostasis, pancreatic β-cells must produce additional insulin. If β-cells cannot produce a sufficient quantity of insulin, type 2 diabetes, a condition characterized by a failure of insulin to properly maintain glucose homeostasis, results.

Insulin resistance can lead to β-cell failure, and reduction in β-cell mass is relentless in patients with insulin resistance and type 2 diabetes. Why β-cells fail in some individuals is a central issue in diabetes research today.

Glycogen synthase kinase-3β (Gsk-3β) is a serine/threonine kinase that inactivates glycogen synthase (GS), thereby inhibiting glycogen synthesis. Insulin inhibits Gsk-3β, and inactivation of Gsk-3β appears to be the major route by which insulin activates glycogen synthesis. Gsk-3β has been shown to affect many cellular processes, including cell proliferation and apoptosis. When elevated, it can impair replication and increase cell death.

Researchers found that mice missing two alleles of the insulin receptor substrate 2 ($Irs2^{-/-}$) had a 4-fold elevation of Gsk-3β activity, a decrease in β-cell proliferation, and an increase in β-cell apoptosis. $Irs2^{-/-}$ mice are insulin resistant and develop profound β-cell loss, resulting in diabetes.

Researchers hypothesized that decreasing Gsk-3β activity would reduce insulin resistance and increase β-cell mass in $Irs2^{-/-}$ mice. To test this hypothesis they crossed insulin resistant $Irs2^{-/-}$ $Gsk-3\beta^{+/+}$ mice with mice haploinsufficient for Gsk-3β ($Irs2^{+/+}$ $Gsk-3\beta^{+/-}$).

Experiment 1

Insulin resistant mice missing two alleles of the insulin receptor substrate 2 ($Irs2^{-/-}$ $Gsk-3\beta^{+/+}$) were crossed with mice haploinsufficient for Gsk-3β ($Irs2^{+/+}$ $Gsk-3\beta^{+/-}$). Fed blood glucose concentration in wild-type ($Irs2^{+/+}$ $Gsk-3\beta^{+/+}$) mice was compared with that in mice deficient in Irs2 and/or haploinsufficient in Gsk-3β.

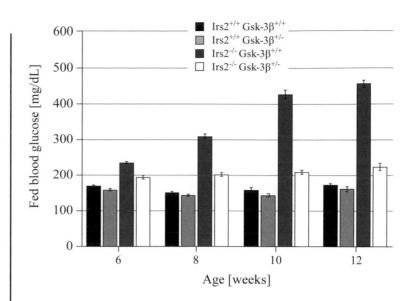

Figure 1 Effects of glycogen synthase kinase-3β genotype and insulin receptor 2 genotype on fed blood glucose concentration at 6, 8, 10 and 12 weeks of age

Experiment 2

β-cell mass in wild-type ($Irs2^{+/+}$ $Gsk-3\beta^{+/+}$) mice was compared with that in mice deficient in Irs2 and/or haploinsufficient in Gsk-3β.

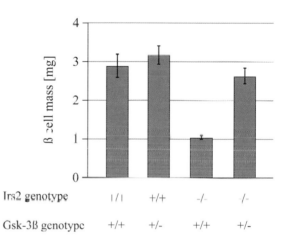

Figure 2 Effects of glycogen synthase kinase-3β genotype and insulin receptor 2 genotype on β-cell mass

This is the type of complex passage that will be found on the MCAT®, but don't panic! With time and practice, it will become easier to interpret a passage in the context of your prior knowledge and gain the new information needed to answer the questions. Similarly to reading CARS passages, as described later in this manual, there are strategies that a reader can use to identify the most important aspects of a passage. As in the given example, it is likely that complex words that you have never seen before will appear in passages. Many students get so hung up on new vocabulary that they forget to apply what they already know. Be confident in your ability to interpret complicated new words and phrases using simpler background knowledge.

An example of the type of narration that a successful test taker uses to understand a research-based passage is given in yellow highlighting on the next page.

Sample Passage I: Successful Narration

Insulin resistance is a condition in which cells exhibit a diminished response to insulin, a hormone that promotes glycogen synthesis. In order to overcome this resistance and maintain glucose homeostasis, pancreatic β-cells must produce additional insulin. If β-cells cannot produce a sufficient quantity of insulin, type 2 diabetes, a condition characterized by a failure of insulin to properly maintain glucose homeostasis, results.

Insulin resistance can lead to β-cell failure, and reduction in β-cell mass is relentless in patients with insulin resistance and type 2 diabetes. Why β-cells fail in some individuals is a central issue in diabetes research today.

Glycogen synthase kinase-3β (Gsk-3β) is a serine/threonine kinase that inactivates glycogen synthase (GS), thereby inhibiting glycogen synthesis. Insulin inhibits Gsk-3β, and inactivation of Gsk-3β appears to be the major route by which insulin activates glycogen synthesis. Gsk-3β has been shown to affect many cellular processes, including cell proliferation and apoptosis. When elevated, it can impair replication and increase cell death. So far there is not enough information to determine the hypothesis or variables of the actual study. This is all background information that the researchers used to develop their question. Think of this section of the passage as the INTRODUCTION. Introduction sections often present two or three phenomena and then give a hypothesis about how they are related. (In this case, the researchers are examining insulin resistance and the activity of Gsk-3β.) Recognizing this standard framework can help with data interpretation. Since the hypothesis of this passage will likely test how Gsk-3β and insulin resistance interact, we should approach any data by asking what they tell us about the relationship between these two variables.

Researchers found that mice missing two alleles of the insulin receptor substrate 2 (Irs2$^{-/-}$) had a 4-fold elevation of Gsk-3β activity, a decrease in β-cell proliferation, and an increase in β-cell apoptosis. Irs2$^{-/-}$ mice are insulin resistant and develop profound β-cell loss, resulting in diabetes. Irs2$^{-/-}$ mice are insulin resistant and develop profound β-cell loss, resulting in diabetes. Irs2$^{-/-}$ is a symbolic description of the genotype. Whenever you see it, think of the associated phenotype: high Gsk-3β activity and insulin resistance. These two aspects of the phenotype are related, since insulin normally inhibits Gsk-3β activity. The overall result of insulin resistance and high Gsk-3β activity will be very low rates of glycogen synthesis.

Researchers hypothesized that decreasing Gsk-3β activity would reduce insulin resistance and increase β-cell mass in Irs2$^{-/-}$ mice. The hypothesis is easy to find and is clearly related to the background research presented by the passage. The independent variable is level of Gsk-3β activity, and the dependent variables are β-cell mass and insulin resistance in Irs2$^{-/-}$ mice. To test this hypothesis they crossed insulin resistant Irs2$^{-/-}$ Gsk-3β$^{+/+}$ mice with mice haploinsufficient for Gsk-3β (Irs2$^{+/+}$ Gsk-3β$^{+/-}$). The unfamiliar term "haploinsufficient" can be interpreted using background information and the symbol for the genotype. "Haplo" means half, as in haploid cells. The genotype shows a +/− which, like the "half,"

indicates one dominant and one recessive allele. Notice that the same name (Gsk-3β) is used for both the enzyme and its related genotype. You can tell them apart based on context and the fact that the genotype is italicized.

Experiment 1

Insulin resistant mice missing two alleles of the insulin receptor substrate 2 (Irs2$^{-/-}$ Gsk-3β$^{+/+}$) were crossed with mice haploinsufficient for Gsk-3β (Irs2$^{+/+}$ Gsk-3β$^{+/-}$). Fed blood glucose concentration in wild-type (Irs2$^{+/+}$ Gsk-3β$^{+/+}$) mice was compared with that in mice deficient in Irs2 and/or haploinsufficient in Gsk-3β. Now we have moved into the METHODS section. The variables in the hypothesis have been operationalized for the purposes of the experiment. Level of Gsk-3β activity has been operationalized as different genotypes that will be associated with different levels of Gsk-3β. Presumably haploinsufficiency for Gsk-3β will be associated with a lower level of Gsk-3β activity. We also know from the passage that the Irs2$^{-/-}$ genotype is associated with high levels of Gsk-3β activity. Insulin resistance has been operationalized as fed blood glucose concentration, since insulin resistance is associated with a failure in blood glucose homeostasis.

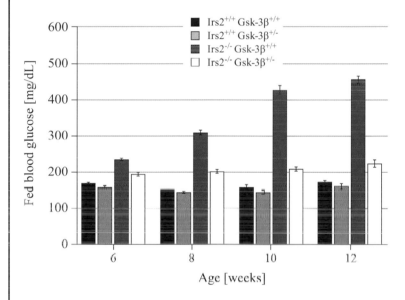

Figure 1 Effects of glycogen synthase kinase-3β genotype and insulin receptor 2 genotype on fed blood glucose concentration at 6, 8, 10 and 12 weeks of age

Once a passage presents a figure, you have moved into the RESULTS section and the primary focus for the rest of the passage will usually be data interpretation. The interpretation of graphical data will be talked about in more detail for Figure 2, but we can get a general sense of the results by considering each category of the independent variable. In an experiment involving genotype, wild type is almost always a control group. In this case, it provides a baseline for fed blood glucose in mice that are not insulin resistant and have normal levels of Gsk-3β. The next group is haploinsufficient for Gsk-3β, meaning that it has lower levels of Gsk-3β, but is wild type for insulin receptor substrate. The graph indicates that this genotype is no different from wild type. The

GO ON TO THE NEXT PAGE.

third group is wild type for Gsk-3β and is missing the two alleles for insulin receptor substrate—that is, it has normal levels of Gsk-3β and is insulin resistant. As expected based on the background research, fed blood glucose levels are much higher than in the previous two groups. Finally, the fourth group allows the researchers to observe blood glucose level in mice who are both insulin resistant and have lowered levels of Gsk-3β. As hypothesized, the result of this genotype is lowered fed blood glucose compared to the group that is insulin resistant and has normal levels of Gsk-3β. However, blood glucose is still elevated compared to the groups that are wild type for insulin receptor substrate.

Experiment 2

β-cell mass in wild-type (Irs2$^{+/+}$ Gsk-3β$^{+/+}$) mice was compared with that in mice deficient in Irs2 and/or haploinsufficient in Gsk-3β. The independent variable in this experiment is the same as in the previous one, but now the other dependent variable of interest, β-cell mass, is being examined. This passage does not contain an interpretation of what the results mean – information you would expect to find in a DISCUSSION section. Most MCAT® passages will not include this information. Instead, the questions will require test-takers to develop their own interpretation of the results.

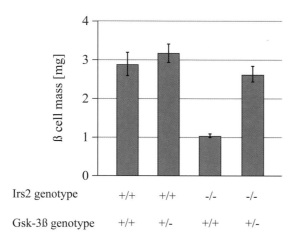

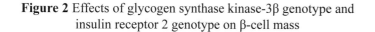

Figure 2 Effects of glycogen synthase kinase-3β genotype and insulin receptor 2 genotype on β-cell mass

STOP.

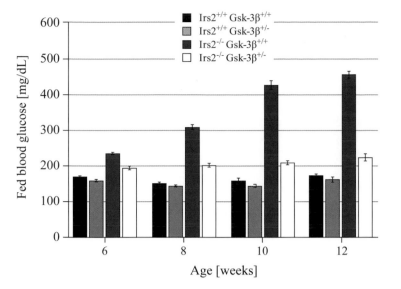

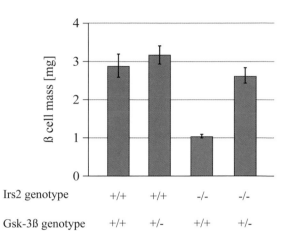

Figure 1 Effects of glycogen synthase kinase-3β genotype and insulin receptor 2 genotype on fed blood glucose concentration at 6, 8, 10 and 12 weeks of age

Figure 2 Effects of glycogen synthase kinase-3β genotype and insulin receptor 2 genotype on β-cell mass

As you can see in Figure 2, research-based passages often use graphs to present the data. This means interpreting these graphs to determine the important findings of the study. Like the passages themselves, the graphs appear intimidating but will get easier to interpret with practice. Use the following method to systematically interpret and extract information from figures:

1) Read the figure and axis titles.

2) Determine what the data suggest.

3) Look at the range of error.

To illustrate, consider Figure 2, taken from the sample passage.

Read the Figure and Axis Titles

At first, ignore the data and look only at the figure and axis titles, using them to determine the overall purpose of the figure.

In this case, the figure title suggests that the independent variable is genotype, since the effects of genotype are being demonstrated. Because two different genes are being considered, there are four categories of the independent variable: 1) wild type for both, 2) altered for both (+/- for Gsk-3β and -/- for Irs2), 3) wild type for Gsk-3β and altered for Irs2, and 4) altered for Gsk-3β and wild type for Irs2. β-cell mass must be the dependent variable, since the graph shows the effects of genotype on β-cell mass. The independent variable should appear on the x-axis, and the dependent variable should appear on the y-axis. This is the case here, indicating that the figure is intended to show how β-cell mass changes according to changes in Irs2 and Gsk-3β genotype. Notice that the four genotype combinations are each represented on the x-axis.

Determine What the Data Suggest

Only after determining the overall purpose of the passage should you attempt to interpret the data. Keeping in mind the background research and hypothesis of the study, examine the graph to see what differences between groups it indicates. This passage suggested that, relative to wild-type mice, those deficient for Irs2 exhibit reduced β-cell mass. Therefore, you might expect β-cell mass to be lower in Irs2$^{-/-}$ mice. The researchers hypothesized that increased Gsk-3β activity contributes to reduced β-cell mass in Irs2 deficient mice. In other words, if the hypothesis is correct, β-cell mass will be lower in Irs2$^{-/-}$ Gsk-3β$^{+/+}$ mice than in Irs2$^{-/-}$ Gsk-3β$^{+/-}$ mice.

The first column indicates that mice wild-type for both *Irs 2* and Gsk-3β (Irs2$^{+/+}$ Gsk-3β$^{+/+}$) have a β-cell mass of approximately 3 mg. By contrast, as indicated by the third column, mice wild-type for Gsk-3β but missing two alleles of Irs2 (Irs2$^{-/-}$ Gsk-3β$^{+/+}$) have a β-cell mass of just 1 mg. Together, the third and fourth columns indicate that, as expected, β-cell mass is lower in Irs2 deficient mice wild-type for Gsk-3β (Irs2$^{-/-}$ Gsk-3β$^{+/+}$) than in those haploinsufficient for Gsk-3β (Irs2$^{-/-}$ Gsk-3β$^{+/-}$).

Look at the Range of Error

Looking at Figure 2, you may have been tempted to conclude that β-cell mass is higher in Irs2$^{+/+}$ Gsk-3β$^{+/-}$ mice than in Irs2$^{+/+}$ Gsk-3β$^{+/+}$ mice. However, the error bars indicate that this conclusion is not warranted. When interpreting a figure, always look at the range of error if it is given.

The T-shaped bars at the top of each column, called error bars, indicate the uncertainty, or possible error, present in each reported measurement. To determine the full range of error, extend the error bar an equal distance below the reported measurement. Eyeballing the range of error can be useful in making quick assumptions about statistical significance. If the ranges of error for two measurements do not overlap, the difference between them is likely to be statistically significant. If there is considerable overlap, then the difference between the two measurements is not significant. A moderate amount of overlap may indicate statistically significant differences or not, and further statistical testing is needed. Furthermore, the size of the error bars indicates the amount of uncertainty. The larger the error bar, the less precise the data are. In summary, be cautious about concluding that there is a statistically significant difference between groups if the error bars are both large and overlapping.

The MCAT® is unlikely to ask questions about ambiguous error bars. In this figure, the ranges of error for columns one and two overlap considerably. For this reason, it would be inappropriate to conclude that β-cell mass is higher in Irs 2$^{+/+}$ Gsk-3β$^{+/-}$ mice than in Irs 2$^{+/+}$ Gsk-3β$^{+/+}$ mice. However, the range of error for column three clearly does not overlap with any of the other columns. This supports the conclusion that, as expected, this group is significantly different from the others.

This lecture contains everything that you need to know to interpret research-based passages and answer questions involving research skills. With every passage that you read, practice finding the hypothesis and the independent and dependent variables. Eventually it will become second nature.

The rest of this manual discusses the skills needed for success on the CARS section. As you will see, the interpretation of CARS passages draws upon the same critical and logical thinking skills that are required for tackling research-based passages.

Learn Key 3: Most science and psychology passages on the MCAT® describe an experimental scenario. They will have a hypothesis, variables, methods, and data. For each passage, identify each of these components of the experiment. If the passage does not spell out the hypothesis, variables, methods or trends in the data, you may be asked to consider the missing components. As you're reading each research-based question, identify whether you're being asked about the hypothesis, methods, or results. Hold the hypothesis in mind when answering research-based questions.

ii.9 | Ethics of Research

The ultimate purpose of research is to create a model that can then be generalized to the real-world phenomena it is intended to represent. The elements of study design that allow scientists to draw conclusions about actual phenomena based on research were discussed earlier in this lecture. In many cases, *ethical guidelines* necessarily place limitations on the models constructed for the purpose of research. The MCAT® is unlikely to feature questions on research ethics, so consider the following largely background information.

One of the most important components of research ethics is the protection of those who are involved as study participants, whether they are humans or other organisms. Any possible risks to participants must be necessary to the purpose of the study, outweighed by the expected benefits, and minimized as much as possible. Some psychological studies, for instance, involve deception, meaning that the participants are not told the truth about some aspect of the study. In most studies, participants are fully informed of the purpose of the study. In deception studies, there is some risk that people will end up participating in an experiment to which they would not have knowingly consented. It is the responsibility of the researcher to minimize risk by telling the participants as much as possible before the experiment, revealing the true purpose afterwards, and providing an opportunity for the subjects to ask questions. To further protect experimental subjects, deception can be used only if telling participants the whole truth prior to the experiment would make it impossible to test the hypothesis. As a final condition, the deception must be justified by the expectation that valuable scientific knowledge will be gained from the study.

In many cases, animal subjects are used in the place of human subjects when it is clear that the benefits of the study do not outweigh the risks to human participants. Any type of experiment that poses permanent damage to the organism will involve animals rather than humans, but the same fundamental ethical consideration of whether the benefits of the study outweigh the risks applies to animal subjects. Researchers using laboratory animals in their research must follow standard guidelines for humane treatment and justify their research design by the expectation of gaining scientific knowledge with significant benefits.

In addition to protecting the rights of study participants, researchers must follow guidelines of *scientific integrity*, or intellectual honesty. Researchers are expected to act with integrity at every step of the research process, from formulating a research question to drawing conclusions and presenting the results to other researchers and the general public. This means that researchers cannot present the ideas and work of others as their own. They also cannot invent data, take measurements that are biased towards their desired result, or intentionally misrepresent the results of their study. In other words, researchers are required to present the actual data that they obtain, whether or not the results of the experiment are what they had hoped to find. This requirement of researchers extends to *protecting the interests of research consumers*. Researchers have a responsibility to report their results accurately to the public, without misrepresenting the data for monetary or any other type of gain.

MCAT® THINK

Stanley Milgram's studies of obedience to authority provide a prominent example of controversy over research ethics. Milgram recruited subjects to participate in a study about how punishment affects learning. The real purpose of his study, inspired by the Holocaust, was to examine people's willingness to break their moral code when ordered to do so by an authority figure. Milgram found that many people were willing to deliver extreme shocks to another participant (who was in fact an actor and did not actually experience shocks) when told to do so. Even though the participants experienced extreme psychological distress, they continued to obey the authority figure and deliver shocks. In this case, the study could not have taken place if the subjects had known its true purpose. However, some argued that the information gained about obedience to authority was not valuable enough to outweigh the stress experienced by the subjects during the experience and the possibility of lasting psychological effects. In other words, they argued that the study was not acceptable according to ethical standards.

Analysis
Applied research
Basic research
Conclusions
Confidence intervals
Dependent variable
Experimental studies
External validity
Hypothesis
Independent variable
Internal validity
Interquartile range

Median
Measurement/data collection
Measures of central tendency
Measures of dispersion
Mode
Natural science
Negative controls
Observational studies
Positive controls
Precision
Question
Random assignment

Random error
Range
Social science
Standard deviation
Statistical significance
Study design
Systematic error
Temporality
Theory
Uncertainty
Variables

MCAT® THINK ANSWERS

Pg. 37: **C is the best answer.** A machine sampling at 1 Hz takes a reading once every second. The question states that during a single second, an electrical impulse in the AV node can travel 0.5 m or 500 mm, more than 10 times the distance covered by a single electrode. Although it is still possible for a single electrode to detect this activity, it is also possible that the impulse could travel completely through the AV node between readings, so choice A can be eliminated. At 10 Hz, or 0.1 seconds between readings (since there are 10 readings per second), an impulse could travel 50 mm between readings. This is slightly larger than the distance sampled by the electrode, so there is still no guarantee that the signal would be detected. Choice B can be eliminated. A 100 Hz detector, which takes readings every 0.01 seconds, would only allow an AV impulse to travel 5 mm between measurements. This is much smaller than the electrodes' receptive field, so detection is guaranteed. A 1000 Hz sampling rate would also guarantee detection, but the question asks for the minimum sampling rate, making choice C the best answer.

Pg. 45: **D is the best answer.** It is important to know the features and limitations of different research methods, including observational studies like surveys. The main limitation of observational studies is that they cannot demonstrate causality, only correlation. For this reason, a researcher could not correctly conclude that majoring in a social science causes any outcome, and choice D is not supported.

Answers to sidebar on page 41:

Mean: 3.4

Median: 3

Mode: 3

DON'T FORGET YOUR KEYS

1. In an experimental setup, the independent variable is manipulated and the dependent variable is measured and/or observed.

2. Correlated factors do not necessarily indicate a causal relationship.

3. Narrate research-based passages and questions: identify the hypothesis, variables, methods, and results. Interpret the data as it relates to the hypothesis.

Introduction to CARS: Strategy and Tactics

1.1 Introduction

1.2 Studying for the CARS Section

1.3 The Examkrackers Approach: Strategies for Success

1.4 The Examkrackers Method: Test-Taking Tactics

1.1 Introduction

The *Critical Analysis and Reasoning Skills* (CARS) Section of the MCAT® (formerly known as Verbal Reasoning) is composed of nine passages, averaging 500–600 words per passage. Five to seven multiple-choice questions follow each passage for a total of 53 questions. Answers to these questions do not require information beyond the text of the passage. The test taker has 90 minutes to complete the entire section.

Topic Areas Covered by CARS passages

CARS passages are excerpted from books, magazines, journals, and other sources, and they cover a wide variety of disciplines from the humanities and social sciences. These disciplines are laid out in Tables 1.1 and 1.2. All the information that you need to know to answer test questions is contained in the passages and question stems; no outside knowledge is necessary. That said, familiarity with the subject areas will make reading CARS passages more fluid. Use the table as a guide to acquaint yourself with the subject areas by looking up the basic definition and interests of each field. Some students taking the MCAT® may have a broad liberal arts background and feel comfortable with all of these topics; others may need to gain familiarity with several of these areas. A good way to gauge your understanding is to imagine yourself in a conversation with someone who is completely unfamiliar with the topic area. Practice giving a brief definition of the field. In addition, imagine several potential MCAT® topics beyond what is listed in the table. If you can do that, you are ready for whatever the MCAT® throws at you.

THE 3 KEYS

1. Energy, Focus, Confidence, Timing. Remind yourself of these strategies before each practice test and evaluate after.

2. Use the Tactics every step of the way from passage to questions to answer choices.

3. Read CARS passages for the author's view, not your own. Answer CARS questions as though you were the author.

TABLE 1.1 > Humanities Disciplines in CARS Passages

Topic
Architecture
Art
Dance
Ethics
Literature
Music
Philosophy
Popular Culture
Religion
Theater
Studies of Diverse Cultures

TABLE 1.2 > Social Science Disciplines in CARS Passages

Topic
Anthropology
Archaeology
Economics
Education
Geography
History
Linguistics
Political Science
Population Health
Psychology
Sociology
Studies of Diverse Cultures

*These lists are not exhaustive. Other humanities and social science disciplines may be discussed in CARS passages.

Other CARS Strategies

Dogma about the CARS section is abundant and free, and that is an accurate reflection of its value. There are many cockamamie CARS strategies touted by various prep companies, academics, and well-wishers. **We strongly suggest that you ignore them.** Some test prep companies design their CARS strategy to be marketable (to make money) as opposed to being efficient ("raising your score"), the idea being that unique and strange will be easier to sell than commonplace and practical.

If your college professor hasn't taken the MCAT®, why would you take his advice on it?

Some colleges offer classes designed specifically to improve reading comprehension in the MCAT® CARS section. Typically, such classes resemble English 101 and are all but useless at improving your score. They are often taught by well-meaning humanities professors who have never even seen a real MCAT® CARS section. Being a humanities professor does not qualify you as an expert on the MCAT® CARS section. The emphasis in such classes is usually on detailed analysis of what you read, rather than how to eliminate wrong answers and find correct answers. Improvements are predictably miserable.

There are those who will tell you that a strong performance on the CARS section requires speed-reading techniques. This is not true. Most speed-reading techniques actually prove to be an impediment to score improvements by shifting focus from comprehension to reading technique. It is unlikely that you will improve both your speed and comprehension in a matter of weeks. As you will soon see, speed is not the key to a good score on the CARS section. Finishing the CARS section is within the grasp of everyone who follows the advice given in this manual.

A favorite myth among MCAT® students is that copious amounts of reading will improve scores on the CARS section (formerly on the Verbal Section). This myth originated years ago when prep companies having insufficient practice materials suggested that their students "read a lot" rather than use the other companies' materials. The myth has perpetuated itself ever since. "Reading a lot" is probably the least efficient method of improving your CARS score. If you intend to take the MCAT® four or five years from now, you should begin "reading a lot." If you want to do well on the CARS section this year, follow the guidelines given in this manual.

Take Our Advice

Most smart students listen to advice, then pick and choose the suggestions that they find reasonable while disregarding the rest. This is not the most efficient approach for preparing to take the MCAT® CARS section. In fact, it is quite counter-productive. Please abandon all your old ideas about CARS and follow our advice to the letter. Do not listen to your friends and family. They are not experts at teaching students how to score well on the CARS section. We are.

Expected Improvement

Taking the CARS section is an art. Like any art form, improvement comes gradually with lots of practice. Imagine attending a class in portraiture taught by a great artist. You would not expect to become a Raphael after your first lesson, but you would expect to improve after weeks of coaching. The CARS section is the same way. With the tools you will learn here and with regular practice, you will see dramatic improvements over time.

1.3 The Examkrackers Approach: Strategies for Success

The rest of this lecture will examine the CARS section from two perspectives: strategic and tactical. The strategic point of view, presented in this section, will describe the general approach to the CARS section and how to study in order to achieve success. The tactical point of view, presented in the following section, will explain exactly how to tackle the passages and questions.

It is extremely important to have a good strategy before you begin the CARS section. The Examkrackers strategy has four components:

1. Maintain energy.

2. Stay focused.

3. Be confident.

4. Mind timing.

Maintain Energy

Pull your chair close to the table. Sit up straight. Place your feet flat on the floor, and be alert. This may seem to be obvious advice to some, but it is rarely followed. Test-takers often look for the most comfortable position in which to read the passage. Do you really believe that you do your best thinking when you're relaxed? Merriam-Webster's Dictionary gives the definition of relaxed as "freed from or lacking in precision or stringency." Is this how you want to be when you take the MCAT®? Your cerebral cortex is most active when your sympathetic nervous system is in high gear, so do not deactivate it by relaxing. Your posture makes a difference to your score.

One strategy used by the test writers is to wear you down with the CARS section before you begin the Biological section. You must mentally prepare yourself for the tremendous amount of energy necessary for a strong performance on the CARS section. Like an intellectual athlete, train yourself to concentrate for long periods of time. It is crucial to improve your reading comprehension stamina. **Practice! Practice! Practice!** always under timed conditions. **And always give 100% effort when you practice.** If you give less than 100% when you practice, you will be teaching yourself to relax when you take the CARS section, and you will be lowering your score. It is more productive to watch TV than to practice with less than complete effort. If you are not mentally worn after finishing three or more CARS passages, you have not tried hard enough, and you have trained yourself to approach the section incorrectly; you have lowered your score. Even when you are only practicing, sit up straight in your chair and attack each passage.

Sit up straight!

Stay Focused

The CARS section is made up of nine passages with both interesting and boring topics. It is sometimes difficult to switch gears from "archaeological evidence of early human migration" to "economic theories of post-Soviet Russia." In other words, sometimes you may be reading one passage while thinking about the prior passage. Learn to **focus your attention on the task at hand.** Methods to increase your focus will be discussed in the section on tactics.

During the real MCAT®, it is not uncommon for unexpected interruptions to occur. People get physically ill, nervous students breathe heavily, air conditioners break down, and lights go out. At some testing centers, people are taking different standardized tests with different schedules of breaks. Your score will not be adjusted for unwelcome interruptions, and excuses will not get you into medical school, so learn to focus and **ignore distractions.**

Know Key 1: Energy, Focus, Confidence, and Timing allow you to perform at your best and achieve a high score. They are gained through practice. Remember that body position affects energy, focus, and confidence. To gain a feel for MCAT® timing, whenever you practice, check the clock once, halfway through the section. Speed up or slow down as needed.

Be Confident

There are two aspects to confidence on the CARS section: 1) **be confident of your score** and 2) **be confident when you read**.

1) CONFIDENCE IN YOUR SCORE Imagine taking a multiple choice exam and narrowing 50% of the questions down to just two answer choices, and then guessing. On a physics exam, this would almost certainly result in a very low grade. Yet this exact situation describes a stellar performance on the CARS section of the MCAT®. Even those who have earned a perfect score (including many of our own students) guessed on a large portion of the answers. The test writers are aware that most students can predict their grades on science exams based on their performance, and that guessing makes science majors extremely uncomfortable. The CARS section is the most dissatisfying in terms of perceived performance. Realize that even the best test takers finish the CARS section with some frustration and insecurity concerning their performance. A perceived dissatisfactory performance early in the testing day is likely to reflect poorly in scores on the Biological and Psychosocial sections if you let your confidence waver. Instead, assume that you have answered every question of the CARS section correctly and get psyched to ace the Biological section.

You the man!

2) CONFIDENCE WHEN YOU READ The second aspect of confidence concerns how you read CARS passages. Read the passages as if you were a Harvard professor grading high school essays. Read critically. If you are confused while reading the passage, assume that it is the passage writer, not you, who is at fault. If you find a contradiction in the reasoning of the argument, trust in your reasoning ability and that you are correct. The questions will focus on the author's argument, and you must be confident in your understanding of the strong and weak points. In order to identify the strong and weak points, you must read with confidence, even arrogance.

Mind the Timing

Generally speaking, timing can be broken down into three smaller components:

1) **start with a five second break;**

2) **read and attempt every passage and every question, in order;**

3) **check time only once and finish with 5 minutes left.**

1) THE FIVE SECOND BREAK If we observed a room full of MCAT® test takers just after beginning a section, we would see many students read for 20 to 30 seconds, pause, and then begin rereading from the beginning. Why? Because as they race through the first passage, they are thinking about what is happening to them ("I'm taking the real MCAT®! Oh my God!"), and not thinking about what they are reading. They need a moment to become accustomed to the idea that this MCAT® section has actually begun. They need a moment to focus. However, they do not need 20 to 30 seconds! They take so much time because they are trying to do two things at once: calm themselves down and understand the passage. They end up accomplishing neither. This loss of concentration may also occur at the beginning of each new passage, when the test-taker may still be struggling with thoughts of the previous passage while reading the new passage.

If we continued to observe the test-takers, we would see them in the midst of a passage suddenly stop everything, lift up their head, stretch, yawn, or crack their knuckles. Their beleaguered minds are forcing them to take a break. No one has an attention span 90 minutes long. If you do not allow yourself a break, your mind will take one. How many times have you been reading a passage when suddenly you realize that you were not concentrating? You're forced to start the passage over. More time is wasted.

There is a simple method to prevent all this lost time. Instead of taking breaks at random, inconvenient moments, plan your breaks. **Before each passage, including the first passage, take five seconds to focus your thoughts.** Remind yourself to forget the last passage and all other thoughts not related to the task at hand. Remind yourself to sit up straight, concentrate, and focus. For these five seconds, look away from the page, stretch your muscles and prepare to give your full attention to the next passage. Then begin and do not break your concentration until you have finished answering all the questions to that passage. The five second break is like a little pep-talk before each passage.

Unfortunately, most students will not take the five second break. Understand one thing. All students will take breaks during the CARS section. Most will take them without realizing it, and most will take them at inopportune moments. If your goal is to get the highest CARS score of which you are capable, you should take the five second break at planned intervals.

These strategies regarding focus, confidence, and taking a five second break are useful for every section, not just CARS!

---

2) READ AND ATTEMPT EVERY PASSAGE AND EVERY QUESTION, IN ORDER

If you want a 127 or better on the CARS section, you must read every passage and attempt to answer every question. If you want to go to medical school, you should attempt to score 127 on the CARS section. That means you need to read every passage in the order given and attempt every question.

You don't get penalized for missed questions anyway, so why would you leave a question blank?

Skipping around in the CARS section to find the easiest passages is a marketable strategy for a prep company but an obvious waste of time for you. It is a bad idea that makes a lot of money for some prep companies because it is an easy trick to sell. 'Cherry picking' is an unfortunate carryover from SAT strategy where it works because the questions are prearranged in order of difficulty. On the MCAT®, some passages are difficult to read, but have easy questions; some passages are easy to read, but have difficult questions. Some passages start out difficult and finish easy. You have no way of knowing if a passage is easy or difficult until you have read the entire passage and attempted all of the questions, so 'cherry picking' is a waste of precious time and lowers your score.

If you begin reading a passage and are asking yourself "Should I continue, or should I move on to the next passage? Is this passage easy or difficult?", you are not reading with confidence; you are not concentrating on what the author is saying; you are wasting valuable time. Your energy and focus should be on doing well on each passage, not on trying to decide which passage to do first.

...Three One Thousand
..Four One Thousand
...Five One Thousand

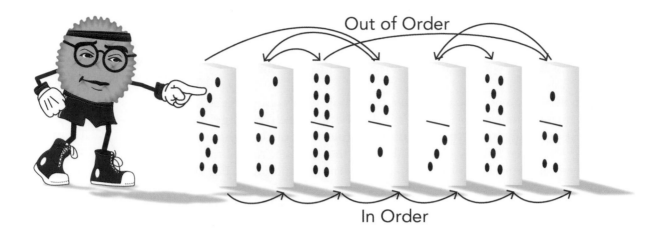

Out of Order

In Order

Hmmm. Let's see. I must knock down all seven dominos. Is it faster and more efficient to knock them down in order, or is it faster to decide which one is heaviest and then run back and forth and knock them down out of order?

---

3) CHECK TIME ONLY ONCE AND FINISH WITH 5 MINUTES LEFT Check your time only once during the CARS section. Constantly checking your time is distracting and not very useful since some passages take longer to finish than others. Instead, **check your time only once, and after you have finished the questions in the fifth passage and associated questions.** You should have about 40 minutes left. A well-practiced test taker will develop an acute sense of timing and will not need to look at the time at all.

Do not spend too much time with the difficult questions. **Guess at them and move on.** Guessing is very difficult for science students, who are accustomed to either being certain of the answer on an exam or getting the answer wrong. Test writers are aware of this, and use it to their advantage. Learn to give up on difficult questions so that you have more time to spend on easier questions. Accurate guessing on difficult questions is one of the keys to finishing the exam and getting a high score. To accurately guess, practice learning to use all of your tools for answering the questions. We will discuss this when we discuss tactics.

Finish the entire section with five minutes to spare, no more, no less. If you have more than five minutes to spare, you missed questions on which you could have spent more time. The stress of exam taking makes you more perspicacious while you take the exam. When you finish an exam, even if you intend to go back and check your work, you typically breathe a sigh of relief. Upon doing so, you lose your perspicacity. The best strategy is to use your time efficiently during your first and only pass through the exam.

Some people have difficulty finishing the exam. These people often think that they cannot finish because they read too slowly. This is not the case. In the next section, we will discuss how finishing the exam does not depend on reading speed: in fact, anyone can finish the exam.

> Many test-takers are able to guess on difficult questions during a practice exam, but when it comes to the real MCAT®, they want to be certain of the answers. This meticulous approach has cost such students dearly on their scaled score. Learn to guess on difficult questions so you have time to answer the easy questions.

Finish the entire section with five minutes to spare.

Use this strategy every time you take a practice CARS section. Before long, it will become second nature.

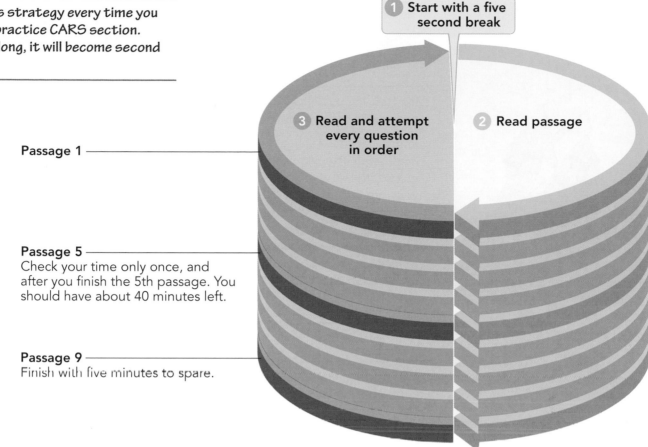

1 Start with a five second break

3 Read and attempt every question in order

2 Read passage

Passage 1

Passage 5
Check your time only once, and after you finish the 5th passage. You should have about 40 minutes left.

Passage 9
Finish with five minutes to spare.

1.4 # The Examkrackers Method: Test-Taking Tactics

The following techniques are designed to increase your pace and efficiency. Practicing them may initially take longer – that is true of learning any skill. Over time these tactics will increase your pace, efficiency, and score. Many students begin to pick and choose CARS methods that they think best suits their own personalities. Please don't do this. Follow our strategies and tactics exactly for each passage and with practice your CARS score will increase.

Reading the Passage

Most test takers have difficulty finishing the CARS section in the 90 minutes allowed. Strangely enough, the vast majority of premeds are capable of reading 5000 words in around 25 minutes. A very slow reader can easily read every word of a 600 word passage in 3 minutes. Try it! It's true! This leaves about 65 minutes to answer the questions, or around 70 seconds per question. In other words, over two thirds of your time is spent answering questions on the MCAT® CARS section, and less than one third is spent reading. If you read TWICE as fast as you do now, you would have about 85 seconds, instead of 70 seconds, to answer each question. So increasing your reading speed has very little effect on your CARS score. If you're not finishing now, you won't be able to finish by reading faster.

90 minutes

| Time spent reading | Time spent answering questions |

It's not your reading speed that you need to improve, it's your efficiency at answering the questions.

Improving your efficiency at answering questions will be more profitable than increasing your reading speed. Improving your efficiency at answering the questions will also give you more time to read the passages. If you increase your reading speed by 10%, a strong improvement, you will only gain 2 and a half minutes on the entire exam. Spread over 53 questions, this allows you less than 3 extra seconds per question. Not too fruitful. If you increase your efficiency at answering questions by 10%, a rather simple task as you will soon see, you gain 6 and a half minutes. This is easily enough time to read one or more entire additional passages!

Work on your efficiency at answering the questions, NOT your reading speed.

So why do so many test-takers fail to finish the CARS section? The answer is that they spend too much time hunting for the answer in the passage, and end up reading the passage many times over. We'll talk more about "looking back" in Lecture 3. For now, just believe us that **you can read every word in the CARS section and easily finish the exam,** so you should.

Have you ever tried skimming through a novel, not reading every word? Try it and see how much you understand. If you do not usually understand much when you skim, why would you skim on the most important test of your life, especially when it won't give you much more time to answer the questions? **Do not skim.**

Have you ever mapped out a novel by writing a brief synopsis alongside each paragraph as you read? Try it. We think you will fall asleep from boredom. You will understand less of what you read, not more. Passages are intended to be read in their entirety as a single work presenting one overriding theme. The MCAT® expects you to understand this theme. The details within the theme are far less important. **Do not distract yourself by taking notes.**

The people that write the MCAT® know that most of us are scientists who like to find the exact answers to questions. Give us a mysterious powder and let us analyze it, and we will tell you exactly what it is. Show us the exact words in a passage as an answer choice and we will probably choose it. Do not fall for this trap. The CARS section tests your ability to detect and understand ambiguities and gray areas, not details. Rely heavily on your main idea and give little weight to details. If you are highly certain of all your answers on the CARS section, you have probably fallen for all of its traps. **Mastering this section is as much an art as a science.** With practice, you will develop a 'feel' for a good MCAT® answer, which will help you move faster through the CARS section. If you teach yourself not to expect the concrete certainty that you get with science questions, you will become more comfortable with the CARS section and your score will increase.

The biggest mistake you can make on the CARS section is to consciously attempt to remember what you are reading. The vast majority of the questions will not concern the details of the passage and will not be answerable by searching the passage for facts. Most questions are about the main idea of the passage. The main idea will not be found in a list of details. In order to learn the main idea, the passage as a whole must be understood. Read the passage the way you would read an interesting novel: **concentrate on the main idea, not the details.**

Remember Key 2: The tactics in this lecture help you read for the main idea in each passage and bring that forward to answer the questions.

Strategies like skimming, taking notes, and skipping around are equally unhelpful on the other sections of the MCAT®.

A tactic often taught by some test prep companies is to read the questions first. Don't do it! You will not remember even one question while you read the passage, much less the 5 to 7 questions that accompany every passage. Not only that, reading the questions first will force you to read for detail, and you will never find the main idea. You will probably end up rereading the passage many times but never straight through. This results in a tremendous waste of time.

Some of the CARS topics will fascinate you and some will bore you. The challenge will be to forget the ones that fascinate you as soon as you move to the next passage, and to pay close attention to the ones that bore you. **Train yourself to become excited and interested in any and every passage topic.** This will increase your comprehension. However, do not become so engrossed in a passage that you slow your pace.

Likewise, **free yourself from outside bias.** We all have outside knowledge and bias that we want to bring into our reading. Although this is natural in real life, do not do it on the MCAT®! CARS passages and questions are designed to be read and answered based solely on the information provided in the passage. If you like or dislike a topic or point of view, your opinion may color your reading. If a topic hits close to home, or if you dislike a subject, it is easy to get distracted, allow your reading to be disrupted, and misunderstand the main idea or author's point of view. Strive to be an open-minded, objective reader for each and every CARS passage. Watch out for incorrect answer choices that are based on commonly held beliefs or even known facts but do not have passage support. The MCAT® may attempt to trick you by presenting topics that have been in the news lately and then offering distractor choices that are true and relevant but beyond the scope of the information presented in the passage.

Do not use fancy speed reading techniques where you search for meaningful words or try to read entire phrases in one thought. This will only distract you from your goal. Read the way you normally read. Your reading speed is unlikely to change significantly in 10 weeks, and your reading speed is not the problem anyway. Finishing the entire section depends on how long you spend answering the questions, not how long it takes you to read the passages. You also cannot assume that the passages are written well enough that you could read just the first and last sentence of each paragraph. They are sometimes barely intelligible even when you read every word.

Read each passage like you are listening to a friend tell you a very interesting story. Allow the details (names, dates, times) to slip in one ear and out the other while you wait with bated breath for the main point. The funny thing about this type of reading is that, when you practice it, you cannot help but remember most of the details. Even if you were to forget some of the details, it only takes about 5 seconds to find a name, number, or key word in a 600 word passage: when you run into a rare question about a detail that you've forgotten, it is easy to find the answer. Another convenient aspect of this tactic is that you are trying to accomplish exactly what the CARS section will be testing: your ability to pick out the main idea. The best thing about this type of reading is that you have practiced it every day of your life. This is the way that you read novels, newspapers, and magazines. Read the passages the way that you read best: read for the main idea.

When I create a great soup, you do not taste the salt, and each spice separately. You must experience the whole soup as a single, wonderful consommé.

Consider a hypothetical political science CARS passage about what social issues are typically important to voters in presidential elections in the U.S. followed by a question about which social issue the author believes is most significant. An incorrect answer choice might involve a controversial issue that featured prominently in recent presidential elections but was not mentioned in the passage. Readers who remember this issue being discussed or feel strongly about it themselves might select this answer. Remember, leave outside information and bias behind!

Aim to clear your cache after every passage, and be a blank slate!

When you read, ask yourself, "What is the author trying to say? What is his point? Is he in favor of idea A or against it? If this author were sitting right in front of me, would he want to discuss idea A or is his real interest in idea B?" **Creating an image of the author in your mind will help you understand him or her.** Use your life experiences to stereotype the author. This will help you make quick, intuitive decisions about how the author might answer each MCAT® question about the passage. Make careful mental note of anything the author says that may not fit your stereotype. Use the stereotype to help guide your intuition on the questions. A typical CARS question might ask, "The author would most likely be in favor of which of the following policies?" For this type of question, your image of the author will guide you to the answer that is most consistent with his or her argument and opinions. Lecture 2 of this manual will demonstrate how creating an image of the author can help you construct the main idea of the passage.

FOLLOW OUR PASSAGE READING TACTICS:

• Don't skim.

• Don't distract yourself by taking notes.

• Concentrate on the main idea, not the detail.

• Don't read the questions first.

• Train yourself to become excited and interested in every passage topic.

• Free yourself from outside bias.

• Don't use fancy speed reading techniques.

• Read each passage like you are listening to a friend tell you a very interesting story. Allow the details (names, dates, times) to slip in one ear and out the other.

• Create an image of the author in your mind.

The Main Idea

As you read the passage, you will construct the main idea that the author is trying to communicate. Then, when you have finished reading a passage, take twenty seconds to state the main idea in the form of one or two complete sentences. Lecture 2 of this manual contains detailed techniques for constructing a main idea. On a timed MCAT®, writing the main idea requires too much time, so spend 20 seconds mentally contemplating the main idea before you begin the questions. After you have completed an entire timed practice exam, scored yourself, and taken a break, go back to each passage and write out the main idea for practice.

Many questions will directly or indirectly test your understanding of the main idea. Consider the following common question type: "Which of the following, if true, would most support the author's argument?" A main idea that includes the major ideas of the passage and the author's opinion will allow you to eliminate answer choices that are irrelevant or contrary to the author's beliefs. Reading the answer choices with your main idea in mind is a powerful way to spot the answer choices that are most in line with the author's beliefs and therefore the strongest answers.

How to Study for the CARS Section

To maximize time available for preparing for the MCAT®, you will want to practice in the most efficient way that will give you the best results. While you learn the Examkrackers method, covered in the next three CARS lectures, use the algorithm below to guide your studying. Through frequent practice using this process, you will learn to analyze passages, questions, and answer choices from every angle. We believe that this is the most effective way to improve your CARS score.

1. Take a CARS test under strict timed conditions and score yourself. Remember to use the test-taking strategies to improve your timing. Early on, you may need to check the time more than once. If you find that you have spent more than 9-10 minutes on a particular passage and its questions, guess and move on.

2. Take a break from CARS for at least one day.

3. Look at the set of questions for the first passage in the CARS exam that you recently finished and examine the questions and answer choices as if you had never read the passage. As Lecture 3 will demonstrate, the questions and answer choices are "tools" that contain extensive information about the author's interests and opinions. Look for clues about the tone (neutral or opinionated?) and topic of the passage.

4. Repeat step 3 for each passage.

5. Take a break from CARS for at least one day.

6. Carefully read the first passage in the same CARS test, and write out a precisely worded main idea in one or two complete sentences being certain that your main idea expresses the author's opinion or stance on the issues.

7. Match your main idea to each question and all the answer choices and see what insights you gain into answering MCAT® questions.

8. For questions that you got wrong, think about what prevented you from selecting the best answer. Did you misinterpret the author's tone or opinion? Did you select an answer choice that took the argument a step too far? Did you rely on outside information or biases that were not supported by passage information? Are you repeatedly missing a certain type of question?

Repeat steps 6, 7, and 8 for each passage.

If you learn our method and use this algorithm for studying, you will see marked improvement in your CARS score. The more you practice, the more you can target your own weaknesses and start to recognize what a strong CARS answer "feels" like. Identifying patterns in the questions that you miss or the incorrect answers that you select will help you avoid the same pitfalls the next time you practice.

"Reading a lot" isn't going to get you a better score on the CARS section. Using the Examkrackers method will. Book clubs, reading, and study groups are a good way to increase your reading comprehension, but are not effective tools for raising your CARS score in a short amount of time.

DON'T FORGET YOUR KEYS

1. Energy, Focus, Confidence, Timing. Remind yourself of these strategies before each practice test and evaluate after.

2. Use the Tactics every step of the way from passage to questions to answer choices.

3. Read CARS passages for the author's view, not your own. Answer CARS questions as though you were the author.

The Main Idea

2.1 Introduction

2.2 Constructing the Main Idea

2.3 A Close Reading: Narrating toward the Main Idea

2.4 Tools for Close Reading on the MCAT®

2.1 Introduction

The main idea is a thematic summary of the passage in one or two sentences. It should reflect the author's opinion (if presented or implied), and it should emphasize minor topics to the same extent that they are emphasized in the passage. It is not a list of topics discussed in the passage, nor is it an outline of those topics. It is a statement about the passage topics, and includes the author's opinion. The main idea does not get bogged down by detail. Instead, it presents the author's overarching point of view, which ties together the most important ideas presented in the passage. A good main idea represents the middle ground that the author eventually reaches after presenting alternative points of view. A good main idea usually does not present an extreme viewpoint. Instead, the main idea, like the passage itself, will settle on a middle ground between opposing perspectives. This idea is explored further in the last lecture of this manual.

In one form or another, 90% of the CARS Section questions will concern the main idea. Notice that the main idea cannot be found by going back to the passage and searching for details. You must concentrate on the main idea while you read the entire passage. If you read for detail and try to remember what you have read rather than processing what you are reading, you will have to guess at 90% of the questions.

It is important to have a clear concept of the main idea before reading any questions. MCAT® CARS Section questions are designed to take your inchoate thoughts concerning the passage and subtly redirect them away from the true main idea. Each successive question embellishes on insidious pseudo-themes steering unwary followers into an abyss from which there is no return. Like a faithful guide, your clearly stated main idea unmasks these impostors and leads you toward the holy grail of CARS Section perfection.

Writing the main idea on paper is an important step toward improving your ability to find the main idea; however, it requires too much time while taking the exam. Instead, a few days after taking a practice exam, go back to each passage and write out the main idea. While taking the exam, pause for 20 seconds after reading a passage and construct the main idea in your head. Say the main idea "out loud" in your head before moving on to the questions.

Most students resist writing out their main idea until they are halfway through the course and the materials. At this point they begin to realize how important the main idea is. Unfortunately, they must start from scratch and begin writing out the main idea with only four weeks until the MCAT®. Don't do this. Start now by going back to used passages and writing out the main idea. **It is very painful at first, but it will get easier, and it will dramatically improve your score.**

The last lecture of this manual will revisit the main idea from the particular perspective of placing ideas in the passage along a continuum between extreme viewpoints.

Remember Key 1: The main idea will reliably help you choose the best answer. If you read passages for the point, you will notice details, identify their purpose, then read on. No need to memorize minutiae.

Because I'm good enough, I'm smart enough and doggone it, people like me!

2.2 | Constructing the Main Idea

A good main idea can be formed as follows:

1. After finishing the passage, write down a list of main topics. Each item should be one to four words long.

2. Choose the most important topics, two or three at a time, and write a short phrase relating them to each other and the passage.

3. Now connect the phrases into one or two sentences which still concern the most important topics but incorporate the other topics as well. Be sure to include the author's opinion if it was given or implied. Try to emphasize each topic to the same extent to which it was emphasized in the passage. This is your main idea. Over time, you will be able to construct the main idea in your head.

Confidence

Often on the MCAT®, passages seem incomprehensible. Don't worry! Remember, most questions are answered correctly by 60% or more of test takers, and only two or three are answered incorrectly by fewer than 40%, so no group of questions will be that difficult. Have the confidence to keep reading. **Do not reread a line or paragraph over and over until you master it.** If a line or paragraph is incomprehensible to you, then it is probably incomprehensible to everyone else, and understanding it will not help your score. Instead, continue reading until you get to something that you do understand. Just get the general sense of what the author is trying to say. Chances are good that this will be enough to answer all the questions. As discussed further in the next lecture, after you read the passage you will have four additional tools to help you answer the questions.

Know Your Author

Become familiar with the author. Who is he or she? Is the author young or old, rich or poor, male or female, conservative or liberal? Do you love or hate this author? Take a guess. Create a picture of the author in your mind. Use your prejudices to stereotype the author. Your harsh judgment of the author is everything to understanding what he is trying to say. The better you understand the author, the easier the questions will be. Read with a critical eye and judge harshly.

Statements presented in the passage will often reflect the author's unique "voice," but they can also represent a counterpoint or a specific example. Knowing your author will allow you to recognize the author's voice. This idea will be explored further later in the lecture.

Once you know the author intimately, when you get to a question, ask yourself "If this author were right here in front of me, how would he or she answer this question?" The way that the author would answer the question is the correct answer.

Details and the Big Picture

There is no reason to remember the details of a passage. They can be found in seconds and are rarely important to answering a question. Instead, focus on the big picture. Ask yourself "What is the author trying to say to me? What's his beef?" The author's 'beef' will be the main idea, and the key to answering 90% of the questions. Read the passage as described in the tactics section of Lecture 1, looking for the author's main point rather than focusing on the details.

STOP!

DO NOT LOOK AT THE FOLLOWING PASSAGE AND
QUESTIONS UNTIL CLASS.

IF YOU WILL NOT BE ATTENDING CLASS, READ THE PASSAGE IN
THREE MINUTES AND ANSWER THE QUESTIONS WHICH FOLLOW.

Passage I

It is roughly a century since European art began to experience its first significant defections from the standards of painting and sculpture that we inherit from the early Renaissance. Looking back now across a long succession of innovative movements and stylistic revolutions, most of us have little trouble recognizing that such aesthetic orthodoxies of the past as the representative convention, exact anatomy and optical perspective, the casement-window canvas, along with the repertory of materials and subject matters we associate with the Old Masters—that all this makes up not "art" itself in any absolute sense, but something like a school of art, one great tradition among many. We acknowledge the excellence which a Raphael or Rembrandt could achieve within the canons of that school; but we have grown accustomed to the idea that there are other aesthetic visions of equal validity. Indeed, innovation in the arts has become a convention in its own right with us, a "tradition of the new," to such a degree that there are critics to whom it seems to be intolerable that any two painters should paint alike. We demand radical originality, and often confuse it with quality.

Yet what a jolt it was to our great-grandparents to see the certainties of the academic tradition melt away before their eyes. How distressing, especially for the academicians, who were the guardians of a classic heritage embodying time-honored techniques and standards whose perfection had been the labor of genius. Suddenly they found art as they understood it being rejected by upstarts who were unwilling to let a single premise of the inherited wisdom stand unchallenged, or so it seemed. Now, with a little hindsight, it is not difficult to discern continuities where our predecessors saw only ruthless disjunctions. To see, as well, that the artistic revolutionaries of the past were, at their best, only opening our minds to a more global conception of art which demanded a deeper experience of light, color, and form. Through their work, too, the art of our time has done much to salvage the values of the primitive and childlike, the dream, the immediate emotional response, the life of fantasy, and the transcendent symbol.

In our own day, much the same sort of turning point has been reached in the history of science. It is as if the aesthetic ground pioneered by the artists now unfolds before us as a new ontological awareness. We are at a moment when the reality to which scientists address themselves comes more and more to be recognized as but one segment of a far broader spectrum. Science, for so long regarded as our single valid picture of the world, now emerges as, also, a school: a *school of consciousness*, beside which alternative realities take their place.

There are, so far, only fragile and scattered beginnings of this perception. They are still the subterranean history of our time. How far they will carry toward liberating us from the orthodox world view of the technocratic establishment is still doubtful. These days, many gestures of rebellion are subtly denatured, adjusted, and converted into oaths of allegiance. In our society at large, little beyond submerged unease challenges the lingering authority of science and technique, that dull ache at the bottom of the soul we refer to when we speak (usually too glibly) of an "age of anxiety," an "age of longing."

Source: Adapted from T. Roszak, The Making of a Counter Culture. 1969 Doubleday.

Answer the following questions without going back to the passage. If you do not know the answer, guess.

YOU MAY NOT LOOK AT THE PASSAGE!

- Is the author male or female?
- Does the author have long or short hair?
- How old is the author?
- What political party is the author a member of?
- Would the author prefer a wild party or a night at the opera?
- Do you think you would like the author?
- What does the author do for a living?

Know Key 2: As with everything you read, each CARS passage is written by a person with an opinion. Even the first few lines of a passage reveal a great deal about the author's view. Be careful not to fall into the trap of thinking a passage is presenting neutral facts. Read every passage for its point, the main idea.

These are the types of questions that you should be able to answer with prejudice if you have read the passage correctly. If you can answer these questions, you have compared the author to people of your past and categorized the author accordingly. This means that you have a better understanding of who the author is, and how he would answer the MCAT® questions about his own passage.

The previous questions were asked to make you realize how you should be trying to understand the author. Do not ask yourself these questions on a real MCAT®. When taking a real CARS section, ask yourself questions that are relevant to the author's main idea and tone – the aspects of the passage that will be most heavily tested. Here are some questions to ask yourself on a real MCAT®:

- What is the author's profession?
- What topic does the author care about the most? Is it connected to the author's profession?
- Does the author like, dislike, or feel ambivalent towards the topic?
- If there are two opposing views in the passage, which one does the author agree with?

The answers to such questions will be helpful for many question types. These include questions about the author's central thesis, what the author would think about a new topic or opinion, and what the author thinks about people who hold opposing viewpoints. Some questions will directly ask about the author's tone. Others will have answer choices that express the same idea but differ in their tone. Understanding whether the author is strongly opinionated or more neutral will allow you to answer these question types easily.

The questions above could be applied to any CARS passage. Here are some questions that you could ask yourself about the passage in this lecture:

YOU MAY NOT LOOK AT THE PASSAGE!

- If the author were sitting in front of you, would he or she want to discuss science or art?
- What emotion, if any, is the author feeling?
- Is the author a scientist?
- Is the author conservative, liberal, or somewhere in the middle?

The answers to these questions are unequivocal. This author is discussing science, not art. Art is used as a lengthy, nearly incomprehensible introduction to make a point about science. The author does not even begin discussing the main idea until the beginning of the third paragraph. "In our own day, much the same sort of turning point has been reached in the history of science." When you read this, you should have been startled. You should have been thinking "Where did science come from? I thought we were talking about some esoteric art history stuff that I really wasn't understanding." This one sentence should have said to you "Aha! That other stuff was just an appetizer; now the author is going to discuss his real interest." Notice that it is at the beginning of the third paragraph that the writing actually becomes intelligible. In other words, the second two paragraphs are much easier to read. This is because the author is interested in this topic and knows what he wants to say. If you spent lots of time rereading the first two paragraphs, trying to master them, you wasted your time. However, as discussed later in this lecture, these paragraphs are still useful in that they provide a window into the author's opinions about his true interest.

The author is frustrated and possibly even bitter. He is so angry that he is name-calling. For instance, he calls the scientific community "the technocratic establishment." The tone of the passage is like that of a whining child. He blames scientists for being too conservative and creating "an age of anxiety," as if the anxiety of most people would be relieved if scientists were less practical. In the last sentence, he even blames us, his reader, for not taking *his* issue more seriously. The author is positively paranoid. Notice that his adversaries move against him "subtly" as if trying to hide their evil intentions. They take "oaths of allegiance" like some kind of cult. This is way overdone when you consider that the author's only complaint is that science is not liberal enough in its approach.

The author is certainly not a scientist. First of all, he writes like a poet, not a scientist: "orthodox world view of the technocratic establishment," "subterranean history of our time," "gestures of rebellion subtly denatured." Secondly, his whole point is that he is upset with scientists. (A separate argument can be made that his point results from a misunderstanding of how science progresses.) And finally, he talks like a member of some pyramid cult, not a scientist: "alternative realities" and "ontological awareness." This author probably flunked high school physics and just can't get over it.

The author is certainly liberal, or anti-establishment. He talks about "liberating us" and "rebellion" among other things.

Now, with this understanding of the author, answer the questions on the next page.

YOU MAY NOT LOOK AT THE PASSAGE!

Passage I (Questions 1–9)

Question 1

The author believes that in "the subterranean history of our time" (paragraph 4) we find the beginnings of a:

- ○ **A.** renewal of allegiance to traditional values.
- ○ **B.** redefinition of art.
- ○ **C.** redefinition of science.
- ○ **D.** single valid picture of the world.

Question 2

The author compares art and science mainly in support of the idea that:

- ○ **A.** the conventions of science, like those of art, are now beginning to be recognized as but one segment of a far broader spectrum.
- ○ **B.** aesthetic orthodoxies of the past, unlike scientific orthodoxies of the present, make up only one tradition among many.
- ○ **C.** artistic as well as scientific revolutionaries open our minds to a more global conception of art.
- ○ **D.** artists of the past have provided inspiration to the scientists of the present.

Question 3

The two kinds of art discussed in the passage are the:

- ○ **A.** aesthetic and the innovative.
- ○ **B.** dull and the shocking.
- ○ **C.** traditional and the innovative.
- ○ **D.** representative and the traditional.

Question 4

The author's statement "How far [new perceptions of science] will carry toward liberating us from the orthodox world view of the technocratic establishment is still doubtful" (paragraph 4) assumes that the:

- ○ **A.** technocratic establishment is opposed to scientific inquiry.
- ○ **B.** traditional perception of science is identical to the world view of the technocratic establishment.
- ○ **C.** current perceptions of science are identical to those of art.
- ○ **D.** technocratic establishment has the same world view as the artistic revolutionaries of the past.

Question 5

Which of the following concepts does the author illustrate with specific examples?

- ○ **A.** Scientific innovations of the present
- ○ **B.** Scientific innovations of the past
- ○ **C.** Aesthetic innovations of the present
- ○ **D.** Aesthetic orthodoxies of the past

Question 6

The claim that the unease mentioned in the fourth paragraph is "submerged" most directly illustrates the idea that:

- ○ **A.** our great-grandparents were jolted by the collapse of academic certainty.
- ○ **B.** we have grown accustomed to the notion that there is more than one valid aesthetic vision.
- ○ **C.** so far, new perceptions of science are only fragile and scattered.
- ○ **D.** the authority of science is rapidly being eroded.

Question 7

Based on the information in the passage, the author would most likely claim that someone who did NOT agree with his view of science was:

- ○ **A.** dishonest.
- ○ **B.** conformist.
- ○ **C.** rebellious.
- ○ **D.** imaginative.

Question 8

Based on information in the passage, which of the following opinions could most reasonably be ascribed to the author?

- ○ **A.** It is misguided to rebel against scientific authority.
- ○ **B.** The world views of other disciplines may have something valuable to teach the scientific community.
- ○ **C.** Art that rebels against established traditions cannot be taken seriously.
- ○ **D.** The main cause of modern anxiety and longing is our rash embrace of new scientific and artistic theories.

Question 9

Adopting the author's views as presented in the passage would most likely mean acknowledging that:

- ○ **A.** it is not a good idea to accept traditional beliefs simply because they are traditional.
- ○ **B.** we must return to established artistic and scientific values.
- ○ **C.** the future is bleak for today's artists and scientists.
- ○ **D.** the scientific community has given us little of benefit.

STOP

Do not worry about the correct answers yet.

YOU MAY NOT LOOK AT THE PASSAGE YET!

The first thing to notice is that only question 5 requires any information from the first two paragraphs, and question 5 was a question about detail, not concept. This is because the first two paragraphs are not about the main idea.

The second thing to notice is that none of the questions require us to go back to the passage, even though some refer us to specific paragraphs. All but question 5 are answerable directly from the main idea. Question 5 is a detail question, but before you run back to the passage to find the answer, look at the possibilities. Chances are that you remembered Raphael and Rembrandt from the first paragraph. These are specific examples of "aesthetic orthodoxies of the past," answer choice D.

Notice that many of the questions can be rephrased to say "The author thinks _____." In fact, the word "author" is mentioned in 7 of them. This is typical of an MCAT® passage, and that is why you must "know your author."

Question 1: Forget about the quote for a moment. Simplify the question to say "The author thinks that we find the beginnings of a:." Choice C describes the main idea. Certainly the author would disagree with A, B, and D. **Choice C is the best answer.**

Question 2: "The author thinks:" that science is like art, and that conventions of both are but part of a larger spectrum. Choice B says science is not like art, the opposite of what the author thinks. Choice C says that scientific revolutionaries are changing science; the author is frustrated because this is not really happening. Choice D says scientists of the present are opening their minds to new ideas; the author complains that they are not. **Choice A is the best answer.**

Question 3: The main idea of the passage contains the theme of traditional vs. innovative. **Choice C is the best answer.**

Question 4: Ignore the quotes until you need them. Without the quotes, the question says "The author's statement assumes that the:." In other words, "The author thinks _____." Choices C and D are exactly the opposite of what the author thinks. Choice A plays a common game on the MCAT®. They take the author's view too far. They want you to think "the author doesn't like the scientists, therefore, he thinks the scientists can't even do science." Even this author would not go that far; A is incorrect. Choice B requires you to realize that the "technocratic establishment" is conservative. **Choice B is the best answer.**

Question 5: The second part of the passage talks about science but does not address any particular innovations of the past or present. The author focuses more broadly on his radical view of how scientific discovery should progress. Choices A and B are not strong answers. Note that choice D refers to "orthodoxies" rather than innovations. The first paragraph lists several technical examples of "orthodoxies" in the old school of art that was dominant in the past. Notice that you do not need to remember any of these specific examples to answer the question. **Choice D is the best answer.**

Question 6: Choice D is out because it disagrees with the main idea, and choice C is the only answer that supports the main idea. This question is best answered by comparing the answer choices with the question. The question asks for an example of "submerged unease." "Jolted" in choice A certainly does not describe submerged unease. "Grown accustomed" in choice B certainly does not describe submerged unease. Choice C could describe submerged unease, and it does describe the main idea. **Choice C is the best answer.**

Question 7: The author is rebellious and imaginative. If you disagree with him, he thinks you are a conformist, which, by the way, is worse than dishonest as far as he is concerned. **Choice B is the best answer.**

Question 8: "The author thinks _____." The whole point of the introduction is that the scientific community should learn from the discipline of art. The other answer choices directly contradict the author's main point. **Choice B is the best answer.**

Question 9: "The author thinks _____." The author is a rebel. He thinks you should always question authority and tradition. Notice that choice D is another example of taking an argument too far. No sane individual could argue that science has provided little benefit. Choice C would be a weak answer even if it had not included 'artists.' It would have been too extreme. **Choice A is the best answer.**

Hopefully, we have demonstrated the power of knowing the author and understanding the main idea. In the next lecture, you will see that answering CARS questions requires the test taker to repeatedly apply the main idea.

2.3 | A Close Reading: Narrating toward the Main Idea

You have a good idea of what the main idea looks like and how important it is to know your author. A close reading of the passage will allow you to find the components of the main idea in order to construct it. Success on the CARS section requires reading every word, a close reading is a way of gaining as much information as possible from the passage. Narrating in your own voice as you read will allow you to construct the main idea.

Close reading is a way of reading interactively, rather than passively. Close reading allows you to notice every clue to the author's opinions. It uses an analysis of language to find meaning and to find the author. A close reading looks at not just what the author says but also how he says it. This technique originates with the study of literature and is highly relevant to medicine. Reading a passage closely is like listening closely to a patient. Just as you attend to the nuance of a passage, physicians attend to their patients—to their histories and thereby their physical states and needs. The ability to construct a narrative is essential for success as a physician, not only to understand the patient's experience, but also to make an accurate diagnosis. A good physician is able to listen to patients; a successful test taker is able to read CARS passages closely.

Reading closely means engaging with the text, asking questions, and considering the author's writing decisions. Construct the main idea by narrating the passage in your own voice: restate information, examine word choice, and parse phrases and sentences—i.e., read in small chunks. The specific skills that you can use to build a narration will be described further at the end of this lecture. Success on the CARS section will come as you develop your own voice. You will learn to trust that your own voice is a reliable guide to interpreting the passage.

Use a close reading to align yourself with the author's opinion. This process is similar to trying on the author's opinion like a set of clothes. For the time that it takes to read the passage and answer the questions, be the author. This process allows you to select the answer that the author would choose. Recall from Lecture 1 how important it is to fully concentrate on each passage. A close reading will help you achieve complete immersion in the passage. Read as though you are deeply interested in the topic. The passage becomes your whole world. Between passages you take that five-second break before moving to the next passage—so that one can become your world!

Remember to read and answer questions with confidence. If you are having problems with energy, focus, confidence, or timing, go back to the basics of this manual. Figure out what part of our strategy you aren't using, and use it.

By doing a close reading of the passage, I get to try on the author's opinion!

Let's now subject the passage you just read to a close reading and narration. This section will give you a better idea of the strategies that a successful test-taker uses to tackle a CARS passage and form the main idea. It will include a focus on connecting words and phrases, which indicate transitions or clarifications. Examples include "however," "but," "indeed," and "on the other hand." Some words and phrases may indicate changes in the author's argument or focus, such as shifts in the time period or topic being considered. These connectors are valuable clues to the main idea.

The original passage is in black type. The MCAT® student's narration is highlighted in yellow. Connecting words and phrases are highlighted in green.

Begin your narration by reading the citation at the end of the passage to gain any information you can. The title often gives a clue to the main idea. The journal may suggest your author's profession or bias.

The Making of a Counter Culture, 1969.
The author wrote a whole book with "Counter Culture" in the title. He is interested in social movements that are opposite of the mainstream.
It is roughly a century since European art
The author cares about art and history. He references a time 100 years ago.
began to experience its first significant defections from the standards of painting and sculpture that we inherit from the early Renaissance.
"Defection" is dramatic. A defector leaves for a good reason. Author, do you like or dislike change?
Notice how much you can determine about your author and his or her opinion from a close reading of the first sentence alone!
Looking back now across a long succession of innovative movements and stylistic revolutions
"Innovative" and "revolutions" are positive words that mean new or change. "Revolutions" is similar to "defections." When I see the author repeating himself, I'm on the right track to the main idea.
most of us have little trouble recognizing
This phrasing is casual and confident, indicating that this is the author's opinion.
that such aesthetic orthodoxies of the past
The author offers the opposites of old and new: orthodoxy and revolution versus tradition and change. I predict that he prefers what is new. He likes change.
as the representative convention, exact anatomy and optical perspective, the casement-window canvas,
This is a list of *examples* of traditional art. The author may be an art historian.
along with the repertory of materials and subject matters we associate with the Old Masters—
Old Masters represent tradition — the author is respectful, but not complimentary. that all this makes up not "art" itself in any absolute sense,
The use of "not art" to refer to traditional art is not positive. The author still prefers the new to the old.
but something like a school of art, one great tradition among many.
The use of "but" indicates that the part of the sentence that will follow will be opposite the first part. Often the author's opinion follows the use of "but." After the "but," the author takes all of art history and shrinks it in significance.
We acknowledge the excellence which a Raphael or Rembrandt could achieve within the canons of that school;
The author is respectful of these classics but not enthusiastic.
but we have grown accustomed to the idea that there are other aesthetic visions of equal validity.
"We" indicates that the author includes himself - this is his opinion and not a counterpoint. The author says that "other" visions are equally valid to the classics.
Indeed, innovation in the arts has become a convention in its own right with us, a "tradition of the new,"

Lecture 4 will help you construct the main idea by building a Spectrum. A Spectrum lays out opposite ideas that appear in a passage, such as change and tradition in this passage.

"Indeed" is casual and the sentence will be in the author's "voice."

Innovation equals convention - the new equals the old? What's going on? Until now, the author treated change and tradition as opposites, and he preferred change; but now he says that change has turned into a convention or tradition.

to such a degree that there are critics to whom it seems to be intolerable that any two painters should paint alike. We demand radical originality, and often confuse it with quality.

The author is using strong opinion words like "intolerable" and "radical," which are negative and indicate that he does not like something here. We know that he likes change. He explains that a constant demand for change can itself become a restrictive tradition.

Yet what a jolt it was to our great-grandparents to see the certainties of the academic tradition melt away before their eyes.

How distressing, especially for the academicians, who were the guardians of a classic heritage embodying time-honored techniques and standards whose perfection had been the labor of genius.

This is different from everything so far. This is a counterpoint. The author is presenting the other side by offering sympathy to those who do not like change.

Suddenly, they found art as they understood it being rejected by upstarts who were unwilling to let a single premise of the inherited wisdom stand unchallenged,

This language is dramatic. The author likes change, but not when it is too extreme.

Now, with a little hindsight, it is not difficult to discern continuities where our predecessors saw only ruthless disjunctions.

The author is pointing out how change can include continuity. The author's main idea is closer to the middle than to the extremes of change or tradition.

To see, as well, that the artistic revolutionaries of the past were, at their best, only opening our minds to a more global conception of art which demanded a deeper experience of light, color, and form.

The author puts down the art of the past, even that of revolutionaries, by using the word "only." The author likes the new.

Through their work, too, the art of our time

Now the author is referencing the present.

has done much to salvage the values of the primitive and childlike, the dream, the immediate emotional response, the life of fantasy, and the transcendent symbol.

This is a list of *examples* to support the previous sentence. It lists the ways that new art is the same, "salvaging" or keeping the best of the old. This paragraph can be given the simple reference - "moderate change."

In our own day, much the same sort of turning point has been reached in the history of science.

What is happening? I thought the author worked in the field of art. Now he is talking about science. Is he an artist or a scientist? Maybe neither; he may be a historian or philosopher.

It is as if the aesthetic ground pioneered by the artists now unfolds before us as a new ontological awareness.

"Pioneered" is a positive word. The author is still the author - he likes the new. This sentence extends the *same* idea from the previous paragraph into the realm of science. I don't know what "ontological" means, but no single word ever matters much because the author will repeat himself to make his point.

when the reality to which scientists address themselves comes more and more to be recognized as but one segment of a far broader spectrum. Science, for so long regarded as our single valid picture of the world, now emerges as, also a school: a *school of consciousness*, beside which alternative realities take their place.

The author is making the *same* point about science that he made about art. The author shrinks the significance of traditional science and prefers "alternative realities" because he likes change. What does the author care more about: science or art? Did the author set up the first half of the passage as an analogy to explain his position on science?

Remember Key 3: Narrate each passage as you read. The eight narrating tools will make every passage interesting and clear. While many passages may seem neutral in tone, hidden in the language of every passage is the author's opinion. Ask yourself if a word or phrase is complimentary or insulting. The author's language reveals whether the author likes or dislikes each idea, and this will lead you to the main idea.

There are, so far,

The passage started with the past, moved to the present, and is now hinting at possibilities for the future.

only fragile and scattered beginnings of this perception. They are still the subterranean history of our time.

The language here is emotional. "This perception" is fragile and scattered. What perception? This likely refers back to a perception of "alternative realities." Is the author happy or sad about the fact that the beginnings are fragile and scattered? These are negative words. The author likes change and is unhappy that "alternative realities" are not yet accepted.

How far they will carry toward liberating us from the orthodox world view

"Liberating us" indicates that the author includes himself and feels restricted by tradition. This is the *same* idea made earlier in the art section.

of the technocratic establishment is still doubtful.

I don't know what "technocratic" means here, but I recognize "establishment." "Technocratic" is associated with the "orthodox world view" from which the author wants us to be "liberated." He does not like "technocratic." Looking back a sentence, technocratic is the mainstream of science, not the "alternative realities."

These days, many gestures of rebellion are subtly denatured, adjusted,

I know that the author likes rebellion and he writes that it is being "denatured." The rebellion is falling apart.

and converted into oaths of allegiance.

The author likes change, so he would not like rebellion turning into allegiance. The author's emotions come through here - frustration, bitterness. This sentence has a tone of disgust. The author is sad that change is not successful.

In our society at large, little beyond submerged unease

This is a similar word to "subterranean." "Little beyond" is negative.

challenges the lingering authority of science and technique,

"Challenges" is like rebellion. This is the type of change that the author likes. Authority reminds me of tradition or convention from the beginning of the passage. The author equates science with tradition which he did not like. He has moved past art and now he does not like science either. He has been consistent through the passage in his love of change.

that dull ache at the bottom of the soul we refer to when we speak (usually too glibly) of an "age of anxiety," an "*age of longing*."

The author is extremely emotional here, showing his tendency for drama and poetic language. We can complete the main idea. The author longs for change in modern times: the acceptance of alternative realities beyond the mainstream of science.

2.4 | Tools for Close Reading on the MCAT®

Narrating the passage can be done using concrete tools that you can apply to any passage to find the author and construct the main idea:

1. Animated voice,
2. Parsing sentences,
3. Reading for the author,
4. Asking questions,
5. Naming,
6. Title for each paragraph,
7. Word choice,
8. Same or different.

These skills are suggestions to help you build the skill of close reading. They are not intended as a list to be memorized! You already have an intuitive feel for how to narrate a passage as narration is thinking along as you read. These techniques will allow you to take that ability further. After reading the following descriptions, go back to the passage narration demonstrated above and find examples of how the skills were used.

Using an *animated voice* as you read is a crucial instrument in your close reading toolbox. When you read a CARS passage, the voice in your head should be excited and engaged, as though you are reading a story to a young child. You will not remember or understand anything that you read in a boring, dull monotone. When you read with animation, you notice each word the author chose and its positive or negative valence. You will have an easier time staying interested which will allow you to listen more closely for the author.

Parsing sentences allows you to consider parts of a sentence separately. Some CARS sentences are so lengthy and convoluted that by the end of the sentence it is impossible to remember the beginning. Note how many times the passage narration above stopped in the middle of particularly complex sentences. Pausing part of the way through is the best way to make sense of your author's point. Once you determine the meaning and significance of a clause, move on to the next until you have read the whole sentence.

Reading for the author from the very first word is the best way to stay oriented and find the author's main idea. Frame your narration in terms of what the author likes and does not like. New information should be evaluated with simple statement like "the author says…" or "the author thinks…" Repeating these phrases will remind you that the CARS section is testing how well you find the author's opinion, not your memory of facts. No matter how disorganized the passage may seem, you will stay in touch with the author.

Asking questions is a tool for building an idea of what the author cares about. The strategy of asking yourself questions about what the author thinks was presented earlier in this lecture. You can also imagine speaking directly to the author. Do you like this? What did you mean by ___? Is this your opinion? Toward the beginning of the passage narration above, asking questions was used as a way to think through the author's opinion of change.

Identifying and *naming* the purpose of a sentence will help you follow the author's argument. Most statements in a CARS passage can be named as one of the following: author's voice, counterpoint, or example. Any statement that feels as though the author is speaking directly to the reader is the author's voice. A coun-

The repetition of a word or idea is like the author holding up a big sign saying, "Look here! This is what I care about!"

As you read each sentence, ask yourself: Is this the same or different from what I read before? Does this support or contradict the points that the author has been making?

terpoint will oppose the author's opinion, such as when the author in this passage considered the feelings of people who were startled by change, and is there to show the opposite perspective. Often the author will move in the direction of the counterpoint, although in this case the author quickly rejected the counterpoint. The main idea often includes a nuance gained from the counterpoint. Noticing lists of examples or evidence is useful when answering questions about whether the passage provided evidence or examples to support a particular idea. Recall from earlier in the lecture that one of the questions associated with this passage asked you to determine which of several choices was most supported by examples. Selecting "aesthetic orthodoxies" would be easier after noting the list of examples provided, as in the passage narration.

At the end of each paragraph, *title the paragraph*. The title should be short and simple – a few words at most. The title will not capture every nuance of the paragraph, as you know, taking lengthy notes is a waste of precious time. Use a simple word or phrase to remember the point of that paragraph. Almost all CARS questions depend on your knowledge of the passage as a whole, and the titles you create will help you construct the author's argument as it develops from the beginning of the passage to its end. A mental paragraph title allows you to "carry forward" the ideas of each paragraph to the next so that new arguments or topics can be connected to previous ones.

Examining *word choice* allows you to find the author's beliefs. The words that appear in a passage were chosen deliberately by the author to convey a certain message. Ask yourself if a word is positive or negative. You do not need to look for adjectives and adverbs to find connotations. All word types, not only adjectives and adverbs but also nouns and verbs, have positive or negative connotations. Ask yourself why the author decided to use one particular word instead. Considering word choice is valuable for evaluating the author's tone. The use of casual or extreme language reveals what the author likes or dislikes. When you do not know a word, don't worry. The author will give you many different opportunities to hear his or her opinion.

In this passage, the author consistently used strongly positive words to describe change. What if he had said "new" instead of "innovative" or "changes" instead of "revolutions" or "begun" instead of "pioneered?" The tone of the passage would have been much more neutral. As it is, these word choices demonstrate the author's passionate approval of change. Word choices like these give you a lot of information about how the author feels and how much he or she cares about the topic of the passage. They can point readers to the main idea.

Use the 8 narrating tools!

- Read in an animated way.

- Focus on the author, rather than the content – "The author likes/dislikes…."

- Parse sentences into manageable pieces.

- Ask questions.

- Name the purpose of each sentence.

- Title each paragraph after reading.

- Consider the author's choice of words.

- Ask yourself if each idea is the same or different from what the author has already said. If different, how different? If opposite, a counter point. If an adjustment, the author is constructing the main idea.

Word choice can also provide information about the author's profession and position. The use of technical jargon in a passage about a scientific discovery might indicate that the author is a specialist within the field discussed.

Noticing transition words such as "but," however," or "yet" will help you find the author's voice and follow the argument, even when the passage is disjointed. Connecting words leaves a trail of bread crumbs that allow you to follow the author's train of thought. Putting emphasis on connecting words also helps you read in an animated way.

As you read, classify each statements as *same or different*. As you read, compare and connect each new sentence and paragraph with what you've read so far. If it is the same, the author is using repetition for emphasis of the main idea. Carrying forward what you've read and comparing it to each new statement will help you navigate a disjointed passage and translate it into an argument you can follow. In the passage narration, repeatedly asking about same or different was helpful in realizing that what seemed like a sudden shift to science was actually just a continuation of the same broad argument about change.

When a statement presents an idea that is different from what you have read so far, ask yourself "how different is it?" Is it a slight adjustment to or does it oppose what has been stated so far? If opposite, it is a counterpoint and likely not the author's opinion. If it is similar to something you have read, but makes a new point, it is an important adjustment to the author's opinion. Pay attention to the way it adds critical nuance to the main idea. Certain words indicate that the author is spending extra time on a certain idea ("furthermore", "in addition") while others mark the shift to a new idea or perspective ("but", "however", or "yet"). Comparing what you have read to each new statement as "same or different" is key to the spectrum, an advanced CARS concept discussed in the last lecture of this manual.

Narrating as you read a passage closely makes it easy to identify the main idea. The main idea is your most powerful tool to finding the correct answers to CARS questions. Now that you have practiced narrating a close reading of the passage, the next lecture focuses on the questions and answers.

Some of these techniques will take a long time to get used to at first, but don't worry. With repeated use and practice, you will get better at using them and finding the main idea quickly.

Once you get comfortable with these techniques, you can even try applying them to passages on other sections of the MCAT®! For example, when multiple experiments and/or graphs are included, ask yourself whether the results of each one point to the same or a different conclusion.

DON'T FORGET YOUR KEYS

1. Success on CARS depends on reading for the main idea, not your memory of the details.

2. From the start, read for the author's opinion. As you read each sentence, ask if the author likes or dislikes....

3. Narrate each passage. Read every word. Most words are positive or negative—nouns, verbs, adjectives, and adverbs—and reveal the author's opinion.

Answering the Questions

3.1 Introduction

3.2 Question Stems

3.3 Answer Choices

3.4 Identifying the Best Answer

3.5 Simplification of the Question and Answer Choices

3.1 | Introduction

For most students, the CARS Section is literally a test of their ability to comprehend what they have read. Such students read a question and choose an answer based on what was said in the passage. If they do not arrive at an answer, they eliminate answer choices based on what was said in the passage. If they still do not arrive at an answer, they search the passage for relevant information that they may have missed or do not recall. If they still do not arrive at a single correct answer choice, which is likely to be about 50% of the time with this method, they repeat the process until they give up and make a random guess in frustration. This method uses only about 50% of the information provided by the test. When you cannot identify an answer, 'thinking harder' (whatever that means) is not an effective strategy. Nor is it effective to search the passage until the answer jumps out at you. Both of these methods simply consume your precious time.

A successful test taker does more than just look for the answer in the passage.

In addition to your understanding of the passage, there are four tools that you can use to answer the questions. These four tools go beyond simply understanding the passage. They force you to consider additional information presented in the question stems and answer choices that is often overlooked or noticed only on a subconscious level.

The Four Tools

1. Looking back,
2. The main idea,
3. The question stems,
4. The answer choices.

Just thinking harder won't work.

Use your four tools.

THE 3 KEYS

1. Question stems are simple at their core. Rephrase complex wording in the question stem to find the question being asked. Look out for when the main idea is presented in the question stem – a gift!

2. Keep your hand on the pulse of the author as you answer the questions. After reading each question stem, restate the main idea and predict an answer.

3. The best answer to CARS questions will both match the passage and answer the question stem.

Looking Back

'Looking back' refers to rereading parts of the passage to search for an answer. Only use 'looking back' when:

1. you are regularly finishing an exam on time,

2. you know what you're looking for, and

3. you know where you can find the answer.

'Looking back' is the most time consuming and least useful of the four tools. Unfortunately, it is the tool most often relied upon by inexperienced test takers. It is true that forgotten details can be found by rereading parts of the passage. However, most questions require an understanding of the main idea, not your memory of details. **The main idea cannot be found by rereading parts of the passage.**

'Word-for-word' and other traps have been set for the unwary test taker looking for the 'feel-good' answer. The 'feel-good' answer is an answer where a section of the passage seems to unequivocally answer the question so that the test taker *feels good* when choosing it. The 'feel-good' answer choice may even use a phrase from the passage word-for-word. This is often a trap. Remember, the CARS Section is ambiguous and a simple clear answer is rarely correct.

Learn to use 'looking back' as seldom as possible. Force yourself to choose the best answer without looking back at the passage. This is a difficult lesson to accept, but it is extremely important to achieving your top score. Looking back at the passage for anything but a detail will take large amounts of your testing time and will allow the test writers to skew your concept of the main idea by directing you toward specific parts of the passage. **If you are unable to finish the test in the time given, it is because you are overusing the 'looking back' tool.** If you are not finishing, do not look back at all until you can regularly finish an entire CARS section with time left over.

Your number one goal is to finish the CARS Section. Difficult questions are worth no more than easy questions. **Do not sacrifice five easy questions by spending a long time answering a single difficult question.** If you usually finish the CARS section with time to spare, you can 'look back' to the passage more often; if you do not usually finish the CARS section, you should stop looking back to the passage until you begin finishing within the allotted time on a regular basis.

'Looking back' is a useful tool. Just use it wisely.

Main Idea

The main idea, discussed in the previous lecture, is the most powerful tool for answering MCAT® CARS questions. After you read the question stem, before you read the answer choices, restate the main idea. This will help keep you in touch with the author and the passage. Three-quarters of all answer choices are wrong, so after reading the questions for any passage, you will have read 18 to 21 misleading answer choices. If you do not stay in regular touch with the main idea, wrong answer choices can interfere with your memory of the passage. After every question stem, restate the main idea before you read the answer choices.

If you're not finishing in time, it is probably because you are using the 'looking back' tool too often and for too long.

If you usually don't have time to finish the CARS section, try taking a practice exam where you read each passage once through and then don't allow yourself to look back at the passage no matter what. You will finish with time left to spare, and your score will probably go up.

As discussed in the Strategy and Tactics Lecture, you can read quickly enough to finish the exam. On the next practice exam, you can use the extra time that you know you will have at the end to take an occasional look back at the passage. But don't look too often or for too long. Looking back is why you weren't finishing the exam in the first place.

It's not bad to use your 'looking back' tool. Just don't overuse it.

For most questions, the best answer is usually aligned with the main idea, except when the question is asking for the *opposite* of the main idea. Either way, having the main idea at hand will consistently help you choose the best answer. Answer the question from the perspective of the author.

MCAT® practice is medical practice. Just as you will align a patient's care with their wishes, align yourself with the perspective of the author as you consider the answer choices.

It can also be helpful to predict an answer to the question stem before looking at the answer choices. Hold a prediction in mind that is aligned with the main idea. By restating the main idea and predicting the answer before reading the answer choices, you will find it much easier to eliminate wrong answers based on how far they deviate from the main idea.

Remember to look out for those questions that ask you to oppose the main idea. Holding the main idea in mind will still be orienting, but here you will choose the answer that is least true, not most true.

Remember Key 1: Most CARS question stems are very simple, even when they are disguised in complex wording. Sometimes the main idea itself is given in one or two of the question stems for each passage. Use this gift to verify your reading of the passage.

3.2 Question Stems

The question stems hold as much information as the passage. Read these question stems and see how much you can learn about the passage without even reading it.

1. The author of the passage believes that the fiction written by the current generation of authors:

2. The overall point made by the passage's comparison of movies to fiction is that:

3. According to the passage, John Gardner concedes that preliminary good advice to a beginning writer might be, "Write as if you were a movie camera." The word concedes here suggests that:

4. The fact that the author rereads Under the Volcano because it has been made into a movie is ironic because it:

5. The passage suggests that a reader who is not bored by a line-by-line description of a room most likely:

6. The passage suggests that if a contemporary writer were to write a novel of great forcefulness, this novel would most likely:

7. The passage places the blame for contemporary writers' loss of readers on the:

Ask yourself some questions about the author. What does the author do for a living? How does the author vote? How old is the author? Is the author male or female? What are the author's interests and beliefs? Look closely at each question stem and see what kind of information you get from it. Why are certain positive, neutral, or negative adjectives used? Who is John Gardner? What can I learn about the passage from these question stems?

Notice that some of the questions that can be asked about the question stems, such as about word choice and the author's opinions, are similar to the kinds of questions used to develop the main idea in Lecture 2. The question stems and answer choices may reveal information that will help you formulate the main idea

The questions give as much information as the passage. On the real MCAT® it is important to always read the passage before answering the questions, but this lecture will ask you to try answering questions without the passages. These exercises will teach you to recognize and use the information held in question stems.

On the CARS MCAT®, the best answer matches the passage and matches the question stem. If it corresponds with one or the other, but not both, it is not the best answer.

and the author's argument. Keep this in mind while completing the exercises in this lecture.

Now, in the space below, write down everything that you can think of that is revealed about the passage from each stem. Write an answer for each of the seven question stems. (Warning: If you read on without writing the answers, you will miss an important opportunity to improve your CARS skills. Once you read on, the effect of the exercise will be ruined.)

1. _____

_____

2. _____

_____

3. _____

_____

4. _____

_____

5. _____

_____

6. _____

_____

7. _____

_____

Information that can be gained from the seven previous question stems:

1. The author of the passage believes that the fiction written by the current generation of authors:

From the first question stem, we immediately know that the passage was about the writing of fiction. The word 'current' suggests a comparison between authors of fiction from the past and the present.

2. The overall point made by the passage's comparison of movies to fiction is that:

From the second question stem we learn that there is a comparison between movies and fiction. We also know that this was central to the author's point. The movies are a 'current' medium, while 'written fiction' might be considered older or in the past. Hmmm. What is the significance of this?

3. According to the passage, John Gardner concedes that preliminary good advice to a beginning writer might be, "Write as if you were a movie camera." The word concedes here suggests that:

In question stem three, you need to wonder, "Who is John Gardner?" A named person will likely be someone whom the author used either to support his point or as an example of someone who has a bad idea. You should decide which. Now, even if the question hadn't asked this, you should have asked yourself about the word 'concedes,' because it provides valuable information about the context of the quote. When you concede, you give in. So 'concedes' here indicates that Mr. Gardner is giving in to a point when he says "Write as if you were a movie camera." Mr. Gardner's argument must be that written fiction is not good when it is like the movies, but it is okay to write like a movie camera when you are a beginning writer. Notice how hesitant the wording is. 'Beginning' is emphasized by the use of both 'preliminary' and 'beginning,' and the word 'might' is also used. At this point, you should be getting a feeling of what this passage was about: movies versus fiction, current fiction versus past fiction, and someone implying that movies do not make good fiction. The author believes something about current fiction and makes a point about fiction and movies. Given three question stems with no passage and not even answer choices to the questions, we can already get a sense of the passage. The remaining question stems will confirm what the passage is about.

4. The fact that the author rereads Under the Volcano because it has been made into a movie is ironic because it:

The fourth question stem indicates that a movie makes the author read a book. The question states that this is ironic. That means that the actual result is incongruous with the expected result. Apparently, according to the author's argument, watching a movie should not make him read the book. Thus, part of the author's argument in the passage must be that movies make people less interested in reading. Based on this question stem, it is also reasonable to assume that the author used John Gardner in question stem #3 to support his argument, so the author probably believes that fiction written like a movie is not good fiction. Extrapolating further from the comparison of movies to fiction and the stated dichotomy between current and past fiction, the author is probably arguing that current fiction is not as good as old fiction.

5. The passage suggests that a reader who is not bored by a line-by-line description of a room most likely:

The fifth passage compares the phrase 'line-by-line description' with the idea of boredom. It is a simple logical jump to equate 'line-by-line description' with past fiction as opposed to current fiction or movies. From our conclusions thus far about the author's argument, it is logical to conclude that someone who is NOT bored by 'line-by-line descriptions' would NOT be bored by past fiction, but would, in fact, appreciate it as the author obviously does.

6. The passage suggests that if a contemporary writer were to write a novel of great forcefulness, this novel would most likely:

Question stem #6 reinforces our conclusion about the author's argument. The 'if' indicates that 'contemporary writers' do not 'write novels of great forcefulness.' Instead, they must be writing novels that resemble movies. The only question is "What would a novel of great forcefulness do?" Answering this question is as simple as seating the author in front of you and asking him. The amazing thing is that we already have a stereotypical idea of this author just by reading six question stems! This guy is a college English professor fed up with the quick fix satisfaction offered by movies. He would love a novel of great forcefulness. Does he think that we would appreciate it? Be careful here. He appreciates the novel because he truly believes that the novel itself is great, not because he thinks he is great or better than everyone else. The answer is yes, he thinks that we would appreciate a novel of great forcefulness as well.

7. The passage places the blame for contemporary writers' loss of readers on the:

This last question stem answers the previous question. The seventh question stem says that current fiction is losing readers. It asks for the explanation. Of course, the author's whole point is to explain why current fiction is losing readership. It is because it is like movies and not forceful like past fiction. What should be revealing and even shocking to you is that we can accurately answer every question without reading the passage. In fact, on this particular passage, we can accurately answer every question without reading the passage OR the answer choices. Most MCAT® passages are like this. Did you realize that there was this much information in the question stems alone? Have you been using this information to answer the questions on the MCAT®? If you haven't, you are capable of scoring many points higher on the CARS Section. You cannot expect to always be able to answer questions without the passage or the answer choices (and you should not try to on the actual test), but you can expect to gain a lot of information about the passage from the question stems.

Compare your answers with the actual answer choices below and choose a best answer.

Question 1

The author of the passage believes that the fiction written by the current generation of authors:

- ○ **A.** lacks the significance of fiction written by previous generations.
- ○ **B.** is, as a whole, no better and no worse than fiction written by previous generations.
- ○ **C.** brilliantly meets the particular needs of contemporary readers.
- ○ **D.** is written by authors who show great confidence in their roles as writers.

Question 2

The overall point made by the passage's comparison of movies to fiction is that:

- ○ **A.** contemporary authors have strengthened their fiction by the application of cinematic techniques.
- ○ **B.** the film of Under the Volcano is bound to be more popular than the novel.
- ○ **C.** great fiction provides a richness of language and feeling that is difficult to re-create in film.
- ○ **D.** contemporary authors would be well advised to become screenwriters.

Question 3

According to the passage, John Gardner concedes that preliminary good advice to a beginning writer might be, "Write as if you were a movie camera." The word "concedes" here suggests that:

   I. Gardner's approach to writing has been influenced by the competing medium of film.
   II. Gardner must have written screenplays at one point in his life.
   III. Gardner dislikes the medium of film.

- ○ **A.** I only
- ○ **B.** II only
- ○ **C.** I and II only
- ○ **D.** II and III only

Question 4

The fact that the author rereads Under the Volcano because it has been made into a movie is ironic because it:

   I.   seems to go against the overall point of the passage concerning fiction and film.
   II. implies that the film version was a box-office failure.
   III. hints that the author was dissatisfied with the novel.

- ○ **A.** I only
- ○ **B.** II only
- ○ **C.** III only
- ○ **D.** II and III only

Question 5

The passage suggests that a reader who is not bored by a line-by-line description of a room most likely:

- ○ **A.** prefers the quick fix of the movies.
- ○ **B.** would be bored by a single shot of a room in a film.
- ○ **C.** has no tolerance for movies.
- ○ **D.** displays the attitude demanded by good fiction.

Question 6

The passage suggests that if a contemporary writer were to write a novel of great forcefulness, this novel would most likely:

   I.   confuse and anger lovers of great literature.
   II. exist in stark contrast to the typical contemporary novel.
   III. win back some of the readers contemporary writers have lost.

- ○ **A.** I only
- ○ **B.** II only
- ○ **C.** I and II only
- ○ **D.** II and III only

Question 7

The passage places the blame for contemporary writers' loss of readers on the:

   I.   competition presented by movies.
   II. writers themselves.
   III. ignorance of the public.

- ○ **A.** I only
- ○ **B.** II only
- ○ **C.** I and II only
- ○ **D.** I, II, and III

STOP

Answers to the Questions

Question 1

Choice A, the answer to question #1, is exactly what we expected: past fiction is better than current fiction. Notice that we can simplify the choices to:

- ○ A. Current fiction is not as good as past fiction.
- ○ B. Current fiction is equal to past fiction.
- ○ C. Current fiction is good.
- ○ D. Current fiction is good.

Simplifying the question and the answer choices can make the best answer easier to find. We'll discuss simplification later in this lecture. The main idea is all you need to answer this question.

Question 2

Choice C, the answer to question #2, is also exactly what we expected. The choices can be rephrased to:

- ○ A. Movies have been good for fiction.
- ○ B. Movies are more likeable than fiction.
- ○ C. Movies are not as good as good fiction.
- ○ D. Authors of fiction should make movies.

When we put these questions to our author, the choice is obvious.

Question 3

The answers to question #3 are not what we expected. We expected a more sophisticated question pertaining to the use of the word "concedes." Although the question told us a lot about the passage, the answer choices match a much simpler question than we anticipated: "Who is John Gardner?" The choices can be rephrased as:

- I. John Gardner has been influenced by movies.
- II. John Gardner wrote movies.
- III. John Gardner dislikes movies.

Clearly John Gardner has been influenced by movies if he is suggesting that writing like a movie might be good advice for a beginning writer. From the answer choices, we can see that if option I is correct, option III is likely to be incorrect. If Gardner dislikes movies, it is unlikely that he would be influenced by them. Option II is incorrect because Gardner can be influenced by movies without having actually written them. Even if option III could be correct, and even assuming that Gardner is like the author, liking good fiction more than movies is not the same as disliking movies. Choice A is the best answer.

Question 4

The answer to question #4 is exactly what we expected. The choices can be rephrased to:

- I. Seeing the movie shouldn't have made the author read the book.
- II. The movie flopped.
- III. The author didn't like the book.

Only option I addresses the 'irony' suggested in the question and pertains to the main idea. The answer is choice A.

Question 5

Choice D, the answer to question #5, is exactly what we expected. The choices can be rephrased to:

- ○ A. If you're patient, you'll prefer the fast pace of movies.
- ○ B. If you're patient, you won't like waiting for action.
- ○ C. If you're patient, you won't have the patience for the fast pace of movies.
- ○ D. If you're patient, you'll like the careful pace of good fiction.

Choices A, B, and C seem to be self-contradictory.

Question 6

Choice D, the answer to question #6, is exactly what we expected. Remember that "a novel of great forcefulness" describes past fiction according to our author, and that our author would expect us to like past fiction. This is consistent with options II and III.

Question 7

Choice C, the answer to question #7, is exactly what we expected. Option I restates the main idea that movies have hurt fiction. Certainly, our author is criticizing current authors, so option II is also true. Option III is not true, based upon our belief that the author would expect us to like a forceful novel. The answer here is choice C.

For practice, try this exercise again for another passage. Read these question stems and write answers in the blank lines given. Keep in mind that the questions can be considered as a set. Information from question stems and answer choices can be used to go back and make better decisions about earlier questions.

1. The passage suggests that most medieval thinkers of the 13th century were:

2. In the late 15th century, Christopher Columbus proposed an alternate passage to the Indies which would take him around the Earth. According to the passage, most of his educated contemporaries probably believed:

3. Based upon the information in the passage, which of the following events most likely occurred before 1300 A.D.?

4. The author probably believes that science in the 13th century:

5. Based upon the information in the passage, an educated person of the 13th century might explain the perpetual motion of the planets as:

6. The 13th century friar Roger Bacon argued that the progress of human knowledge was being impeded by excessive regard for ancient authorities. This information:

7. "Long before the 13th century, Aristotle taught that natural science should be based on extensive observations, followed by reflection leading to scientific generalizations" (paragraph 1). The author would most likely agree with which of the following statements concerning this scientific method proffered by Aristotle?

1. _____

_____

2. _____

_____

3. _____

_____

4. _____

_____

5. _____

_____

6. _____

_____

7. _____

_____

Information that can be gained from the seven previous question stems:

1. The passage suggests that most medieval thinkers of the 13th century were:

From the first question stem, we immediately know that the author has some opinion about "thinkers of the 13th century." Do not ignore the adverb "most." It does not tell us much, but it does hint of some moderation in the tone of the passage. Compare the tone if we were to replace the word "most" with "all": "The passage suggests that all medieval thinkers of the 13th century were:"

Of course, we cannot yet answer the question with any accuracy, but let's just consider some possibilities. Does the author suggest that 13th century thinkers were naïve, well informed, foolish, clever, careful, brash, guided by religion, guided by reason, or what? Keep this in mind.

2. In the late 15th century, Christopher Columbus proposed an alternate passage to the Indies which would take him around the Earth. According to the passage, most of his educated contemporaries probably believed:

The second question stem tells us that we are not dealing with just the 13th century, but with a broader era of history that spans at least until the 15th century.

Again, we cannot answer the question yet, but we can make a reasonable guess. What beliefs might contemporaries have had about Columbus' journey? The words "proposed" and "alternate" show that he was taking a new path. Columbus was sailing into the unknown, so the questions are likely to be about what he might find.

The question stem repeats the theme of "thinkers" with the words "educated contemporaries." We now know not only that the author is discussing educated thinkers from medieval times, but also that he is giving his opinion as to how they thought. He is making some kind of suggestion about what these educated contemporaries probably believed about Columbus sailing around the Earth.

"Educated" is a key word here. Imagine the question stem without the word "educated." "According to the passage, most of his contemporaries probably believed:" How does it change the answer? What is the difference between a "contemporary" and an "educated contemporary"? The question specifically mentions "around the Earth," drawing attention to the question of whether or not the world was thought to be round. Does the author suggest that educated contemporaries believed Columbus would fall off the edge of the world, or does he suggest that they believed that Columbus would find the new world? The word "educated" implies that the author is making the point that the 15th century thinker's thoughts may have been more accurate than we would expect.

We can expect an answer that says "educated contemporaries probably had reasonable expectations about Columbus' journey."

3. Based upon the information in the passage, which of the following events most likely occurred before 1300 A.D.?

Since we are asked to predict the chronology of certain events, the author must be discussing not just educated thought, but the progression of educated thought.

We can begin to narrow in on the time period beginning before the 13th century and ending around 1500 A.D. (Remember that the 13th century is during the 1200s.) We can infer that educated thought was progressing during this time period.

Because the question asks about the early part of the progression of educated thought (before the 13th century) and not the later part (the 15th century), the answer choice should be an event that reflects less highly developed educated thought. Keep in mind that this is the MCAT® and not a high school exam. The answer is not likely to be as simple as "Thinkers were naïve in the 13th century and brilliant by the 15th century."

4. The author probably believes that science in the 13th century:

From this question stem, we see that the author is discussing scientific thought, not just educated thought in general.

Like question #3, this question asks about the early part of the progress discussed in the passage. Again, we will choose an answer choice with this in mind.

We can assume that science in the 13th century was less like modern science than science in the 15th century, but we still do not have enough information from the question stems alone to know how science changed.

5. Based upon the information in the passage, an educated person of the 13th century might explain the perpetual motion of the planets as:

This is almost the same question three times in a row. We might rephrase them as "Which of the following reflects a way of thinking prior to or toward the beginning of the progress in thinking discussed in the passage?" We are still waiting to learn more about the nature and extent of the change. One thing we do know is that the explanation will be different from a modern scientific explanation because there must be a progression to modern science.

6. The 13th century friar Roger Bacon argued that the progress of human knowledge was being impeded by excessive regard for ancient authorities. This information:

Finally we are given a clue about the aspect of change. The stem tells us that Bacon thought thinkers of the 13th century relied too heavily upon ancient thinkers. You should ask yourself, "13th century thinkers relied on ancient thinkers as opposed to relying on what?" In other words, instead of just believing whatever ancient thinkers say, they should have done what? The answer should be obvious to any modern science student: investigate and think for yourself!

Based on our analysis thus far, it appears that Bacon was used to support the author's argument.

The answer to this question will probably be something like "This information supports the author's argument because it is evidence that 13th century thinkers were relying too much on ancient thinkers rather than thinking for themselves."

7. "Long before the 13th century, Aristotle taught that natural science should be based on extensive observations, followed by reflection leading to scientific generalizations" (paragraph 1). The author would most likely agree with which of the following statements concerning this scientific method proffered by Aristotle?

As an MCAT® student with a strong science background, you can see that the method proposed is not only practical, but is the method currently in use by today's scientists. Using the reasoning from question #6, we could infer that the author would disagree with Aristotle because he is an ancient source. It is also possible that the author would agree with this common sense and modern-seeming statement by Aristotle, and that there is some kind of twist to this question that we cannot predict from the question stem alone. We know the author thought early thinkers relied too heavily on ancient sources, but, in this case, it may have been a good thing. The MCAT® is tricky like this.

We now have enough information to revisit and answer the earlier questions.

1. REVISITED: Based on information from question #6, the passage suggests that most medieval thinkers of the 13th century were too trusting of the work of the ancient thinkers, which impeded progress.

2. REVISITED: We already answered this to some extent, but the new information confirms: In the late 15th century, Christopher Columbus proposed an alternate passage to the Indies which would take him around the Earth. According to the passage, most of his educated contemporaries probably believed his trip was at least possible.

3. REVISITED: We still have no clue as to what events the answer choices will include, so we can only give a general answer. Based upon the information in the passage, the event that most likely occurred before 1300 A.D. was one that, though perhaps more impressive than many modern students would expect, did not require too much advanced science.

4. REVISITED: The author probably believes that science in the 13th century was not completely primitive but not advanced either, or (based on question #6) that it relied upon ancient knowledge with few innovations.

5. REVISITED: Based upon the information in the passage, an educated person of the 13th century might explain the perpetual motion of the planets as similar to the way ancient thinkers would have explained it, which is also somehow less scientific than Renaissance science or modern science.

6. REVISITED: As previously stated, the answer to this question is likely something like: This information supports the author's argument because it is evidence that 13th century thinkers were relying too much on ancient thinkers rather than thinking for themselves.

7. REVISITED: The author may disagree with the statement presented in the question stem, based on disapproval of reliance on ancient sources. Another strong possibility is that the author would agree that natural science should be based on extensive observations, followed by reflection leading to scientific generalizations – and that there is some kind of twist to this question that we cannot predict from the question stem alone.

Compare your answers with the actual answer choices below and choose a best answer.

Question 1

The passage suggests that most medieval thinkers of the 13th century were:

- ○ **A.** impractical mystics.
- ○ **B.** good empirical scientists.
- ○ **C.** somewhat superstitious.
- ○ **D.** confident of the veracity of Aristotelian physics.

Question 2

In the late 15th century, Christopher Columbus proposed an alternate passage to the Indies which would take him around the Earth. According to the passage, most of his educated contemporaries probably believed:

- ○ **A.** Columbus would fall off the edge of the earth.
- ○ **B.** the trip was possible in theory.
- ○ **C.** the sun was the center of the universe.
- ○ **D.** in Aristotelian physics.

Question 3

Based upon the information in the passage, which of the following events most likely occurred before 1300 A.D.?

- ○ **A.** Spectacles for reading were invented.
- ○ **B.** Nicholas of Cusa conceived the idea of an infinite universe.
- ○ **C.** Scientists abandoned Aristotelian physics.
- ○ **D.** Raw sugar was refined.

Question 4

The author probably believes that science in the 13th century:

- ○ **A.** laid the groundwork for modern science.
- ○ **B.** was the beginning of a scientific revolution.
- ○ **C.** is underestimated by modern historians.
- ○ **D.** was more practical than theoretical.

Question 5

Based upon the information in the passage, an educated person of the 13th century might explain the perpetual motion of the planets as:

- ○ **A.** propelled by a mysterious prime mover.
- ○ **B.** *impetus* resulting from an initial, tremendous push.
- ○ **C.** movement due to lack of any opposing force.
- ○ **D.** a violation of Aristotelian physics.

Question 6

The 13th century friar Roger Bacon argued that the progress of human knowledge was being impeded by excessive regard for ancient authorities. This information:

- ○ **A.** weakens the claims made by the author because it is an example of a direct criticism of Aristotle's scientific presuppositions.
- ○ **B.** weakens the claims made by the author because it demonstrates that religion still dominated science in the 13th century.
- ○ **C.** strengthens the claims made by the author because it is evidence that 13th century thinkers were not questioning the scientific suppositions of Aristotle.
- ○ **D.** strengthens the claims made by the author because Aristotle was Greek, not Roman.

Question 7

"Long before the 13th century, Aristotle taught that natural science should be based on extensive observations, followed by reflection leading to scientific generalizations." (lines 3-5) The author would most likely agree with which of the following statements concerning this scientific method proffered by Aristotle?

- ○ **A.** This method had a stultifying effect on 15th century science.
- ○ **B.** This method was faithfully practiced by most thirteenth century thinkers.
- ○ **C.** Practice of this method led to the *first major break with Aristotelian physics* (paragraph 2) in the fourteenth century.
- ○ **D.** Extensive scientific observations of the thirteenth century resulted in gross inaccuracies in the interpretation of Aristotelian physics.

STOP

Answers to Questions

Notice that, although there was less information in the question stems for this passage than in the previous exercise, the lack of information was made up for by information in the answer choices. In other words, for this passage, much of the information was in the answer choices. Still, the point is that you need to use all of the information to answer a question, not just the words in the passage. In the next section we will discuss extraction of information from the answer choices. For now, let's consider the answers to this passage.

Question 1: Choice D is just what we thought: too much trust in ancient sources. Notice that while choices A and C are criticisms of 13th century thinkers, they do not relate to the point about placing trust in ancient sources. They are also potentially more extreme than the passage in the characterization of early thinkers as "impractical" or "superstitious."

Question 2: Choice B is, again, exactly what we might predict. Notice that choices C and D are what we expect from early thinkers, not later thinkers. Choices C and D also do not answer the question as precisely, since they do not refer to Columbus' trip. Choice A does not represent the theme that 15th century thinkers were advancing in educated thought.

Question 3: Choice A is the best answer. Our limited knowledge from only the question stem allows us to narrow the answer to A or D, but it may not be enough to choose between the two. Choice B is a theoretical advance. Recall from question #6 that early thinkers were relying on ancient thinkers rather than innovative thought. Choice C is wrong since the question refers to early thinkers. Again, question #6 tells us that early thinkers were embracing ancient thinkers, not abandoning them.

Question 4: This one is very tough. Choice D is the best answer, and makes sense given our idea that there was little innovative thinking going on. However, choices A and B seem to be possibilities. "Modern" science cannot have arrived by the 15th century, so perhaps we can eliminate choice A. The weakness of choice B is the word "revolution," but it is still not a bad answer based on only the information in the question stems. Based on our analysis of the question stems, choice C seems unlikely.

There is no need to be concerned if we cannot answer a question with absolute certainty based on only the question stems. We still have the passage and the analysis of answer choices (discussed in the next section) to consider. A close reading of all answer choices of all questions in this passage will reveal an underlying theme that is simply not in the question stems. The underlying theme is that science at the beginning of this period of scientific progression was more practical than theoretical. Of course, reading the passage would make this theme even more apparent.

Question 5: Choice A is the best answer. Choices B and C are close to how we would explain planetary motion today, so they are wrong answers for how an early thinker would explain it. It turns out that choice B is specifically described in the passage as an example of 14th century thought and thus must be a wrong answer. Choice D contradicts the idea that 13th century thinkers were relying on ancient thinkers without thinking for themselves.

Question 6: Choice C is the best answer and fits well with what we predicted.

Question 7: The other question stems and answer choices have established the idea that the author is contrasting early and late thinkers, with more progressive late thinkers being roughly identified with the fifteenth century. The author would not say that the 15th century was "stultified," so choice A is not a likely answer. On the flip side, 13th century (early) thinkers must not have been practicing the modern method described in the question stem, so choice B is not a strong answer. Choice C makes the most sense given our idea that there could be some kind of twist in the correct answer choice, given the fact that in the question stem a very early thinker describes the modern scientific method. The twist is that Aristotle's advice to base knowledge on observation led to the evidence that his own theory of physics was wrong. Thus, by following Aristotle's own early advice, the late thinkers broke with Aristotle—an irony that makes for a tricky MCAT® question.

Answer Choices

Each MCAT® question has four possible answer choices. One of these will be the best answer and the other three we will call *distractors*. Typically, when a CARS question is written, the correct answer choice is written first and then distractors are created. Because the correct answer is written to answer a specific question and a distractor is written to confuse, the two can often be distinguished without even referencing the question. In other words, with practice, a good test taker can sometimes distinguish the best answer among the distractors without even reading the question or the passage. This is a difficult skill to acquire and is gained only through extensive practice.

Begin by learning to recognize typical distractor types. Among other things, an effective distractor may be: a statement that displays a subtle misunderstanding of the main idea, a statement that uses the same or similar words as in the passage but is taken out of context, a true statement that does not answer the question, a statement that answers more than the question asks, or a statement that relies upon information commonly considered true but not given in the passage.

In order to help you recognize distractors, we have artificially created five categories of **suspected distractors**. It is unlikely, but not impossible, that the best answer choice might also fall into one of these categories. Thus, you must use this tool as a guide to assist you in finding the best answer, rather than as an absolute test.

- Round-About: a distractor that moves around the question but does not directly answer it
- Beyond: a distractor whose validity relies upon information not supplied by (i.e., information *beyond*) the passage
- Contrary: a distractor that is contrary to the main idea
- Simpleton: a distractor that is very simple and/or easily verifiable from the passage
- Unintelligible: a distractor that you do not understand

The Round-About

Round-about distractors simply do not answer the question as asked. They may be true statements. They may even concur with the passage, but they just don't offer a direct answer to the question. A *roundabout* is the answer you expect from a politician on a Sunday morning political talk show: a lot of convincing words are spoken but nothing is really said.

Here's a manufactured example of a roundabout:

13. In mid-afternoon in December in Montana, the author believes that the color of the sky most closely resembles:

    A. the most common pigment according to typical winter sky patterns.

This roundabout can be restated so that the question stem and answer choice, put together, say that "The color of the sky in December looks like the color of the sky in winter." This is typical of a roundabout distractor. Be wary of answer choices that simply restate the question stem or provide no new information.

Beyonds

A distractor will often supply information beyond that given in the question and passage without substantiating its veracity. These distractors are called beyonds. While reading a beyond, you will typically find yourself thinking something like "This answer sounds good, but the passage was about the economics of the post Soviet Union. I don't remember anything about the Russian revolution."

As you answer each question, align yourself with the author. BE the author! The best answer is usually the one the author would choose, unless asked for the opposite, i.e. what would weaken the argument.

Think of round-abouts as the kind of answer a politician would give. It sounds really good but it doesn't answer the question.

Beyonds can also play upon current events. A passage on AIDS may have a question with an answer choice about cloning. Cloning may be a hot topic in the news, but if it was not mentioned in the passage or in the question, be very suspicious of it in an answer choice.

Remember that some question stems directly ask you to assume new information as true. In this case only, the best answer can include information that is outside the scope of the passage.

Contraries

A *contrary* distractor contradicts the main idea. If the question is not an EXCEPT, NOT, or LEAST, the answer choice is extremely unlikely to contradict the main idea. **Most answer choices support the main idea in one form or another.**

Suppose that the author argues passionately for the importance of extending healthcare access to all people living in the United States. An answer choice describing restrictions on healthcare access for certain social groups is unlikely to be the best answer unless the question stem specifically asks for a situation that the author would *oppose* or be *least* likely to support.

Simpletons

If the best answers on the CARS Section were simple, direct, and straightforward, everyone would do well. Instead, the correct answers are vague, ambiguous, and sometimes debatable. An answer choice that is easily verifiable from a reading of the passage is highly suspect and often incorrect. These answer choices are called *simpletons*. Simpletons are not always the wrong answer choice, but you should be highly suspicious when you see one.

Simpletons often have extreme wording like *always, never, and completely.* Be very cautious of choosing answer choices that contain words like these unless the main idea is similarly extreme. It is not impossible for the best answer to contain extreme words, but it is unlikely.

Here's a manufactured example of a simpleton:

> **13.** In mid-afternoon in December in Montana, the author believes that the color of the sky most closely resembles:
>
> **B.** cotton balls floating on a blue sea.

If this were the answer, everyone would choose it. This is unlikely to be the best answer.

Unintelligibles

Unintelligibles are answer choices that you do not understand. Whether it is a vocabulary word or a concept, avoid answer choices that you do not understand. These are likely to be traps. Strangely enough, many test takers are likely to choose an answer that confuses them. This is apparently because the MCAT® is a difficult test and students expect to be confused. Test writers sometimes purposely use distractors with obscure vocabulary or incomprehensible diction in order to appeal to the test taker who finds comfort in being confused. As a general rule, do not choose an answer that you don't understand unless you can positively eliminate all other choices. Be confident, not confused.

Here's a manufactured example of an unintelligible:

> **13.** In mid-afternoon in December in Montana, the author believes that the color of the sky most closely resembles:
>
> **C.** shades reminiscent of stratocumulus clouds.

Remember Key 2: Stay in touch with the passage and the author as you go through the question set. After you have read a few questions you have read many misleading, wrong answers. To stay oriented to the passage and the author, restate the main idea after reading each question stem.

Unless stratocumulus clouds were defined and discussed in the passage, this is unlikely to be the best answer. Be suspicious of answer choices including obscure vocabulary.

3.4 | Identifying the Best Answer

The best answer in the CARS section will fulfill two criteria: it will match the passage and it will answer the question being asked. One way to rule out wrong answer choices is to look for answers that fulfill one of these two criteria but not the other.

Familiarize yourself with the typical look and feel of strong answer choices. This will become easier with practice. The best answer choice contains a *softener*. Softeners are words that make the answer true under more circumstances, such as *most likely*, *seemed*, *had a tendency to*, *almost always*, *usually*, etc. An answer choice with a softener is not necessarily correct; it is just more likely to be correct than an answer choice with more extreme language.

Also pay attention to positive, neutral, and negative words when evaluating answer choices. The best answer will match the tone of the passage and the main idea. Just as the words chosen in the passage can lead you to the main idea, particular words in the answer choices can help you eliminate answer choices that are contradictory to the author's opinion or tone. Suppose a question asks for the author's opinion about a topic that was discussed in the passage from a fairly balanced perspective. An answer choice containing a strongly positive or negative opinion is unlikely to be the best answer.

For some tricky questions, the best answer must fulfill multiple criteria. A typical question stem might ask a variation of the following: "Which of these assertions from the passage is most supported by evidence?" Any answer choice that is NOT asserted in the passage can be eliminated. Any answer choice containing an assertion that is not supported by evidence in the passage can also be eliminated. The best answer will 1) contain a passage assertion and 2) be supported by some type of evidence, such as a list of examples or a quote from an expert. Being aware of the multiple conditions in the question stem will allow you to quickly hone in on the best answer by eliminating choices that fail to meet one or both of these conditions.

3.5 | Simplification of the Question and Answer Choices

It is often helpful to simplify the question and answer choices in terms of the main idea. Most test-takers already subconsciously simplify the question stems to some extent. The jump to doing it intentionally is not too difficult, and this technique makes it easier to evaluate how well the answer choices match the passage and question stem.

Re-examining the questions and answer choices from our original seven AAMC question stems in section 3.2, we have a passage with the following main idea:

"Great fiction provides a richness of language and feeling that is difficult to recreate in film. Contemporary authors emulating film have lost this richness and their audience with it."

This is a nice, complete main idea, but it can be difficult to understand all at once. It is helpful to simplify it as follows: past fiction, current fiction, and movies.

• Past fiction is good,

• Current fiction is bad, and

• Current fiction is like movies.

Remember Key 3: The best answer matches the main idea of the passage and answers the question well. This means that wrong answers can be ruled out when they match only the passage or only the question, but not both.

When analyzing the question stems and answer choices, restate them in terms of these ideas, keeping in mind that this is a simplification. Replace intimidating or complex words and phrases with simpler language aligning with major ideas discussed in the passage. For instance, any reference to "a great, forceful novel" or "a line-by-line description" can be replaced by "past fiction." "The passage suggests" can be replaced by "the author thinks." This technique is much like using the concept of an ideal gas to approximate the behavior of a real gas and then accounting for the characteristics of a real gas when more details are needed. Simplifying the answer choices makes it easy to evaluate each one in terms of the main idea of the passage.

Think back to the Examkrackers method for studying for the CARS section presented at the end of Lecture 1. Now you have covered many of the techniques that will help you get the most out of every CARS practice section. After taking a break for one day, examine the question stems and consider what they tell you about the passage, as demonstrated in this lecture. What does each question stem tell you about the main idea of the passage? The author's opinion? What the author is like, and what he or she cares about? Do the questions stems tell you anything about the passage argument? Sometimes the question stems will build on each other, providing a more complete picture of the author and the passage. Whenever possible, consider what the answer to the question might look like. Then move on to the answer choices. Examine the answers alongside the insights that you gained from analyzing the question stems, and compare them to what you thought the best answer would look like. Identify incorrect answers that fall into the categories described in this lecture. At the end of your analysis, go over the questions and answer choices one more time and restate each of them in simpler terms.

The idea behind this in-depth exercise is that eventually asking yourself these kinds of questions as well as simplifying questions and answers will become less strenuous. In fact, it will become second nature. This will go a long way toward choosing the best answers and improving your score.

Compare the following restatements with the original seven AAMC questions (if you want to practice, fold the page so you cannot see the restatements):

Original Question	Restatement

Question 1

The author of the passage believes that the fiction written by the current generation of authors:

- **A.** lacks the significance of fiction written by previous generations.
- **B.** is, as a whole, no better and no worse than fiction written by previous generations.
- **C.** brilliantly meets the particular needs of contemporary readers.
- **D.** is written by authors who show great confidence in their roles as writers.

Question 1

The author believes that current fiction is:

- **A.** not as good as past fiction.
- **B.** equal to past fiction.
- **C.** good.
- **D.** good.

Question 2

The overall point made by the passage's comparison of movies to fiction is that:

- **A.** contemporary authors have strengthened their fiction by the application of cinematic techniques.
- **B.** the film of Under the Volcano is bound to be more popular than the novel.
- **C.** great fiction provides a richness of language and feeling that is difficult to re-create in film.
- **D.** contemporary authors would be well advised to become screenwriters.

Question 2

The author compares movies to fiction in order to show that:

- **A.** movies have been good for fiction.
- **B.** movies are more likable than fiction.
- **C.** movies are not as good as good fiction.
- **D.** authors of fiction should make movies.

Question 3

According to the passage, John Gardner concedes that preliminary good advice to a beginning writer might be, "Write as if you were a movie camera." The word concedes here suggests that:

- I. Gardner's approach to writing has been influenced by the competing medium of film.
- II. Gardner must have written screenplays at one point in his life.
- III. Gardner dislikes the medium of film.

Question 3

John Gardner says, "Write like the movies," therefore:

- I. he has been influenced by movies.
- II. he wrote movies.
- III. he dislikes movies.

Question 4

The fact that the author rereads Under the Volcano because it has been made into a movie is ironic because it:

- I. seems to go against the overall point of the passage concerning fiction and film.
- II. implies that the film version was a box-office failure.
- III. hints that the author was dissatisfied with the novel.

Question 4

The author sees a movie that causes him to read a book. This:

- I. weakens his argument.
- II. means the movie was bad.
- III. means the author did not like the book.

Original Question	Restatement
Question 5	**Question 5**
The passage suggests that a reader who is not bored by a line-by-line description of a room most likely:	The author says that if you like past fiction:
○ **A.** prefers the quick fix of the movies.	○ **A.** you will like movies.
○ **B.** would be bored by a single shot of a room in a film.	○ **B.** you will be bored by past fiction.
○ **C.** has no tolerance for movies.	○ **C.** you won't like movies.
○ **D.** displays the attitude demanded by good fiction.	○ **D.** you will like past fiction.
Question 6	**Question 6**
The passage suggests that if a contemporary writer were to write a novel of great forcefulness, this novel would most likely:	If a new novel were like old fiction:
I. confuse and anger lovers of great literature.	I. people who like old fiction would not like the new novel.
II. exist in stark contrast to the typical contemporary novel.	II. the new novel would not be like current fiction.
III. win back some of the readers contemporary writers have lost.	III. people would like to read it.
Question 7	**Question 7**
The passage places the blame for contemporary writers' loss of readers on the:	No one reads current fiction because:
I. competition presented by movies.	I. movies are just as good.
II. writers themselves.	II. current fiction writers write bad fiction.
III. ignorance of the public.	III. people are ignorant.

You have four tools for finding the correct answer: looking back, the main idea, the question stems, and the answer choices. Use all of them in order to get your best MCAT® score. The fourth tool is the most difficult to master. When evaluating the answer choices for distractors, keep in mind that there are no absolutes, just suspects. When necessary, restate complicated questions using simplified concepts from the main idea.

Use the following questions and answer choices to practice using your four tools.

While the questions in this lecture are derived from real passages, only the questions and answer choices are given, not the passages! Through practice using only the questions and answers, you will learn how to use the wording of questions and answer choices to find information about the main idea and the author that can guide you to the best answer.

Passage I (Questions 1–7)

Question 1

According to the passage, the production of music is:

- **A.** always technical, never emotional.
- **B.** either technical or emotional.
- **C.** always emotional, never technical.
- **D.** neither technical nor emotional.

Question 2

A study found that as compared to musicians in African societies, a greater proportion of musicians in Western societies have paid employment. Based on information in the passage, this finding can likely be explained by the fact that:

- **A.** music is more recreational in African societies.
- **B.** more musicians receive training in Western societies.
- **C.** there is a greater demand for music in Western societies.
- **D.** Western societies have a larger population than that of African societies.

Question 3

Which of the following findings would most *weaken* the claim that time lines are relatively unique to African music?

- **A.** Popular American songs usually have a quick tempo.
- **B.** Asian music is often improvised.
- **C.** European dance can inspire the pace of the associated music.
- **D.** African musicians train composers all over the world.

Question 4

It has been said that music can bring together even the most bitter of rivals. Which of the following definitions of music proposed in the passage would best support this claim?

- **A.** Music is the language of emotions.
- **B.** Music reveals a group of people organizing and involving themselves with their own communal relationships.
- **C.** Music is a social event.
- **D.** Music is a public performance that takes place on social occasions when members of a group or a community come together for the enjoyment of leisure.

Question 5

In order to emphasize the improvisation of African music, the author quotes a Fante drummer discussing a "hidden rhythm." The author's point is that:

- **A.** music cannot be seen.
- **B.** music can be dictated by feelings.
- **C.** only composers understand rhythm.
- **D.** African musicians are guided by spirits.

Question 6

Based on the passage, it is reasonable to conclude that improvisation in music is affected by all of the following EXCEPT:

- **A.** the individual player.
- **B.** the community.
- **C.** the mood of the player.
- **D.** the instruments available.

Question 7

Suppose a professor defines African music as entirely driven by feeling. Would the author be likely to agree with the professor?

- **A.** Yes, because the author discusses how emotion guides African music.
- **B.** Yes, because the author believes that all music is inherently emotional.
- **C.** No, because the author describes other factors that influence African music.
- **D.** No, because the author argues that Western music is more emotional than African music.

STOP

Answers to Questions
Before you look at the answers, let's discuss them.

Question 1: Even without reading the passage, choice B is the most likely answer. It is always possible that the passage argues an extreme viewpoint, but common sense tells us that music is probably emotional in quality. The word "production" clues us in to the possibility that technical, non-emotional aspects of music are also considered in the passage. We can also choose choice B according to the simple logic that the best answers on the MCAT® usually do not contain extreme words like "always" and "never." The other questions stems and answer choices may shed more light on this question.

Question 2: The first question indicated that the passage is concerned with the quality of music. Is another theme of the passage the training and employment of musicians? Possibly, but this question may also just be another way to talk about music itself. We also now know that the passage involves a comparison between the music of Western and African societies. Choice A is a strong choice because it provides a plausible answer to the question and also relates back to the quality of music. Choices B and C sound very similar to each other. Both are out of the scope of the passage if we assume that the main idea relates to the quality of music itself. Choice D sounds like a roundabout distractor: it does not actually provide an answer to the question. Choice A seems like the best answer.

Question 3: Presumably the passage defined time lines, but we can infer from the question stem that they have something to do with the timing or pace of music. The best answer will establish that places other than Africa pay attention to timing in music. Choice A seems like a possible answer. Improvisation does not directly involve timing, so choice B is not a likely answer. Choice C is similar to choice A and is another possible answer. If African musicians train other composers, thus spreading African music throughout the world, time lines may very well still be unique to African music. Choice D can be eliminated. We cannot distinguish between choices A and C with the information given. It turns out that the passage defines time lines as pulsations related to movements that set the tempo, so choice C is the best answer.
Note that "time lines" may be a "technical" aspect of the production of music. Based on the fact that none of the answer choices discuss emotion, they are at least not an emotional aspect of music. This reasoning further supports choice B as the best answer to Question 1.

Question 4: This question does not require any information from the passage. To answer it, simply ask: Which answer choice shows how music can bring together people who dislike each other? Choice A can be eliminated because it does not relate to the social nature of music (although it does further establish that the passage discusses the emotional nature of music). Choice B describes music as a process that allows people to develop relationships, so it is a strong answer. Choice C is a simpleton distractor: compared to choice B, it does not specifically answer the question. Choice D describes music as a social experience, but choice B is a better answer because it refers to building relationships rather than simply enjoying a leisure activity.

Question 5: Choice A is a simpleton distractor preying on the test-taker who interprets "hidden" too literally – we already know that music cannot be seen. Choice B refers back to the theme of emotion in music and seems compatible with a "hidden rhythm," so it is a likely answer. Choice C is unrelated to the question stem or any of the concepts that we have seen so far, so it can be eliminated. Similarly, there is no reason to believe that the passage discussed spirits playing a role in music among African musicians. Based on the available information, choice B is the best answer.

Question 6: We may not know the author's views on improvisation, but we do know that it is an aspect of music. Mood, or emotion, is likely involved, so choice C can be eliminated. Since a previous question indicated that the passage defines music as having a social quality, it is likely that the community could also have an influence, and choice B can be eliminated. It is reasonable to assume that the individual player can be influenced by his or her emotions and the surrounding community. This would be consistent with the question stem and answer for Question 5. Choice A can be eliminated, leaving choice D as the most likely answer. Notice that it stands out from the others as a topic that has not been referenced in previous questions and answer choices.

Question 7: Now that we have a rigorous understanding of the passage, this question is easy to answer. The author discusses both emotional and non-emotional aspects of music, so he or she would not agree with the statement in the question stem. Choices A and B can be eliminated. The author is also probably most interested in African music than in Western music since multiple question stems reference African music. This makes choice C a more likely answer than choice D.

The best answers are: 1. B, 2. A, 3. C, 4. B, 5. B, 6. D, 7. C.

STOP HERE UNTIL CLASS!

(DO NOT LOOK AT THE FOLLOWING QUESTIONS UNTIL CLASS.

IF YOU WILL NOT BE ATTENDING CLASS, GIVE YOURSELF 30
MINUTES TO COMPLETE THE FOLLOWING SET OF QUESTIONS.)

Passage I (Questions 1-7)

Question 1

When a beaver senses danger, it will instinctively slap its tail on the water, warning other beavers. According to the passage, this is not "a true form of communication" because it:

- ○ **A.** is instinctive.
- ○ **B.** is not language.
- ○ **C.** is unidirectional.
- ○ **D.** lacks emotion.

Question 2

According to the passage, which of the following are reasons that apes are better communicators than monkeys?

    I. Apes are capable of a greater variety of facial expressions.
    II. Apes are capable of a greater variety of sounds.
    III. Apes have a greater intelligence with which to interpret signals.

- ○ **A.** I and II only
- ○ **B.** I and III only
- ○ **C.** II and III only
- ○ **D.** I, II, and III

Question 3

Suppose researchers selected three adult chimpanzees from a wild troop and taught them sign language. Based on information in the passage, if the researchers returned to the same troop four years later, which chimpanzees in the troop might they expect to be using sign language?

- ○ **A.** Only the chimpanzees that were originally taught sign language
- ○ **B.** Only the chimpanzees that were originally taught sign language and their offspring
- ○ **C.** All chimpanzees in the troop
- ○ **D.** No chimpanzees in the troop

Question 4

According to the passage, which of the following is the most important difference between humans and chimpanzees that explains why humans developed language and chimpanzees did not?

- ○ **A.** Genetic makeup
- ○ **B.** Personal relationships
- ○ **C.** Intelligence
- ○ **D.** The ability to produce a variety of sounds

Question 5

Which of the following would most weaken the author's claim that chimps are the most intelligent communicators in the animal world?

- ○ **A.** Through whistling and clicking alone, two dolphins are able to work together to perform coordinated movements.
- ○ **B.** A wolf's howl can be heard by another wolf from several miles away.
- ○ **C.** Ants have more developed chemical messages than any other animal.
- ○ **D.** A honey bee instinctively performs a complicated series of movements that signals the location of a pollen source to the rest of the hive.

Question 6

The author most likely believes that by studying chimpanzee behavior, humans may learn:

- ○ **A.** that chimpanzees communicate as effectively as humans.
- ○ **B.** new ways of communication.
- ○ **C.** how ancestors of humans developed speech.
- ○ **D.** why chimpanzees cannot speak.

Question 7

The author claims that "The modern chimp may be making the first steps toward language" (paragraph 2). Based on the context of this claim in the passage, the author might also agree with which of the following statements?

- ○ **A.** Modern chimpanzees will one day develop their own spoken language.
- ○ **B.** Given the right training, modern chimpanzees are capable of speech.
- ○ **C.** Specific social behaviors of chimpanzees may prevent them from developing a universal language.
- ○ **D.** Modern chimpanzees are evolving more fluid communication skills.

Next ▶

Passage II (Questions 8–16)

Question 8

According to the passage, a universally accepted scientific theory:

○ **A.** cannot be proven wrong.
○ **B.** is not a fundamental truth.
○ **C.** usually replaces a religious belief.
○ **D.** is no better than a religious belief as a predictor of natural phenomena.

Question 9

The author believes that the view that "You can't argue with science" is:

○ **A.** not scientific.
○ **B.** held only by top scientists.
○ **C.** generally correct.
○ **D.** true concerning matters outside of religion.

Question 10

The author mentions the Scopes Monkey Trial in order to support the claim that:

○ **A.** religion and science are contradictory.
○ **B.** the functions of science and religion are often misunderstood.
○ **C.** science will eventually triumph over religion.
○ **D.** when science and religion are in conflict, most people will believe religion.

Question 11

Einstein once said, "Whether you can observe a thing or not depends on the theory which you use. It is the theory which decides what can be observed." This quote best supports the author's claim that:

○ **A.** science is an imperfect description of nature.
○ **B.** science is not based on fact.
○ **C.** religion is more reliable than science.
○ **D.** religion and science are similar.

Question 12

Dawkins claims that "Religion is, in a sense, science; it's just bad science" (paragraph 4). Dawkins' point is that:

○ **A.** religion attempts to answer the wrong questions.
○ **B.** religion does not provide answers.
○ **C.** the answers provided by religion are unreliable.
○ **D.** religious people are less honest than scientists.

Question 13

If during a speech Dawkins said, "The argument that religion and science answer different types of questions is just false," which of the following statements made by Dawkins in the same speech would most weaken his own claim?

○ **A.** Religions throughout history have attempted to answer questions that belong in the realm of science.
○ **B.** Religion is science; it's just bad science.
○ **C.** Science, then, is free of the main vice of religion, which is faith.
○ **D.** Most religions offer a cosmology and a biology, a theory of life, a theory of origins, and a reason for existence.

Question 14

According to the passage, which of the following properly belongs to the realm of science, but NOT to the realm of religion?

○ **A.** Healthy skepticism
○ **B.** Reliable prediction
○ **C.** Close observation
○ **D.** Peer review

Question 15

With which of the following statements might the author agree?

○ **A.** Science proves that God does not exist.
○ **B.** Science proves the existence of God.
○ **C.** God responds to prayer with a gentle guiding hand.
○ **D.** God reveals himself through the lawful harmony of the universe.

Question 16

According to the author, science and religion:

○ **A.** ask the same questions, and provide conflicting answers.
○ **B.** ask the same questions, and provide compatible answers.
○ **C.** ask different questions, and provide conflicting answers.
○ **D.** ask different questions, and provide compatible answers.

Passage III (Questions 17–23)

Question 17

The author of the passage believes that the modern art held in high esteem by today's art critics:

- ○ **A.** has a weaker impact on contemporary society than did classical art.
- ○ **B.** should not be judged in the same context as classical art.
- ○ **C.** makes a clear statement about today's society.
- ○ **D.** is a testament to the extraordinary skills of modern artists.

Question 18

The comparison of sculpture and architecture (paragraph 2) best supports the author's claim that:

- ○ **A.** modern artists have had to use new technologies in order to stay connected to their audience.
- ○ **B.** modern art is more recognizable than classical art.
- ○ **C.** art must address the social problems faced by contemporary society.
- ○ **D.** function restrains novelty and dictates beauty.

Question 19

The author would most likely agree that truly great works of art:

- ○ **A.** comment on important contemporary social issues.
- ○ **B.** are beautiful to look at.
- ○ **C.** express the inner feelings of the artist.
- ○ **D.** stimulate novel thoughts.

Question 20

It has been said that art not only mimics reality, but reality also mimics art. Which of the assertions from the passage would best support this claim?

- ○ **A.** Beauty is not in the eye of the beholder, but is an absolute reality to be discovered by the artist.
- ○ **B.** Great men in history have been inspired to great deeds by great art.
- ○ **C.** No mere child could recreate The Statue of David.
- ○ **D.** Classical artwork was carefully planned and crafted.

Question 21

Artwork resembling modern abstract art, but painted by a chimpanzee, recently sold alongside famous works at a prestigious London auction house for over $25,000. Based on this information, the author might agree with which of the following statements?

- ○ **A.** Chimpanzees are capable of expressing emotion.
- ○ **B.** Some chimpanzees may be great artists.
- ○ **C.** Some modern art resembles the scribbling of a chimpanzee.
- ○ **D.** Great artwork does not require great minds.

Question 22

Picasso is credited with saying "If there were only one truth, you couldn't paint one hundred canvases on the same theme." This statement best supports which of the following assertions from the passage?

- ○ **A.** If we find classical art beautiful, it is because we see hints of perfection in otherwise common and familiar forms.
- ○ **B.** The modern artist invites us to share a reality that is uniquely his own.
- ○ **C.** There is beauty in truth.
- ○ **D.** Upon a closer inspection, we see that the Discobolus by Myron portrays the discus throw rather than the discus thrower.

Question 23

The passage places the blame for the average person's lack of interest in modern art on:

- I. a lack of talented modern artists.
- II. obtuse subject matter.
- III. the ignorance of the average person.

- ○ **A.** I only
- ○ **B.** II only
- ○ **C.** I and II only
- ○ **D.** I, II, and III

STOP

Do not look at the answers yet, just read on.

Passage I

Question 1: From a layman's perspective, the beaver is "communicating" to other beavers. Thus, we know that the word "true" here is going to be important. The author has apparently distinguished "true communication" from our everyday understanding of the word. From question 2 we see that apes and monkeys both "communicate" according to the passage. Apes and monkeys do not have language, so we can assume that "true communication" does not require language. We can get rid of choice B. Choice D seems poor as well, since presumably a beaver in danger would not be emotionless. Of course you might make the argument that all animals lack emotion, but then there is question 2 again, where apes are animals and apes are communicating, so communication is possible for animals. Since the author is interested in communication (a human quality) in animals, it seems likely that the author would also believe that animals can feel emotion (another human quality). So now we are left with choice A or C. The tail slap is instinctive, as per the question, and it seems to be unidirectional. So which one would be a reason that it is NOT "true" communication? We can think of many examples of communication that are unidirectional: television, a smile, a letter, etc… This weakens choice C. Choice A is the best answer.

Question 2: Common sense tells us that having greater intelligence and being better at producing sound and facial expressions would make us better communicators, so the question is really asking, "At which of these an ape is better than a monkey?" From question stem 5 we see that chimps, which are apes, are "the most intelligent communicators in the animal world," so we know that option III must be part of the answer. Thus choice A is incorrect. We cannot be certain about sound or facial expressions, so it is difficult to narrow this one down just yet.

Question 3: This question is basically asking us, "In the wild, which other chimpanzees, if any, does the author think a signing chimpanzee would teach sign language? And would the signing chimpanzee even retain his sign language?" This question is about social interactions within the troop. We do not have enough information to answer it yet.

Question 4: At first glance, all the answers seem to be possible. As usual, it is important to read the question stem carefully. The stem does not ask for "the only reason" why humans developed language and chimps did not; it is asking for the "most important" reason, and the most important reason "according to the passage." All of the answers may be legitimate reasons why chimps did not develop language and humans did, but which one does the author believe is the most important? Is this author most concerned with genetics, social relationships, intelligence, or ability to produce sounds? Question 3 clearly lends support to choice B. Question 5 seems to strengthen choice C, since it points out the importance of intelligence in communication. Question 2 mentions sound in an answer choice, but we do not know whether it is the best answer choice. Genetics seems to have no support from any other question, so choice A seems wrong.

Question 5: This question can be answered with common sense. The question asks about intelligence. Which answer choice has to do with intelligence? Only choice A.

Question 6: Choice A is false according to common sense and based on other questions. For example, question 4 points out that chimpanzees did not develop language while humans did, and question 5 presents chimps as "the most intelligent communicators **in the animal world**," implying that they are still not as skilled as humans. Choice B seems highly unlikely: since it has been established that chimpanzees communicate less effectively than humans, why would humans learn new communication methods from them? Choice D is wrong because the author's interest lies in communication, not in chimps themselves. In other words, when it comes right down to it, he wants to learn about communication, not about chimps. Choice C satisfies this criterion. Notice that this question also emphasizes behavior. The passage is looking more and more to be about communication as it is affected by social interactions. This provides more support for choice B in question 4.

Question 7: It is important to keep your common sense. Does the author really believe that chimps will be speaking one day? No, of course not. Choices A and B are incorrect. That leaves choices C and D. Both are tempting, but choice C is the better answer because the social behavior aspect of choice C fits so neatly with the rest of the questions. Choice C also strongly suggests that the answer to question 4 is B.

We now have enough information to revisit and answer the earlier questions.

Passage I

Question 2 REVISITED: We know that option III is true. The only hint for choosing option I or II, and it is quite a small hint, is the sense in the questions that the passage was concerned with signs, supporting option I, and not really as concerned with sounds, lacking support for option II. It would be difficult to be confident about this without reading the passage, but, hey, that's why you read the passage. Choice B is the best answer.

Question 3 REVISITED: Now that we understand that the passage is about social behavior as well as communication, and that (according to the answer to question 7) the social behaviors of chimps prevent them from developing a universal language, we know that the chimps are not going to teach all their troop mates to use sign language. Choice C is wrong. There is no evidence in the question stems that the chimp would lose his ability to use sign language, so choice D is unlikely. The question is, "Would the adults teach signing to their offspring?" This is very tough to answer without reading the passage, but there is a hint. What are the "first steps toward language" that the author talks about in question 7? The chimps are teaching their offspring, but not their peers—this is another social behavior standing in the way of language development. Choice B is the best answer.

Question 4 REVISITED: From questions 6 and 7 we see that the answer must be choice B.

Passage II

Question 8: As an MCAT® student strong in the sciences, you know that choice A is false and that choice B is true. Choice C is possible. Choice D seems unlikely. The answer is probably choice B, but we'll have to come back.

Question 9: Again, as an MCAT® student strong in the sciences, you know that choices B, C, and D are false. Furthermore, choice C is not a good MCAT® answer because it is incredibly vague. Choice A is the best answer. Now it is easy to go back and answer question 8.

Question 8 REVISITED: In the light of question 9, the best answer is choice B. Also, since we now know that choice D is wrong, we know that the author is taking a kind of middle ground between science and religion.

Question 10: Choices A and C do not represent the tone that questions 8 and 9 present. They are incorrect. Choice B seems most closely related to the middle ground tone of the questions and answers to 8 and 9. The Scopes Monkey trial refers to the trial of John Scopes for illegally teaching evolution in public school. He was convicted. Obviously,

it was discussed in the passage, so being familiar with it before the MCAT® is unnecessary. The trial was a conflict between science and religion, but it in no way supports the conclusion drawn by choice D. However, it could support an argument that the roles of religion and science are misunderstood. Choice B is the best answer.

Question 11: Choice B implies that a quote from Einstein is used to support a claim that science is not based upon fact. It also implies that the author believes science is not based upon fact. Notice that this further supports the answer to 9 by ruling out choice B. Einstein was certainly a top scientist, and he believed that science could be questioned.

Because choice D from Question 8 was incorrect, the author probably would find choices B and C to be incorrect as well. The question does not draw any connection between religion and science, so choice D seems unlikely. Choice A seems to be a middle ground again and works especially well with the assertion in question 8 that a scientific theory is not a fundamental truth. Choice A is the best answer.

Question 12: Dawkins is not the author, or he would not have been named in the question. Dawkins must be used to support the author's point. The aggressive, confrontational tone of Dawkins' comment is in strong contrast to the moderate tone of the author as revealed by the questions so far. Still, since this question is about Dawkins, rather than the author, it is difficult to answer without reading more questions. We'll have to come back.

Question 13: This question is a logic problem that can be answered by common sense alone. Choice A most weakens Dawkins' claim. Dawkins claims in the question stem that religion and science do not answer different questions, so they must either answer the same question or no questions at all. Choice A indicates that Dawkins believes that certain questions belong in the realm of science and not in the realm of religion. This means that he believes that religion and science do not answer the same questions. This is a contradiction and weakens his argument. The best answer is choice A.

Question 12 REVISITED: From question 13 we see that Dawkins does not believe choice A. Question 12 also seems to indicate that Dawkins believes religion does provide answers, just answers that are somehow not as good as those provided by science. This fits best with choice C. The honesty of religious people is not addressed, leaving no evidence for choice D. Choice C is the best answer.

Question 14: Choice B fits nicely with choice D in question 8 being incorrect. Skepticism, close observation, and peer review are not addressed by any other question, so choices A, C, and D are not supported.

Question 15: Based upon questions 8 and 9, the author would have difficulty arguing that science proves anything. Choices A and B are incorrect. These answer choices are also weakened by the fact that they are stated much more strongly than the moderate tone of the other questions and correct answers. Choice C might be possible, but choice D goes much better with question 14. Based upon questions 8 and 14, the author seems to feel that science is a reliable predictor. Choice D allows for such predictions (in accordance with "lawful harmony") and for God, while choice C seems likely to interfere with the predictive powers of science.

Question 16: Question 14 tells us that the author believes that science and religion ask different questions. The tone of the questions tells us that he believes the answers are compatible. Choice D for question 15 accounts for both the different questions asked by science and religion and the compatibility of science and religion. Choice D is the best answer.

Passage III

Question 17: Why does the question include the modifying phrase "held in high esteem by today's art critics"? To what other kind of modern art might the question refer? Is there modern art that today's art critics consider bad? Is there bad modern art? Apparently, the question writer wants to be clear that he is talking only about good modern art and not about bad modern art. Choice A is the only answer that makes sense using this distinction. With this distinction, choice A can be rephrased as "Even good modern art is worse than classical art," while the importance of the distinction is lost with choices B, C, and D. For instance, choice B: "Even good modern art should not be judged in the same context as classical art." Choice C: "Even good modern art makes a clear statement about today's society." Choice D: "Even good modern art is a testament to the extraordinary skills of modern artists." For the MCAT®, it is important to develop this sense or feeling of whether or not the answer choice fits the question stem. Choice A is the best answer because it fits with the question stem while the other choices do not. Based upon this answer we have learned quite a bit about the author. Now we know that the author has something against modern art and is in favor of classical art. Since choices B, C, and D are weak answers, we can assume that the author thinks it is acceptable to judge modern art and classical art in the same context, that modern art does not make a clear statement about today's society, and that modern art is not a testament to the skills of the modern artist.

Question 18: The question asks about a comparison. The best answer will should address a comparison. Choice D indicates that function behaves in two different ways: 1) It restrains novelty and 2) It dictates beauty. How might this work with sculpture and architecture? How does function apply to architecture? Architecture has a specific function as housing or shelter. Might this function restrain novelty (or new ideas) in architecture? It seems logical. A roof can be made to look differently, but it still must have certain characteristics in order to function like a roof. Might this function also dictate beauty in architecture? Perhaps since the roof is required, what is beautiful in architecture must include a roof. On the other hand, sculpture does not seem to have a function in the same sense. Could a comparison to sculpture and architecture demonstrate how function restrains novelty and dictates beauty? It would seem so. Choice D is a possibility. Choices A, B, and C do not address the comparison quite as well. In addition, choices A and B seem to favor modern art, contradicting the negative feel toward modern art in question 17. Choice D seems to be the best answer, but we cannot be certain yet.

Question 19: The word "truly" is important here. It indicates that the author distinguishes between great works of art and "truly" great works of art. Might that mean that he disagrees with art critics about what is and is not great art? This would support our answer for question 17. Since the author does not seem to be enamored with modern art, and he does seem to like classical art, it is unlikely that he would think that "truly" great art must comment on important contemporary social issues. Choice A is probably out. We will revisit this question after the next question.

Question 20: This question can be answered by common sense. Only choice B answers the question. Only choice B is an example of reality mimicking art. The other choices simply do not address the premise of the question. Choice B is the best answer. This question is important because it gives us four examples of what the author thinks in the four answer choices (all "assertions from the passage"). Even if we had read the passage, these answer choices would be valuable because they sum up the author's ideas in the question writer's words. What the question writer thinks the author said is even more important than what the author thinks he said. Choice A tells us that the author believes beauty is a reality rather than a matter of opinion. This verifies choice B for question 19.

Question 19 REVISITED: From question 20, choice A, we know that the author believes that beauty is not a matter of opinion. This indicates that choice B in question 19 must be the best answer.

Question 21: Clearly choices A and B are wrong; this passage is not about chimps, it is about art. Choice D would indicate that the author thinks that modern art by chimps is "great artwork." Instead, common sense and the author's attitude toward modern art in question 17 tell us that the best answer is choice C.

Question 22: The quote says there is more than one reality and that art is the painter's idea of reality. Only choice B matches the quote. Choice B is the best answer. Again we have four examples of what the author thinks in the four answer choices. Especially revealing is choice A, which verifies that the author likes classical art and tells us why. This strongly supports choice B in question 19.

Question 23: From previous questions we know that the author likes classical art more than modern art. Choice A in question 22 tells us that classical art is beautiful because of the true beauty discovered in its common and familiar subject matter, while choice B tells us that the modern artist is sharing his own reality that is "uniquely his own," i.e., not a common familiar subject matter. Therefore the subject matter of modern art must be a key reason that the author finds modern art less beautiful. Option II is likely to be a part of the strongest answer. On the other hand, there is no hint that the author has an issue with the talent of the modern artist; he is instead focused on the very nature of modern art. This leaves only choice B.

Answers:	4. B	8. B	12. C	16. D	20. B
1. A	5. A	9. A	13. A	17. A	21. C
2. B	6. C	10. B	14. B	18. D	22. B
3. B	7. C	11. A	15. D	19. B	23. B

These exercises are NOT intended to convince you to not read the passage. You should always read the passage. However, the exercises should show you that the questions and answer choices contain a large amount of information. If you achieved a higher score without even reading the passage, you probably haven't been taking advantage of the wealth of information in the question stems and answer choices.

DON'T FORGET YOUR KEYS

1. Question stems are simple at their core. Rephrase complex wording in the question stem to find the question being asked. Look out for when the main idea is presented in the question stem – a gift!

2. Keep your hand on the pulse of the author as you answer the questions. After reading each question stem, restate the main idea and predict an answer.

3. The best answer to CARS questions will both match the passage and answer the question stem.

Advanced CARS Skills

4.1 Introduction

4.2 A Practical Approach to Constructing the Main Idea: The Spectrum

4.3 Building the Spectrum Step by Step

4.4 Spectrum Tips

4.5 Identifying Passage and Question Types

4.1 Introduction

This lecture will help you achieve an even higher score on the CARS section. First you will learn how to best construct the author's main idea and organize the passage, using the Spectrum. Next you will learn to recognize CARS passage and question types to more easily find the main idea and predict the best answer.

The skills gained from the preceding three lectures will come together in this last chapter. In particular, reading for the author's voice and narrating the passage are helpful when building a Spectrum.

THE 3 KEYS

1. Use a Spectrum to organize passage ideas and locate the author's opinion.

2. The main idea is usually on the same side of the Spectrum where the author began.

3. After reading each question stem, notice the question type. Proceed accordingly. Every question type is easier with the main idea in mind.

*← ANONYMITY

FAME →

Motivation is internal
authentic, genuine

Motivation is often exter...

Greater personal freedom

Life is "on di...

Secretive, mysterious

Associated w...

Rebellious in current culture

Conforming...

MAIN IDEA:

Maintain a separation ... identity
and actions creates...

4.2 A Practical Approach to Constructing the Main Idea: The Spectrum

The **Spectrum** is a practical tool that will help you organize the range of opinions in a CARS passage in order to discover the main idea. This section will explain why you need the Spectrum and how to build one.

Why is the Spectrum called the Spectrum? Think of the electromagnetic spectrum of visible light. The passage presents a range of opinions – shades of grey between two more extreme opinions. By writing similar ideas together vertically and noting distinctions horizontally along the spectrum of opinions, it becomes easier to see the difference between the shades of gray. The main idea is usually a nuance of the more extreme ideas.

Why do you need the Spectrum?

CARS passages can be disorganized and needlessly complex. They present a range of opinions, including the one the author believes. Narrating the passage will help you find the author's voice. Building a Spectrum will help you organize ideas that zig and zag between one idea and its opposite. The Spectrum allows you to see a pattern and locate the author.

Why is the AAMC testing your ability to organize information and determine the author's opinion? Very simply, this is a critical skill in medicine. By nature, natural speech does not lend itself to perfect organization. Central to your success will be your ability to listen to patients, organize what you hear, and discover the nuance of each patient's concerns.

The Spectrum is a tool designed to make it easy to follow and organize a CARS passage in order to locate the author's main idea. Students who use the Spectrum report that many CARS questions that had seemed very difficult became clear and easy, once the main idea and the contrast between ideas are clearly organized in the Spectrum. The Spectrum can serve as a quick visual reference, helping you stay oriented when answering questions.

What is a Spectrum and how do you build one?

Put simply, a Spectrum is a tool used to organize the range of ideas and opinions in a confusing CARS passage. Authors usually present their own opinion, but they also discuss opposing ideas, as well as views in between and views at ideological extremes. When you build a Spectrum, you will write down all of the important ideas in simple terms and sort them into a continuum that stretches from one extreme to the opposite extreme.

A Spectrum starts as two lines drawn on a piece of paper in the shape of a big letter "T": a long horizontal line with a vertical line down the middle (see below). You can easily make each Spectrum on the scrap paper provided by the testing center.

Begin reading the passage. Within the first few sentences, identify an idea that the author seems to like, or a pair of opposing ideas, one of which the author seems to favor over the other. Write the idea on one side, or the pair of ideas on opposite sides of the Spectrum. Put a large asterisk on the top of side that the author seems to favor from the beginning so you remember where the author began. Usually the author will remain on that side, but the author's main idea will be an adjustment or nuance, somewhere closer to the middle.

As you continue through the passage, collect ideas that represent the two sides—what the author likes and what the author does not like—and look for the author's opinion, which will usually lie closer to the middle. Write them into the Spectrum in your own words, using short phrases of one to three words. Locate the ideas horizontally with the extreme ideas at the sides and the more moderate views closer to the center but still on one side or the other.

Once you see a pattern emerge on each side, vertically, give a title to the theme of each side.

By the end of the passage, you have in front of you an organized picture of what the author thinks and likes, and what the author does not like. The written Spectrum allows you to see the pattern on each side, and to locate the author's main idea. The main idea is usually on the side the author presented in the first few sentences, but it will be less extreme, located toward the middle of the Spectrum.

Here is a model spectrum, showing where each type of opinion or idea goes:

The ends of the Spectrum are ideas that are as different as apples and oranges. The passage's author will almost never take a stance on one of the extremes: instead, he or she will argue a position just off center.

| FIGURE 4.1 | Model Spectrum |

The CARS Spectrum should remind you of the spectrum of electromagnetic radiation in physics. Just as the visual spectrum contains all possible colors, the CARS Spectrum encompasses all possible viewpoints between two extremes.

TITLE DESCRIBES PATTERN   TITLE DESCRIBES PATTERN

Idea(s) author likes
Opinion author likes
Terms that go with this opinion

Opposite idea(s)
Opposite opinion(s)
Terms that go with opposite opinion

Extreme opinion

Opposite extreme

Main idea:
The author's opinion will be closer to the middle but on the side where the author began.

Remember Key 2: The author reveals likes and dislikes in the first few sentences. Put an asterisk on one side of the Spectrum to remind yourself of the author's side. When the author gives the main idea later in the passage, it will be a nuanced, moderate version of the author's opening ideas. The main idea will be on the same side of the Spectrum where the author began, towards the middle.

To review:

1. **Draw** a big letter "T".

2. **Read for opinions and their opposites**: what does the author like and dislike? When possible, put the ideas into your own words – one- to three-word phrases – and write them into one side or the opposite side of the Spectrum. Always choose a side, but locate the ideas horizontally – extreme views at the ends and more moderate views on one side closer to the middle. If you do not find an opposite opinion in the passage, create it yourself on the opposite side of the Spectrum.

3. **Star ★ the side where the author began**. Within the first few lines of the passage, notice the language to identify which side the author favors, and place a large asterisk on that side of the Spectrum. As the passage zigs and zags, presenting multiple opinions, this mark will help you remember the side your author is on.

4. **Locate the main idea**. Continue sorting as you read, placing those ideas the author likes on one side and those the author does not favor on the other. Read for the author's opinion. The main idea is usually a nuanced version of the author's more extreme idea, but not an opposite. This is the main idea. It is usually an adjustment or slight contrast to where the author began. It usually falls on the side with the asterisk but toward the middle.

5. **Find the vertical pattern on each side**. Once you have collected a few phrases on each side, look for a pattern and write a one- or two-word title for each side of the Spectrum.

Once you get comfortable making a Spectrum, you will find that it increases your understanding of the passage and your grasp of the main idea. This clarity and the Spectrum itself make answering the questions much easier. In the next section, you will create your first Spectrum.

4.3 | Building the Spectrum Step by Step

Sample Spectrum

In this section, we'll go through the *Counter Culture* passage from Lecture 2 one paragraph at a time, building a Spectrum as we go. Here's the first paragraph:

> It is roughly a century since European art began to experience its first significant defections from the standards of painting and sculpture that we inherit from the early Renaissance. Looking back now across a long succession of innovative movements and stylistic revolutions, most of us have little trouble recognizing that such aesthetic orthodoxies of the past as the representative convention, exact anatomy and optical perspective, the casement-window canvas, along with the repertory of materials and subject matters we associate with the Old Masters—that all this makes up not "art" itself in any absolute sense, but something like a school of art, one great tradition among many. We acknowledge the excellence which a Raphael or Rembrandt could achieve within the canons of that school; but we have grown accustomed to the idea that there are other aesthetic visions of equal validity. Indeed, innovation in the arts has become a convention in its own right with us, a "tradition of the new," to such a degree that there are critics to whom it seems to be intolerable that any two painters should paint alike. We demand radical originality, and often confuse it with quality.

TRADITION	CHANGE
Old art	New art
Orthodoxy	Innovation
Old masters	Other visions
One kind of art	Many styles
	New just to be new

The first sentence sets up a contrast: "defections" from Renaissance art. Simplify this as *new art* and *old art*. "Defections" is a positive term – people defect from things that are oppressive or stifling – it seems likely that the author favors new art over old art. From the start, place a big asterisk (a big star) on the new art side of the spectrum.

Continuing through the paragraph, more opposites seem to fit with old art and new art: orthodoxy/innovation and Old Masters/other visions. Notice the contrast between the idea that Renaissance art is the only kind of art and the idea that there are many possible styles of art (you can restate this as one kind of art/ many styles). The author also discusses art that is highly original but of low quality: it is new just for the sake of being new. The author likes new art, but not to this extreme.

Look at the second paragraph:

> Yet what a jolt it was to our great-grandparents to see the certainties of the academic tradition melt away before their eyes. How distressing, especially for the academicians, who were the guardians of a classic heritage embodying time-honored techniques and standards whose perfection had been the labor of genius. Suddenly they found art as they understood it being rejected by upstarts who were unwilling to let a single premise of the inherited wisdom stand unchallenged, or so it seemed. Now, with a little hindsight, it is not difficult to discern continuities where our predecessors saw only ruthless disjunctions. To see, as well, that the artistic revolutionaries of the past were, at their best, only opening our minds to a more global conception of art which demanded a deeper experience of light, color, and form. Through their work, too, the art of our time has done much to salvage the values of the primitive and childlike, the dream, the immediate emotional response, the life of fantasy, and the transcendent symbol.

Up until this point, the author has spoken in mostly positive terms about new art. But the first few sentences of this paragraph seem to say the reverse: the Old Masters represent a "classic heritage" while the innovators were "upstarts" who were "distressing" to those who cared about art. Summarize these ideas as *classics/rebels*. This turn around might at first confuse, but remember that the passage author will often zig and zag between a broad range of opinions. The author began with the author's opinion and will present his or her nuanced view as the passage continues. By placing the asterisk earlier to identify the author's side, you will stay oriented when the passage begins to zig and zag. The last two sentences of the paragraph show the author returning to his preference for new art and change: the artistic innovators were "opening our minds" (*change opens minds*). Add the ideas from this paragraph to the Spectrum.

TRADITION	CHANGE
←	→ *
Old art	New art
Orthodoxy	Innovation
Old masters	Other visions
One kind of art	Many styles
Classic heritage	New just to be new / Distressing upstarts
	Change opens minds

A pattern has emerged on each side and you can now title each side according to its theme.

Here are the third and fourth paragraphs of the passage:

> In our own day, much the same sort of turning point has been reached in the history of science. It is as if the aesthetic ground pioneered by the artists now unfolds before us as a new ontological awareness. We are at a moment when the reality to which scientists address themselves comes more and more to be recognized as but one segment of a far broader Spectrum. Science, for so long regarded as our single valid picture of the world, now emerges as, also, a school: *a school of consciousness*, beside which alternative realities take their place.
>
> There are, so far, only fragile and scattered beginnings of this perception. They are still the subterranean history of our time. How far they will carry toward liberating us from the orthodox world view of the technocratic establishment is still doubtful. These days, many gestures of rebellion are subtly denatured, adjusted, and converted into oaths of allegiance. In our society at large, little beyond submerged unease challenges the lingering authority of science and technique, that dull ache at the bottom of the soul we refer to when we speak (usually too glibly) of an "age of anxiety," an "age of longing."

> *Source: Adapted from T. Roszak, The Making of a Counter Culture. 1969 Doubleday.*

In these paragraphs, the topic of the passage seems to change. Suddenly the author is talking about science instead of art. When this happens, your job is to make a connection where at first you might not see one. Remember that this Spectrum shows ideas along the continuum between classic, revered tradition and radical change. The contrast between *one kind of art* and *many styles* is cropping up again here, in a claim about science. Science, the author says, is not the "single valid picture of the world" anymore; it is just one reality among many alternatives (*science=reality/many realities*). The author sees this idea "liberating us" from the "technocratic establishment" (*tech establishment/liberation*). Notice that the author is writing with passionate language, revealing that he cares a great deal about this topic, science. The author does not seem confident that the revolution will turn out the way it did in the art world. The author's tone is concerned, or even heartbroken. How far the change will go is "doubtful" (*change in science doubtful*).

You have finished the passage, and now you can complete the Spectrum to construct the main idea. You now know that the author primarily cares about science. The author included the paragraphs on art to set up the main idea: the need for rebellion against scientific orthodoxy. You know, from his example of the revolution in the art world, that the author favors change. You also know, from the final paragraph, that he is doubtful about whether science will see the change he wants. The final version of the Spectrum, including the main idea, looks like this:

TRADITION	CHANGE
←	→ *
Old art	New art
Orthodoxy	Innovation
Old masters	Other visions
One kind of art	Many styles
Classic heritage	New just to be new / Distressing upstarts
Science = reality / Tech establishment	Change opens minds / Many realities / Liberation
	Change in science / doubtful

Main idea: Our view of science is changing but not fast enough.

The main idea can usually be phrased simply, like the one shown above. Putting the main idea into as few words as possible makes it portable, so you can easily bring it along when answering the questions.

Spectrum checklist

Remember:

1. Draw the Spectrum – a big letter "T".

2. Read for opposite ideas. Write them into the Spectrum using short phrases in your own words.

3. From the first paragraph of the passage, mark the author's side with a large asterisk at the top of that side.

4. Read for the author's main idea. Usually it will be an adjustment of the opening opinion, so it should be written into the Spectrum on the side with the asterisk but closer to the middle.

5. Look for the vertical pattern and title each side of the Spectrum by its theme.

4.4 Spectrum Tips

Here are tips on how to use the Spectrum to your advantage on MCAT® day.

1. **Do I need the spectrum for each passage?** Begin each passage with a new Spectrum. If you find the passage is simple and you can locate the main idea easily, you can stop filling out the Spectrum.

2. **How do I find contrasting opinions and opposites?** As you read each sentence, ask yourself if the author likes or dislikes this idea, then ask yourself if it is the same or different from what you have already read. If it is the same, you do not need to add it to the Spectrum. If it is different, ask yourself if it slightly different or very different from anything you have already read. If it is very different, it may be an opposite idea. If it is slightly different, it is likely the nuance you are looking for, often the author's main idea.

3. **What if there is no opposite idea to the author's opinion?** Sometimes the author will provide his or her opinion without explicitly stating the opposite in words. In that case, you can derive the opposite opinion yourself and add it to the Spectrum.

4.5 Identifying Passage and Question Types

Identifying passage and question types will help you determine which techniques are best for answering the question. As we go through the passage and question types, we will explain how to address each one.

Passage Types

Passages come in one of two varieties.

PERSUASIVE PASSAGES The author's opinion in *Persuasive Passages* is front and center in the passage. The author's side is clear from the beginning, and the opposing position is stated explicitly. The style is assertive, even passionate. To construct the main idea, line up opposing ideas on the Spectrum and watch for how the author refines his or her opinion as the passage goes on.

DESCRIPTIVE PASSAGES The author's opinion in *Descriptive Passages* is more subtle than those in persuasive passages. To determine what the author likes, notice the words the author chooses to describe facts, events, ideas, and findings. The tone will give away the stance the author takes, which will be closer to the center of the Spectrum than in argumentative passages. The style of descriptive passages tends to be somewhat toned down. You may need to infer the opposite of what the author likes and write it on the other side of the Spectrum.

Question Types

Now we will consider the four question types on the MCAT®. Remember, after you read each question stem, restate the main idea to yourself. This habit will help keep your finger on the pulse of the author. Regardless of question type, the main idea will always help you answer the question. Since three-quarters of the answer choices are wrong, by the time you get to the final questions on any given passage, you have read twelve to twenty-one statements that can confuse your memory of the passage. To stay oriented, always restate the main idea *after* reading the question stem, *before* you read the answer choices. This habit will minimize confusion from wrong answer choices. The best answer is the one the author would pick. As you read the question stem and answer choices, keeping the author's opinion in mind will help you choose the best answer.

Main Idea Questions

Main idea questions ask you to choose the main idea when given other perspectives or ideas also discussed in the passage. The AAMC calls these "comprehension" questions. Do you know which ideas the author liked, and which the author describes but rejects? Do you understand the difference between the author's main idea and the opposing view?

Main idea questions may appear to concern a particular detail from the passage. The details are often less important than finding the answer choice most closely aligned with the main idea. Remember, first read the question stem and restate the main idea to yourself. Simplify the answer choices to compare them to the main idea. Which one matches best?

Argument Questions

Argument questions address how the author supported the main idea. They may ask how strongly the author supported the main idea. The AAMC calls this skill "reasoning within the text."

The Spectrum can help you remember how the details in the passage relate to the main idea or its opposite. These questions ask: whether a particular detail, quotation, example, or statistic supports the main idea or its opposite.

When answering these questions, start by reading the question stem. Then restate the main idea to yourself. Answer the question first in your own words *before* you look at the answer choices. Then find the answer choice that best matches the answer you predicted on your own.

Sometimes argument questions ask you to judge how strongly the author supported his or her argument. Did the author provide examples and supporting evidence, or did the author state the opinion without backing it up? Was the evidence strong and convincing, or weak and vague?

Some argument questions will ask you to compare the strength of support given for two ideas. Was each idea supported? Which set of supporting details in the passage served as more credible evidence? To succeed on these questions, your original narrated reading of the passage will help. When reading, as you encounter details in the passage, notice what idea they support. Notice the strength of the evidence. Did the example given strengthen the argument?

New Context Questions

The next two question types test a third skill that the AAMC calls "reasoning beyond the text."

The first of these two types is *new context* questions. Here you will apply the author's main idea to a new situation. In these questions, the main idea always remains intact. Your job is to figure out what the author would think about this situation, based on the author's main idea. As an example, you might be given a list of choices and asked to decide which one your author would approve or disapprove of. Do not let your own knowledge and opinions cloud your reasoning. Remember, answer the question as the author would.

To answer these questions, first read the question stem and then restate the main idea. Identify which answer choices are aligned with the main idea and which oppose it.

Restating the main idea keeps your hand on the pulse of the author!

Know Key 3: Ask yourself what the question type is before answering each question. For Main Idea and New Context questions, simply apply the main idea. For Argument questions, recall which points were followed by strong evidence and which had weak or no support. (Usually the main idea is well-supported.) For New Information questions, imagine that you are the author. Ask which piece of information challenges the author's assumptions such that the main idea no longer follows. Regardless of question type, the main idea will always orient you toward the best answer.

New Information Questions

New information questions give new information that might undermine the author's main idea and ask you to reconsider the author's argument in light of this new information. In other words, they ask you to pretend that some new idea is true and see how the main idea is affected. Would the main idea be strengthened, weakened, or unaffected by this information? Most of the time, the new information will weaken the main idea.

If the new information is in the question stem, restate the main idea and then decide whether the new information strengthens or weakens the main idea *before* you look at the answer choices.

If the new information is in the answer choices, you are likely being asked to choose which piece of information would most weaken or contradict an assumption the author made. An assumption would be something the author believes (but did not say in the passage) in order to build the main idea. These are the hardest questions and usually appear once or twice per passage. For a very high score on the CARS section of the MCAT®, new information questions require the most practice. Remember, always read and simplify the question stem, restate the main idea, and then simplify the answer choices.

As you begin each CARS question, considering the question type will help you choose an approach and more quickly find the best answer.

You are now equipped with the skills, strategies, and mindset to be successful on the CARS section. It bears repeating: CARS practice *is* medical practice. Every passage author, like every patient, presents a unique viewpoint and experience. Think of each author, passage, and question as a patient and his or her case. Attend fully, reading every word. Listen for the point.

In the first lecture, you gained a mindset for confronting unfamiliar information whose use extends beyond the CARS section. Maintaining energy and focus, gauging time, and staying confident applies to your future work as a physician far beyond your preparation for the MCAT®.

Next, you learned the Examkrackers approach to reading passages: how to narrate passages, picture the author, and read for the main idea. As a physician, you will learn to attend fully to each patient, listening closely for his or her experience.

In the third lecture, you discovered the Examkrackers approach to finding CARS MCAT® questions and answers. You honed your ability to use the language of questions and answers to read for the main idea and anticipate the best answer. Language and tone are your window to the author. In medical practice, you will learn to read your patients closely in order to hear what is being asked of you and choose the best approach.

This final lecture offers the Spectrum as a tool to organize the passage and find the author's view to construct the main idea. The Spectrum allows you to see the author's opinion sits along a continuum of ideas. Once you locate the author's nuanced view, you can easily apply that idea in various contexts. You also learned to recognize passage and question types in order to more efficiently answer them. As a doctor, you will be the connection for your patient to the whole of medical science. You will organize what you observe and hear in order to know the patient and provide care that best fits each patient.

Practice for the CARS MCAT® is the practice of empathy. These skills are only truly mastered through practice. Give every word of every passage your full attention, listening carefully to what your author has to say. Imagine the author as the passage unfolds. When you're confused, ask the author questions, then read for his or her answer. You are building the skill of answering questions in line with the author's beliefs, just as you will come to align the care you provide to each patient's wishes.

Keep your eyes on the prize as you study for the CARS MCAT®! The skills you build here will both increase your score and carry forward.

MCAT® practice is medical practice.

Toward your success!

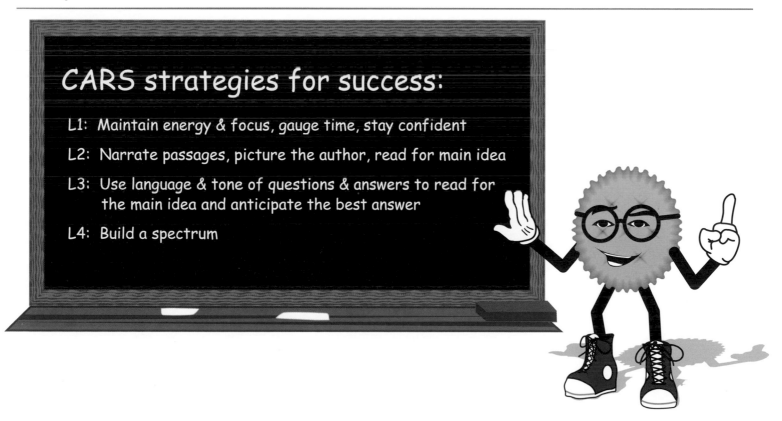

CARS strategies for success:

L1: Maintain energy & focus, gauge time, stay confident

L2: Narrate passages, picture the author, read for main idea

L3: Use language & tone of questions & answers to read for the main idea and anticipate the best answer

L4: Build a spectrum

DON'T FORGET YOUR KEYS

1. Use a Spectrum to organize passage ideas and locate the author's opinion.

2. The main idea is usually on the same side of the Spectrum where the author began.

3. After reading each question stem, notice the question type. Proceed accordingly. Every question type is easier with the main idea in mind.

STOP!

DO NOT LOOK AT THESE EXAMS UNTIL CLASS.

30-MINUTE IN-CLASS EXAM FOR LECTURE ii

Passage I (Questions 1 - 4)

Neuro-Linguistic Programming (NLP) is a controversial theory about the connections between thought, language, and behavior. NLP involves attempting to improve people's communication skills by teaching them about the relationship between eye-movements and thought. Proponents of NLP claim that when right-handed people look up to their right, they are likely to be visualizing a "constructed" (i.e., imagined) event, while when they look up to their left they are likely to be visualizing a "remembered" memory (i.e., an event that has actually happened to them).

A recent experiment was performed to assess the validity of NLP eye movement as an indicator of lying. As part of the study, participants were first given the experimenter's cellular phone. They were then instructed to go into a private office, hide the phone in either their pocket or bag, and return to the briefing room. When asked what they did inside the office, participants either lied or told the truth, according to whether they had been assigned to the lying or not-lying group. No significant differences were observed in participants' eye movements between the lying and not-lying conditions.

In a second experiment, one group of participants was informed of the patterns of eye movement that NLP practitioners believe to be associated with lying while a control group was not. Both groups were presented with video clips and asked to assess whether the speaker was lying. They were also asked to rate their levels of confidence on a scale from 1 (not at all confident) to 7 (very confident). The results are displayed in Table 1.

	NLP-training condition (N=21)	Control condition (N=29)	p-value
Mean correct	16.33	16.59	0.81
Mean confidence	4.65	4.58	0.67

Table 1 Mean number of correct judgments and rated confidence with and without NLP training

This passage was adapted from "The Eyes Don't Have It: Lie Detection and Neuro-Linguistic Programming." Wiseman R, Watt C, ten Brinke L, Porter S, Couper S-L, et al. *PLoS ONE.* 2012. 7(7) doi:10.1371/journal.pone.0040259 for use under the terms of the Creative Commons CC BY 3.0 license (http://creativecommons.org/licenses/by/3.0/legalcode).

Question 1

The findings described in the passage support the conclusion that:

○ **A.** only trained practitioners can effectively use NLP to detect lies.

○ **B.** NLP training is not effective at detecting lying.

○ **C.** NLP training is inconsistent in effectively detecting lies.

○ **D.** NLP training increases confidence among lie detectors.

Question 2

If experimenters modified the experiment so that participants in the first experiment were informed of NLP techniques prior to their participation in the experiment, how might this affect the data collected?

○ **A.** Accuracy in collected data would be decreased by introducing systematic error.

○ **B.** Accuracy in collected data would be decreased by introducing random error.

○ **C.** Precision in collected data would be decreased by introducing systematic error.

○ **D.** Precision in collected data would be decreased by introducing random error.

Question 3

The researchers conducted a follow-up study of NLP to test the hypothesis that there are some situations in which NLP is effective. What is the greatest impediment to studying this hypothesis?

○ **A.** The hypothesis would require a large number of experiments.

○ **B.** The hypothesis is not falsifiable

○ **C.** The findings of the passage experiments disprove this hypothesis.

○ **D.** Testing the hypothesis would require deception.

Question 4

According to the design of the experiments described in the passage, which of the following can be classified as independent variables?

    I. Rated confidence

    II. NLP instruction

    III. Lying or telling the truth

○ **A.** I only

○ **B.** II only

○ **C.** II and III only

○ **D.** I, II, and III

Passage II (Questions 5 - 9)

Stress describes the state of an organism when, under the influence of internal or external stimuli, the dynamic equilibrium of the organism is threatened. Stimuli can include combinations of physical or mental forces. The adaptive response to stress activates the components of the sympathoadreno-medullary (SAM) system, releasing key peripheral mediators, including the catecholamines epinephrine and norepinephrine.

Catecholamines work in concert with the autonomic nervous system to regulate the cardiovascular, pulmonary, hepatic, skeletal muscle, and immune systems. Excessive catecholamine signaling is known to have cytotoxic effects on the heart, stomach, and brain. A recent study investigated the effects of SAM activation on liver toxicity in movement-restrained mice, which are known to experience psychological and physical stress. Blood samples were collected every 30 minutes from immobilized mice over a period of six hours. Samples were analyzed for levels of *aspartate transaminase* (AST), a marker for hepatocyte apoptosis. Results of the experiment are shown in Figure 1.

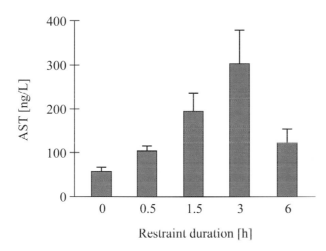

Figure 1 Mean AST concentrations (ng/L) in blood drawn at specific time points, measured in hours (h), during the restraint stress procedure

The experimenters also tested the efficacy of several compounds in preventing liver toxicity during restraint-induced stress. The restraint experiment was repeated using mice randomly assigned to pre-treatment with one of four different drugs. Liver tissue was then collected and analyzed for cell death markers following restraint treatment. Among the tested drugs, only the compound prazosin significantly lowered apoptosis to levels comparable with unrestrained animals.

This passage was adapted from "The Role of Alpha-1 and Alpha-2 Adrenoceptors in Restraint Stress-Induced Liver Injury in Mice." Zhu Q, Gu L, Wang Y, Jia L, Zhao Z, Peng S, Lei L. *PLoS ONE*. 2014. 9(3) doi:10.1371/journal.pone.0092125 for use under the terms of the Creative Commons CC BY 3.0 license (http://creativecommons.org/licenses/by/3.0/legalcode).

Question 5

Suppose that the mean AST levels at 0 and 3 hours depicted in Figure 1 were found to be significantly different, with a p-value of 0.01. Which of the following best explains the meaning of this finding?

- ○ **A.** There is a one percent chance the alternate hypothesis is correct; the difference between groups cannot be due to random chance.
- ○ **B.** There is a one percent chance the alternate hypothesis is correct; the difference between groups could be due to random chance.
- ○ **C.** There is a one percent chance the null hypothesis is correct; the difference between groups cannot be due to random chance.
- ○ **D.** There is a one percent chance the null hypothesis is correct; the difference between groups could be due to random chance.

Question 6

A third experiment was performed to investigate whether daily antioxidant intake could mimic the protective effects of prazosin. Liver tissue samples from mice treated with antioxidants were compared with those of untreated and prazosin-treated mice. Which of the following best describes the role of the prazosin-treated group?

- ○ **A.** Positive control
- ○ **B.** Negative control
- ○ **C.** Independent variable
- ○ **D.** Dependent variable

Question 7

Which of the following can be determined from Figure 1?

  I. The central tendency of each data set

  II. The most common value in each data set

  III. The dispersion of each data set

- ○ **A.** I and III
- ○ **B.** I and III
- ○ **C.** I only
- ○ **D.** I, II, and III

Question 8

Which of the following best explains why the second experiment described in the passage involved random assignment to experimental groups?

- ○ **A.** To ensure significance is found between groups
- ○ **B.** To increase subjectivity
- ○ **C.** To neutralize the influence of variability within the subject population
- ○ **D.** To eliminate bias by ensuring that all data is continuous rather than categorical

Suppose the researchers also found a statistically significant relationship between body fat percentage and stress-induced liver damage. Given the passage information, which of the following could NOT be possible?

○ **A.** A correlational test proved that hepatocyte apoptosis is dependent on body fat percentage.

○ **B.** High body fat percentages were correlated with lower risk of hepatocyte apoptosis.

○ **C.** Low body fat percentages were correlated with lower risk of hepatocyte apoptosis.

○ **D.** A chi-squared analysis revealed significant deviation from expected liver toxicity at extremely low body fat percentages.

Passage III (Questions 10 - 14)

Rechargeable batteries are composed of electrochemical cells whose reactions are electrically reversible. Recent research has focused on the use of lithium/sulfur cells in rechargeable batteries. These cells are composed of a lithium anode, a carbon-sulfur cathode, and an electrolytic solution through which lithium ions pass from the anode to the cathode. The cathode in this battery is in liquid form. When lithium arrives at the cathode, it reacts with sulfur as shown in Reaction 1. Before forming the final product, a number of aqueous lithium polysulfide (PS) intermediates are generated as shown in Reaction 2.

$$2 \, Li^+ + S^{2-} \rightarrow Li_2S$$

Reaction 1

$$Li_2S_{8(aq)} \rightarrow Li_2S_{6(aq)} \rightarrow Li_2S_{4(aq)} \rightarrow Li_2S_{2(s)} \rightarrow Li_2S_{(s)}$$

Reaction 2

Performance of the lithium/sulfur cell is affected by the properties of these PS intermediates. When PS dissolves into the liquid electrolyte, it is able to more readily react with non-conductive sulfur. Reducing the electrolyte volume/sulfur weight (E/S) ratio affects cell performance in two ways: it suppresses Reaction 2, which prevents lithium sulfide from precipitating, and it also increases the solution's viscosity. Researchers sought to determine the E/S ratio that would result in the highest capacity retention, meaning maintained capacity over the course of multiple cycles, in the lithium/sulfur cell. They looked at how battery capacity changed per cycle in lithium/sulfur cells that had E/S ratios of 5, 10, and 15. Results are shown in Figure 1.

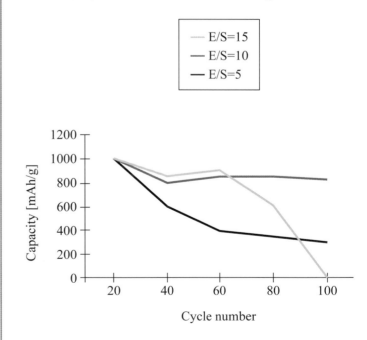

Figure 1 Capacity retention relative to cycle number

This passage was adapted from "Improved Cyclability of Liquid Electrolyte Lithium/Sulfur Batteries by Optimizing Electrolyte/Sulfur Ratio." Zhang, S. *Energies*. 2012. 5(12) doi:10.3390/en5125190 for use under the terms of the Creative Commons Attribution 3.0 License (http://creativecommons.org/licenses/by/3.0/legalcode).

Question 10

Given only the results presented in Figure 1, which additional E/S ratio would the researchers most likely choose to test?

○ **A.** 4
○ **B.** 9
○ **C.** 16
○ **D.** 25

Question 11

When designing the study, it was likely most important for the researchers to control for which of the following properties of the electrolyte solvent?

○ **A.** Molar mass
○ **B.** Density
○ **C.** Polarity
○ **D.** Volume

Question 12

Researchers noted that the voltmeter they were using to measure charge capacity showed a reading of 10mV even when disconnected. This error is most likely to affect the measurements':

○ **A.** accuracy.
○ **B.** precision.
○ **C.** accuracy and precision.
○ **D.** type of measurement scale.

Question 13

According to Figure 1, which E/S ratio has the worst long term cycling efficiency?

○ **A.** E/S = 5
○ **B.** E/S = 10
○ **C.** E/S = 15
○ **D.** E/S = 5 and E/S = 15 are equally inefficient.

Question 14

Suppose the researchers later find that E/S ratio is closely correlated with conductivity and that conductivity affects capacity retention. Which of the following best describes the implications of this finding?

○ **A.** Conductivity is a confounding variable that threatens internal validity.
○ **B.** Conductivity is a confounding variable that threatens external validity.
○ **C.** Conductivity is a biased variable that threatens internal validity.
○ **D.** Conductivity is a biased variable that threatens external validity.

Passage IV (Questions 15 - 18)

Congenital nephrogenic diabetes insipidus (NDI) is a disease characterized by failure of the kidney to concentrate urine in response to the antidiuretic hormone arginine vasopressin (AVP). Symptoms include excessive urination and thirst, despite normal production of AVP. AVP binds to the AVP receptor (Avpr2) on kidney cells and a series of biochemical events results in the insertion of a six-transmembrane water channel, aquaporin 2 (Aqp2), into the outer surface of the kidney cell.

NDI is inherited as an X-linked mutation of the Avpr2 gene or an autosomal mutation of the Aqp2 gene. In vitro experiments suggest recessive Aqp2 mutations result in retention of the protein in the endoplasmic reticulum. A mouse with a valine for phenylalanine substitution at position 204 (F204V) in the Aqp2 gene was used to study NDI. The DNA sequence of the Aqp2 wild type (wt) gene versus the Aqp2-F204V mutant is shown in Figure 1.

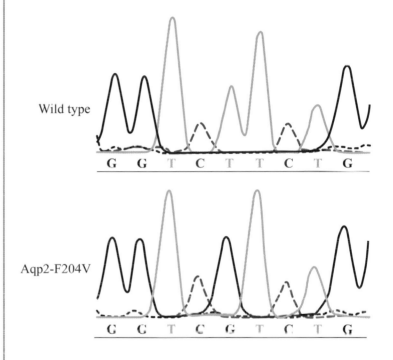

Figure 1 DNA sequence of the Aqp2 wild type gene versus the Aqp2-F204V mutant

The synthetic AVP analog, 1-deamino-8-D-arginine vasopressin (dDAVP, also called desmopressin), is a potent agonist of Avpr2. Controlling for water and food intake, the researchers measured the urine osmolality before and after the administration of dDAVP in $Aqp2^{F204V/F204V}$, $Aqp2^{F204V/wt}$, and wild type mice. The results are shown in Figure 2.

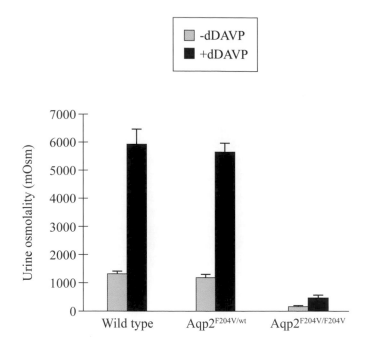

Figure 2 Urine osmolality before and after the administration in dDAVP in Aqp2$^{F204V/F204V}$, Aqp2$^{F204V/wt}$, and wild type mice

Immunoblots of protein extracts from the mouse kidneys (Figure 3) revealed three different forms of Aqp2: non-glycosylated protein at the 29 kDa band, a complex glycosylated protein as a smear between 35 and 45 kDa, and a short-lived intermediate form of 31 kDa representing core, high-mannose glycosylation of Aqp2.

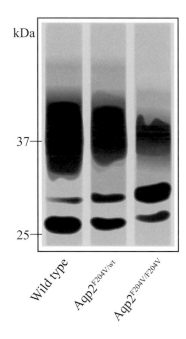

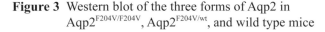

Figure 3 Western blot of the three forms of Aqp2 in Aqp2$^{F204V/F204V}$, Aqp2$^{F204V/wt}$, and wild type mice

Question 15

What experiment or combination of experiments listed below would have supported the hypothesis that the Aqp2 mutation results in the protein being retained in the endoplasmic reticulum?

   I. Examine fluorescent Aqp2 antibody localization in renal tissue extracted from Aqp2$^{F204V/wt}$ mice

   II. Examine fluorescent Aqp2 antibody localization in renal tissue extracted from Aqp2$^{F204V/F204V}$ mice

   III. Examine fluorescent Aqp2 antibody localization in renal tissue extracted from wild type mice

○ **A.** I only

○ **B.** I, II and III

○ **C.** II and III

○ **D.** II only

Question 16

According to information contained in the passage, scientists could most likely conclude that:

○ **A.** Aqp2 F204V confers a heterozygous advantage for controlling urine osmolarity.

○ **B.** two functional copies of the Aqp2 allele are needed for proper urine osmolarity control.

○ **C.** sense mutations render Aqp2 incapable of regulating water reabsorption.

○ **D.** conservative mutations in Aqp2 alter the secondary structure of aquaporin.

Question 17

The response to dDAVP of the Aqp2$^{F204V/F204V}$ mice illustrated in Figure 1 is most likely attributed to:

○ **A.** the Aqp2$^{F204V/F204V}$ mice drinking much less water.

○ **B.** dDAVP binding to another receptor on the outer surface of the kidney cell.

○ **C.** residual activity of the mutant Aqp2 channel.

○ **D.** an increased intake of solutes.

Question 18

Based on the passage, which of the following is the best description of the pattern of expression of Aqp2 forms?

○ **A.** The 29 kDa form is expressed in the Aqp2$^{F204V/F204V}$ mice, the 31kDa form is expressed in the Aqp2$^{F204V/wt}$ mice and the 35-45kDa form is expressed in the wild type.

○ **B.** The 31 kDa form is expressed in the Aqp2$^{F204V/F204V}$ mice and Aqp2$^{F204V/wt}$ mice, while the 35-45kDa form is expressed in the wild type.

○ **C.** The 31 kDa form is expressed in the Aqp2$^{F204V/F204V}$ mice, a mix of the 3 forms are expressed in the Aqp2$^{F204V/wt}$ mice, and the 35-45kDa form is expressed in the wild type.

○ **D.** None of the above

Questions 19 through 21 are NOT based on a descriptive passage.

Question 19

Enthalpies of hydration for common ions are shown in the table below:

Ion	$H_{hydration}$ (kJ/mol)
H^+	-1130
Li^+	-520
Na^+	-406
K^+	-322
Rb^+	-297
Cs^+	-276

Which conclusion is best supported by these data?

- ○ **A.** Larger ionic radii lead to more favorable solute-solvent interactions.
- ○ **B.** Addition of pure sulfuric acid to water is expected to slightly raise the temperature of the solution.
- ○ **C.** Atoms with completely filled p orbitals will react more favorably with water than those that do not have completely filled p orbitals.
- ○ **D.** Smaller ionic radii lead to more favorable solute-solvent interactions.

Question 20

A child learns that he will receive an ice cream reward when a specific tone is played, so he starts salivating and runs to the door to retrieve it. On day 15 of the trial, the tone sounds. He starts salivating and runs to the door, but he does not receive an ice cream. When the tone sounds on day 16, it would be expected that the boy would:

- ○ **A.** start salivating.
- ○ **B.** not experience increased salivation.
- ○ **C.** no longer associate the tone with ice cream.
- ○ **D.** wait for the tone to sound again then start salivating.

Question 21

Chemists interested in purifying a solution of two chemotherapeutic drugs are LEAST likely to use which separation technique?

Drug	Molecular weight	Net molecular charge	Boiling point
A	350 amu	+2	50°C
B	150 amu	-2	55°C

- ○ **A.** Size-exclusion chromatography
- ○ **B.** Ion-exchange chromatography
- ○ **C.** Distillation
- ○ **D.** All the above can be used

STOP. IF YOU FINISH BEFORE TIME IS CALLED, CHECK YOUR WORK. YOU MAY GO BACK TO ANY QUESTION IN THIS TEST BOOKLET.

30-MINUTE IN-CLASS EXAM FOR LECTURE 1

Passage I (Questions 22-28)

The digital revolution has manifested itself in a range of cultural changes that are in many ways far more radical than the ones unleashed by the invention of the printing press over five hundred years ago, and they have made their presence felt far more swiftly. While those earlier changes took centuries before their impact was fully realized, the digital revolution has redefined our communicative world in decades. And whereas the invention of moveable type preserved the basic form of the codex, the digital revolution has altered the most fundamental ways that it is possible to think about the materiality of writing, and about the relation between books and texts.

That is the upside. But if the extraordinarily rapid and wide-ranging changes unleashed by the digital revolution have shaken up our most entrenched assumptions about important forms of cultural production and reception in critically exciting ways, it is equally true that it is hard to think of a time when the humanities were so badly besieged on any number of levels, the most serious of which has been a jarring shift in research priorities towards market-driven applied knowledge: a retrenchment that has foregrounded all over again the question of how to make the case for the value of the humanities.

History repeats itself, but never in quite the same way. The single most important aspect of this history may be the fact that the humanities emerged in their modern form during an age not unlike our own, in which leading activists resisted any vision of reform that was not driven by a central recognition of the importance of applied knowledge. For utilitarians such as Thomas Love Peacock (a poet himself in earlier days), the poet was "a waster of his own time, and a robber of that of others," whose cultivation of poetry had been "to the neglect of some branch of useful study," in stark contrast with the tendency of "the thinking and studious" to draw on "the materials of useful knowledge" in order to prepare for "the real business of life."

Scientists within and outside of universities have been equally outraged by what they regard as an unprecedented attack on the idea of curiosity-driven abstract research. In December 2012, hundreds of leading scientists in lab coats marched to protest being muzzled by a government that is mistrustful of any sort of research that is not in step with their business agenda. Five months later, John McDougall, the businessman who serves as President of Canada's National Research Council, made headlines by insisting that "innovation is not valuable unless it has commercial value." McDougall's comments were part of an announcement of a broader shift in the organization's focus towards research that the government deems "commercially viable."

The crisis that forces us to make the case for the humanities today in the face of similar pressures to focus on "useful knowledge" that is suited to "the real business of life" can best be answered with a clearer understanding of the ways that ideas about the humanities were forged in the crucible of this spirit of intellectual reaction which defined itself in terms of the unique importance of more "serious" forms of knowledge. For early nineteenth-century theoreticians, the arts constituted a central aspect of a larger struggle for social progress, but like today, these arguments were themselves sharpened by the need to challenge a utilitarian emphasis on the primacy of applied knowledge.

This passage was adapted from "'Imagining What We Know': The Humanities in a Utilitarian Age." Keen P. *Humanities*. 2014. 3(1) doi:10.3390/h3010073 for use under the terms of the Creative Commons CC BY 4.0 license (http://creativecommons.org/licenses/by/4.0/legalcode).

Question 22

Based on the information presented in the passage, which of the following changes would the author consider the best remedy to the current state of the humanities?

- **A.** An understanding that the materiality of writing need not affect the content that it conveys
- **B.** An increase in public sector funding for the basic sciences
- **C.** A recognition that applied research can be better contextualized through the lens of the humanities
- **D.** A hearkening back to the primacy of applied knowledge

Question 23

Which of the following is LEAST supported by information presented in the passage?

- **A.** The digital revolution has changed the nature of the humanities.
- **B.** Studying the humanities makes for a better-rounded person.
- **C.** There is a historical precedent to the current changes in the humanities.
- **D.** Research funding is harder to acquire for research in the humanities.

Question 24

How would Thomas Peacock most likely view a biologist studying the mechanism of a particular class of ion pumps in amoebas?

- **A.** The scientist is engaged in a valuable enterprise that benefits society.
- **B.** The scientist's pursuit of knowledge for knowledge's sake is a pointless endeavor.
- **C.** The scientist ought to spend more time studying the humanities.
- **D.** The scientist should instead study business.

 Next ▶

Question 25

Based on the passage, it is reasonable to infer that the author believes which of the following about John McDougall's statements?

○ A. McDougall raises legitimate concerns about the financial solvency of certain kinds of research.

○ B. McDougall supports the plight of leading scientists facing budgetary constraints.

○ C. McDougall is misinformed about the commercial viability of certain kinds of research.

○ D. McDougall has misaligned priorities regarding research funding.

Question 26

Which of the following statements best articulates the author's views on the role of academia outside of the humanities?

○ A. Academia outside of the humanities is a more practical course of study.

○ B. Academia outside of the humanities is more financially burdened than the humanities.

○ C. Academia outside of the humanities is a less worthy pursuit than the humanities.

○ D. The author does not express an opinion about academia outside of the humanities.

Question 27

Which of the following statements, if true, would most weaken the author's argument?

○ A. Research in the humanities is better funded now than it has ever been.

○ B. The digital revolution had little effect on the humanities.

○ C. The humanities have not lost any ground to the basic sciences.

○ D. The situation of the utilitarians was markedly different from that of the humanities today.

Question 28

Which passage topic could be considered a more "serious" form of knowledge, as defined in paragraph 5?

○ A. Entrenched assumptions that went unchallenged prior to the digital revolution

○ B. Applied research with market implications

○ C. The study of topics in the humanities

○ D. Research into fundamental questions of the basic sciences

Passage II (Questions 29-35)

The unreflective arrangement of persons in social gatherings has been an object of scholarly attention since the rise of the social sciences. Recent theory has suggested that attention to issues of location in "social space," apart from the implicit psychological concerns with intention and meaning that pervade the classical tradition, may help lead to the unifying paradigms that sociology has long sought in vain.

The propensity of persons to collect in the back of the church has occasioned frequent anecdotal observation by clergy and students of churches. In popular culture, the back pew of the church functions as a counterpoint, not for the front pew, but for the pulpit. Analogous to their placement in the sanctuary, those in the back are often seen to operate at more of a critical distance from the core of church life than those further forward. Those who are marginal to the church, the unknown and perhaps undesirable, are also perceived to be residents of the rear pews.

With regard to religious congregations, moreover, some would claim that group structures may not be as evident in favor of more focused, even purposive, considerations. Unlike many settings in which interaction is observed, worship is a highly intentional activity. For its participants, it involves not only relating to one another but also more importantly relating to God. In theory, for Protestant Christians (and Muslims), worship begins with the individual, and may be engaged in entirely as a solitary activity. The concerns of group life, although affirmed, are secondary, and to suggest that group structures may play a role in worship may be thought to understate or even belittle the unique spiritual character of worship.

On the other hand, certain features of Christian worship suggest that congregations may be highly susceptible to structurating forces, or influences that organize a group in a particular manner. In addition to a clearly designated front region of the church, from the standpoint of the participant, each pew is also in the front region of all the pews behind it. The inhabitants of the front pew of the church are, as it were, on display to all the worshippers behind them, whereas the inhabitants of the rear pew are in the same sense on display to none. In terms of body language, movement, attention— all the ritual behaviors that make up impression management—the rearmost worshippers form the audience for many and perform for none (or very few), whereas the frontmost worshippers perform for many and form the audience for none (or very few). Those in the rear pews, moreover, in churches of large enough size, are less susceptible to surveillance from those formalized leaders in front who face the body of worshippers.

Those in the front pews enjoy a front region that includes fewer of their fellow worshippers and more of the formal, intentional front performance of the worship setting. Depending on whether one's goal is to focus on the formal worship experience, the front offers fewer distractions, the rear more enticements, from the intentional act of worship. In this way, the physical setting of worship, in fixed pews facing forward, tends to promote a differentiation of worshippers on a front-to-rear axis that corresponds in many ways to the characterization of front and backstage behavior.

Although the importance of such issues for national religious policy or cultural issues of religiosity may be minimal, their value for the concrete practice and congregational experience of religion is clear and direct. They have potential implications for liturgical practice, the placement and projection of homilies, readings and other verbal elements, temporal spacing of religious services, and movement and placement of seating options. Understanding patterns of church sociation also provides valuable instrumental knowledge to religious researchers who survey congregations and to those who design and build church worship settings.

This passage was adapted from "Sitting in Church: Regionalization in Worship Settings." Sullins DP. *SAGE Open*. 2012. doi: 10.1177/2158244012461921 for use under the terms of the Creative Commons CC BY 3.0 license (http://creativecommons.org/licenses/by/3.0/legalcode).

Question 29

Which of the following best describes an assumption made by the author in the passage?

- ○ **A.** Attending a sermon is considered a social event.
- ○ **B.** Popular culture accurately depicts religious practices.
- ○ **C.** Individuals' worship practices primarily depend on their religion.
- ○ **D.** Preachers alter their sermons depending on where individuals are sitting.

Question 30

Which of the following statements about worshippers is most strongly implied by the passage?

- ○ **A.** Worshippers purposefully sit near individuals with similar practices.
- ○ **B.** Individuals likely sit in similar pews even if they attend a new church.
- ○ **C.** Worshippers have more positive experiences when sitting near similar individuals.
- ○ **D.** Individuals feel pressured to sit in the back if they are new to a church.

Question 31

Which of the following people would the author most expect to sit in the front region of church, as the concept is described in the fifth paragraph?

- ○ **A.** Someone who is short in stature and needs to be closer to see the pastor
- ○ **B.** Someone who enjoys attention even if not particularly religious
- ○ **C.** Someone who does not want to be distracted during worship time
- ○ **D.** Someone who is close friends with the pastor

Question 32

Sociologists determine that those seated in the front rows of their churches are more likely to donate money during worship. This finding would most strongly undermine the author's claim that:

- ○ **A.** the physical arrangement of worshipers has more to do with individual rather than group considerations.
- ○ **B.** individuals seated in the back pews are seen as the least desirable members of a congregation.
- ○ **C.** the back rows form an audience for those seated in the pews closest to the front.
- ○ **D.** those in the back rows are not as closely surveilled by those leading worship.

Question 33

Which of the following situations in the theatre industry is most analogous to the one described in the passage regarding religious event attendance?

- ○ **A.** A musical theatre fan who is running late sits in the back of the auditorium so as not to disturb the performance.
- ○ **B.** The star of a show admits she loves getting attention from the audience.
- ○ **C.** Whenever an audience member in the front row laughs, the rest of the audience laughs too.
- ○ **D.** Crew members purposefully wear black so they do not draw attention to themselves.

Question 34

Which of the following passage assertions is LEAST supported by evidence in the passage?

- ○ **A.** In popular culture, the back pew of the church functions as a counterpoint for the pulpit.
- ○ **B.** Unlike many settings in which interaction is observed, worship is a highly intentional activity.
- ○ **C.** Christian worship congregations may be highly susceptible to structurating forces.
- ○ **D.** The physical setting of worship tends to promote a differentiation of worshippers.

Question 35

The author's argument about seating patterns in religious settings imply that he or she would be likely to *support* which of the following?

- ○ **A.** Encouraging church members to sit in the back if they do not plan on participating
- ○ **B.** Creating churches for different kinds of worshippers
- ○ **C.** Updating existing practices based on the congregation present
- ○ **D.** Requiring church members to sit as close as possible to the front

 Next ▶

Passage III (Questions 36-42)

The 1918 Spanish influenza pandemic has been blamed for as many as 50 million deaths worldwide, earning it the designation as the "greatest medical Holocaust in history" and "the mother of all pandemics." Like all major disasters, the full story of the pandemic includes smaller, less noted episodes that have not attracted historical attention. The story of the 1919 influenza epidemic in Bristol Bay, Alaska is one such lost episode. It is an important story because the most accessible accounts—the Congressional Record and the Coast Guard Report—are inconsistent with reports made on the scene. This historical oversight must be remedied.

In the spring of 1919, the adult Native population in Bristol Bay was decimated by influenza. The Native Alaskan population in the region at the time numbered approximately 1,000 people, living a subsistence lifestyle in sod huts and traveling to fish camps in the spring. Weather conditions preclude travel in and out of the region from September to May, and the Native Alaskan population, along with a few federal/territorial employees and salmon industry winter watchmen, was completely isolated from the outside world for 8 to 9 months each year. Because of its remoteness, the region escaped the first wave of the 1918 pandemic. However, as the ice melted in 1919 and preparations for fishing season began, the dead, the dying, and the orphaned were discovered in appalling numbers.

Two major institutions recorded attempts to mitigate the disaster. The Coast Guard, according to its reports on its efforts in the 1920 Congressional Record and its own Annual Report, was authorized and funded to respond. The Alaska Packers Association (APA) responded incidentally to preparations for the salmon fishing season, maintaining private company reports from several sites in the bay. A startling contrast exists between the reports of the rescue. The Bureau of Fisheries of the Department of Commerce, reporting independently, confirmed only the APA reports, calling the Coast Guard efforts "the saddest repudiation of a benevolent intention."

The contradictions between the Coast Guard and the APA reports are startling. The Coast Guard's annual summer mission had long included incidental rescue and medical care, but Congress had allocated an additional $100,000 specifically for the purpose of feeding, supplying, and caring for Native Alaskan residents of Alaskan coastal communities during the pandemic. The Coast Guard reported to Congress that it provided such aid and claimed responsibility for saving innumerable lives, burying the dead, and dispatching starving dogs that were feasting on human remains in Bristol Bay villages. The report characterized the Coast Guard as tireless and heroic, and Congress accepted the report uncritically, praising the Coast Guard for its efforts. However, the Coast Guard report was inaccurate. It was the key governmental agency charged and funded to mitigate the disaster, but it largely failed to respond to the tragic circumstances it encountered.

In spite of all efforts, the loss of life in the region was stupefying. At the end of the 1919 fishing season, 238 orphans remained of 800 to 1,000 adult Native Alaskans formerly inhabiting Nushagak Bay. The salvage of the children, however, is well remembered. The Native Health Corporation was built at the site of the old hospital, and a school and orphanage grew out of the orphaned remnants of the three tribes inhabiting the region.

This passage was adapted from "Influenza in Bristol Bay, 1919: 'The Saddest Repudiation of a Benevolent Intention.'" deValpine M. *SAGE Open*. 2015. doi: 10.1177/2158244015577418 for use under the terms of the Creative Commons CC BY 4.0 license (http://creativecommons.org/licenses/by/4.0/legalcode).

Question 36

Which of the following facts presented in the passage provides the greatest support for the claim that the Coast Guard's rescue effort was unsuccessful?

○ **A.** The Congressional Record and Coast Guard Report are inconsistent with observations made on the scene.

○ **B.** Alaskans did not feel that the Coast Guard helped as much as they could have.

○ **C.** The total number of deaths after the 1919 fishing season was extremely high.

○ **D.** The report by the Bureau of Fisheries of the Department of Commerce characterized the Coast Guard reinforcements as inadequate.

Question 37

Based on information in the passage, the author would most likely agree with which of the following statements about medical emergencies?

○ **A.** Pandemics often garner more attention than is necessary.

○ **B.** External medical help during emergencies does not help the situation.

○ **C.** The spread of pandemics is unavoidable.

○ **D.** Research is required to properly allocate resources when responding to medical emergencies.

Question 38

Which of the following, if true, would best support the passage implication that proper documentation of historical events is paramount to the safety of society?

○ **A.** Descriptions of foreign aid during times of war often cannot be found in written records.

○ **B.** Countries without written records are often not discussed in history classes.

○ **C.** Countries are usually biased when reporting about past civil wars.

○ **D.** Leaders who try to erase history are often overthrown.

Question 39

Which of the following most resembles a "repudiation of benevolent intentions" (paragraph 3)?

- ○ **A.** A student rejecting a classmate's party invitation when she realizes she was only invited so that she would not feel left out.
- ○ **B.** A mother paying her financially-unstable son an allowance that he spends on video games.
- ○ **C.** A movie star donating her proceeds from her latest film to a charity.
- ○ **D.** A high school senior tutoring younger students so that she can add the activity to her resume.

Question 40

In the first paragraph, the author most likely compares the Spanish Influenza to the Holocaust in order to:

- ○ **A.** shock the readers.
- ○ **B.** offend the readers.
- ○ **C.** establish a central thesis.
- ○ **D.** stress the seriousness of the pandemic.

Question 41

Based on information in the passage, which of the following conclusions is most likely to be true?

- ○ **A.** Countries need to save more money for emergency situations.
- ○ **B.** The government should communicate with affected countries after emergencies seem to have passed.
- ○ **C.** Different populations can be affected differently by the same disease.
- ○ **D.** Animals play a large role in transmitting influenza.

Question 42

Which of the following qualities would the passage author most admire in an individual or organization?

- ○ **A.** Truthfulness
- ○ **B.** Selflessness
- ○ **C.** Confidence
- ○ **D.** Intelligence

STOP. IF YOU FINISH BEFORE TIME IS CALLED, CHECK YOUR WORK. YOU MAY GO BACK TO ANY QUESTION IN THIS TEST BOOKLET.

STOP

30-MINUTE IN-CLASS EXAM FOR LECTURE 2

Passage I (Questions 43-49)

Is it good medical practice for physicians to "eyeball" a patient's race when assessing their medical status or even to ask them to identify their race? This question was captured in a 2005 episode of "House M.D.," Fox television's medical drama. In the episode, a black patient with heart disease refuses a hospital physician's prescription for what is clearly intended to represent BiDil, the drug approved by the United States Food and Drug Administration only for "self-identified" African-Americans. Dr. House, on seeing the patient for follow-up, insists on the same prescription. The patient again refuses, telling House, "I'm not buying into no racist drug, OK?" House, a white physician, asks, "It's racist because it helps black people more than white people? Well, on behalf of my peeps, let me say, thanks for dying on principle for us." The patient replies, "Look. My heart's red, your heart's red. And it don't make no sense to give us different drugs."

Racial categories, with shifting meanings and culturally determined parameters, have always shaped medical practice and thinking, leading to vigorous debates about their use in epidemiology, public health, and medical research journals. Throughout the 20th century, race had no standard definition in medical, epidemiological, or health services research. In epidemiology, race vaguely referred to "persons who are relatively homogenous with respect to biologic inheritance."

In the early 20th century in the United States, shades of blackness were assumed to affect medical outcomes. This view generated supposed facts, and once a "fact" was linked to race rather than unhealthy living and working conditions, it resisted further challenge and became part of clinical judgments. Even though retrospective data made it clear that syphilis was more likely to attack the cardiovascular rather than the neurological system in both blacks and whites, it was assumed that since African-Americans did more labor than "brainwork," they were more at risk for cardiovascular complications. Black cardiovascular deaths, in turn, were often labeled syphilitic in origin without the benefit of autopsy, or misread when postmortem studies were done.

These days, researchers rely on respondents' self-identification to collect data on race and ethnicity. Every research grant must report its study population in these terms, leading to their universal use in recruitment of research subjects. It becomes almost "natural" to use these same variables in the subsequent analysis and theoretical framing of the research. As genetic findings assume an increasingly prominent place in biomedical research, some have concluded that self-identified race/ethnicity, routinely collected in biomedical research studies, is a reasonable proxy for genetic homogeneity and may lead to important insights into health disparities.

But the debate remains. Even given the history of the use of racial categories, are they nevertheless useful in the physician's office? Does a quick administrative assessment of race help to diagnose a presenting ailment, or accurately assess future risk of illness? Physicians face huge demands for time efficiency and product output, often being called upon to process as many as six patients per hour. No wonder that rapid racial assessment is an attractive means to figure out what to do with a presenting patient.

There is, in the end, no substitute for an inquiry into family history and the biological and cultural histories of specific populations serviced by a particular treatment center. Clinicians will make better educated patient evaluations if they familiarize themselves with the history of the particular communities that they serve. Cultural competency instruction should be modified to include information on the history of racial categories, current controversies about their biological significance, and the limits of their utility.

This passage was adapted from "Racial Categories in Medicine: How Useful Are They?" Braun L, Fausto-Sterling A, Fullwiley D, Hammonds EM, Nelson A, et al. *PLoS Medicine*. 2007. 4(9) doi:10.1371/journal.pmed.0040271 for use under the terms of the Creative Commons CC BY 3.0 license (http://creativecommons.org/licenses/by/3.0/legalcode).

Question 43

Which of the following statements is best supported by evidence from the passage?

- A. Racial categories have remained unchanged since the 20th century.
- B. Only physicians still place weight on racial categorization.
- C. African-Americans are at increased risk of dying from syphilis attacks on the cardiovascular system.
- D. Racial categories have been used as a shorthand to represent genetic makeup.

Question 44

According to the author, which of the following categorizations would be most useful for medical care?

- A. The shade of the patient's skin
- B. The patient's profession
- C. The patient's geographical origin
- D. The patient's medical history

Question 45

The author's apparent attitude toward prescribing a drug only for "self-identified" African-Americans (paragraph 1) is that:

- A. it is a useful method when physicians are pressed for time.
- B. it is not a common conflict in the clinic, but is dramatized for television.
- C. it has the potential to revolutionize the pharmaceutical industry.
- D. it sometimes occurs regardless of a patient's self-identification.

Next ▶

Question 46

If a new study found that treating patients based on racial categories resulted in similar clinical outcomes as treating patients based on their family history, the author would most likely react by:

- ○ **A.** admitting that the patient's outcome is the only important factor, and physicians should categorize patients however they can to best treat them.
- ○ **B.** arguing that factors other than clinical outcome should also be measured in this study.
- ○ **C.** admitting that racial categorizations should become standard in clinical care.
- ○ **D.** ignoring the study because racial categorizations should never be used.

Question 47

Given the information in the passage, it is reasonable to assume that effective cultural competency training:

- ○ **A.** will completely replace the racial categorization system.
- ○ **B.** will be taught in medical schools all over the nation.
- ○ **C.** can improve care only in unique populations.
- ○ **D.** will emphasize skill in taking a social history.

Question 48

The author describes an episode of the television show "House M.D." in order to:

- ○ **A.** seem culturally competent to readers.
- ○ **B.** keep the tone of the passage lighthearted.
- ○ **C.** humanize the topic of racial categorizations.
- ○ **D.** emphasize how common similar patient-physician encounters are.

Question 49

The author most likely puts quotations around "eyeball" in the first paragraph:

- ○ **A.** because it is a slang term.
- ○ **B.** because it is a quote from television.
- ○ **C.** in order to incorporate new terminology.
- ○ **D.** in order to convey disapproval of the practice described.

Passage II (Questions 50-56)

The conservatives condemn abortion in all its ramifications, and the liberalists give credence to it. The argument of the conservatives is based on the fact that life is sacred and the fetus is a living entity that has the right to live. To conservatives, life is sacrosanct and should not be taken, even at the time of conception. The liberalists are of the opinion that the fetus is not yet a living being because it lacks consciousness. As such, aborting it is not a crime. Some are clamoring for abortion's legalization, while others are calling for its prohibition due to its adverse effects on society and especially on women.

Various definitions of abortion have been proposed. Abortion has been described as the "termination of unwanted pregnancy" or the interruption of pregnancy prior to the time that the fetus can live independently. Better still, it can be more accurately described as the removal of the "non-viable" human being from the mother's womb by human intervention, whether by killing it before removal from the womb, or by exposing it to certain death outside the womb.

Both Christianity and Islam unequivocally condemn the taking of life in whatever form and, more importantly, that of the unborn. The Qur'an says that "whosoever killed a human being… it shall be as if he has killed all mankind." The Bible is emphatic on this issue, saying "you shall not kill." This shows that both Christianity and Islam regard abortion as an abominable and unlawful act. Both religions reject the presupposition that a just-fertilized ovum solely consists of a small group of undifferentiated cells that are not yet a person. The notions that a pre-embryo has no human shape or distinguishable organs, cannot sense its environment, and is not sentient have no bearing on these religion's views.

Two types of abortion can be identified. The first type, which is spontaneous or accidental, occurs naturally as a result of certain pathological conditions, often beyond the control of the pregnant woman and the physician. The second type, which is self-induced, involves the deliberate interruption of pregnancy by artificially inducing the loss of the fetus. It is a voluntary and intentional act, and as a result, it poses a moral question because human life is involved.

Various reasons can be adduced for procuring an abortion. Abortions may be sought out for health reasons, especially in situations where the pregnancy threatens the life of the mother. This could be due to ill health or to the mental and psychological condition of the woman. Similarly, there have been reported cases of rape or incest resulting in pregnancy. In these situations, bringing the fetus to term could lead to other social and moral dilemmas, particularly that of the societal acceptability of a child whose paternal bloodline is in doubt or not known at all. There are also cases where a new child could lead to further impoverishment of the family. In a situation where the woman is poor or has been divorced and saddled with the responsibility of caring for many mouths, an addition to the family may be a problem. Abortion may be procured in this situation. However, whatever the reason(s), abortion is an odious and murderous act. There is an urgent need for a solution to this social dilemma. To some people, abortion is a health service for women, despite the fact that every abortion means the loss of an unborn baby, often without even a funeral service.

This passage was adapted from "Christo-Islamic Perspectives on Abortion and the Challenges of Globalization." Obasola KE. *Review of European Studies*. 2014. 6(1) doi: 10.5539/res.v6n1p76 for use under the terms of the Creative Commons CC BY 3.0 license (http://creativecommons.org/licenses/by/3.0/legalcode).

Question 50

Based on passage information, how would the liberalists respond to the arguments about abortion presented in paragraph 3?

O **A.** The arguments are invalid, because forgoing an abortion could ultimately lead to the mother's death.

O **B.** The arguments are invalid, because the fetus is not yet alive.

O **C.** The arguments are invalid, because the child's life outside the womb may be a death sentence.

O **D.** The arguments are invalid, because the church does not create the law.

Question 51

The author uses the phrase "funeral service" in the final paragraph in order to:

O **A.** highlight the absurdity of the argument against abortion, as parents do not have funerals for aborted fetuses.

O **B.** rhetorically contrast the idea of abortion as a "health service" with a more sinister "service."

O **C.** remind the reader that an abortion marks the end of life.

O **D.** emphasize the solemn and malignant nature of abortions.

Question 52

Which of the following circumstances would most closely compare to the author's definition of abortion?

O **A.** Transferring bacteria from a petri culture to a plastic slide by way of a pipette

O **B.** Transplanting a petunia bud to a different flower bed with the use of gardening tools

O **C.** Leaving a kitten outside overnight in cold weather by locking the cat door

O **D.** Terminating transcription by artificially administering a DNA polymerase inhibitor

Question 53

Which of the following, if assumed to be true, would most strengthen the author's argument?

O **A.** Children of incest have a heightened occurrence of birth defects.

O **B.** Women who are denied abortions have a decreased income 5 years after the birth.

O **C.** Children born into poverty have an increased likelihood of having a positive impact on society.

O **D.** Women who undergo abortions have an increased chance of cervical cancer.

Question 54

Would the author be more likely to condemn or accept spontaneous abortion?

O **A.** Condemn, because a living entity was prematurely killed.

O **B.** Condemn, because the mother's sin likely caused the death of the child.

O **C.** Accept, because the circumstances were beyond human control.

O **D.** Accept, because the sacred life would ascend to heaven.

Question 55

If it was discovered that a fetus moves in response to its mother's voice beginning at 20 weeks post-conception:

O **A.** conservatives would support abortions before 20 weeks because the fetus is not living until it can respond to outside stimuli.

O **B.** liberalists would not support abortions later than 20 weeks because consciousness would be developing at that point.

O **C.** conservatives and liberals would not likely change their opinions because most proponents and opponents already do not support abortions after 12 weeks.

O **D.** conservatives and liberalists would not likely change their opinions because movement in the womb does not necessarily reflect consciousness or viability.

Question 56

The author believes that the well-being of the mother is:

O **A.** an important consideration in the abortion decision-making process.

O **B.** more important than the well-being of the fetus.

O **C.** secondary to the life of the unborn fetus.

O **D.** a benchmark of the well-being of the fetus.

 Next ▶

Passage III (Questions 57-63)

Backers of regulations that limit access to regular ballots for American voters who lack certain types of photographic identification (ID) have floated the idea that such increases in the cost of voting might actually increase overall voter turnout. However, not enough research has been performed to conclusively support this belief. This tension must be explored in the context of fundamental economic concepts that can be used as a tool for thinking critically about the relationship between voter ID laws and electoral participation. Because data that are suited to empirical analyses of this relationship are lacking, complementary techniques, such as modeling and simulation, are useful for testing unverified hypotheses about voter ID rules from the political discourse. Very recent studies have begun to fill this gap and can be used to outline an agenda for future research.

Voter ID laws are the latest product of an ongoing tension in the United States between ensuring the right to vote for all citizens and protecting the franchise against in-person voter fraud. Under these laws, only people who can present photo identification such as a valid driver's license are permitted to vote. Proponents assert that these laws make the American electoral system less vulnerable to malfeasance, while opponents argue that they create new barriers to the polls, especially for minority and disadvantaged populations.

Viewed through this lens, voter ID laws are an obvious and significant source of political conflict, insofar as they represent intentional changes to election procedures, which have the capacity to affect the composition and/or size of a given voter turnout. They have been called "the election administration story" of recent American political contests. This story, which is fraught with hostility and inflammatory rhetoric, centers on interrelated issues. There is the descriptive matter of who does not possess the requisite identification under the applicable state laws. The point in question here is whether certain classes of individuals lack approved modes of ID at higher rates than comparison groups. If this condition proves to be true, then voter ID laws unduly burden—that is, disparately impact—some members of the population relative to others. Such a situation is self-evidently antithetical to core democratic values, namely, equality.

Unlike for the foregoing "who possesses ID" question, empirical evidence for the present "turn-out" question does not point to a relatively general conclusion. To the contrary, some studies find that voter ID laws have a depressive, albeit small, effect on political participation; others find that simply lacking requisite ID significantly reduces turnout; still others find no or statistically insignificant turnout effects from voter ID laws; at least one finds that voter ID laws have an unexplained positive influence on turnout; and yet another, in line with the pro-voter ID argument, purports to show that voter ID laws can boost turnout by promoting confidence in the integrity of the electoral system. In that context, the current state of this literature is decidedly mixed. This outcome is perhaps a reflection of the heterogeneity in the states, elections, and data sources that have been probed to date, and the claims that voter ID laws could increase voter turnout or leave it unaffected run counter to the widely accepted economic theory of democracy that states that voting costs and electoral participation are inversely related.

This passage was adapted from "Can Voter Identification Laws Increase Electoral Participation in the United States? Probably Not—A Simple Model of the Voting Market." Weaver R. *SAGE Open*. 2015. doi: 10.1177/2158244015580379 for use under the terms of the Creative Commons CC BY 4.0 license (http://creativecommons.org/licenses/by/4.0/legalcode).

Question 57

According to the passage, the decisive factor in determining whether an individual is allowed to vote in an election should be his or her:

- ○ **A.** voter identification.
- ○ **B.** citizenship.
- ○ **C.** past electoral participation.
- ○ **D.** ability to pay for a driver's license.

Question 58

Based on information in the passage, which of the following individuals would have difficulty casting his or her vote as a result of the implementation of voter identification laws?

  I. An 18-year-old man who has never driven a car

  II. An elderly woman whose favorite candidate lost the last election

  III. A busy mom in charge of carpool duty

- ○ **A.** I only
- ○ **B.** III only
- ○ **C.** I and II only
- ○ **D.** II and III only

Question 59

Some countries have strict voter identification laws and experience very high voter turnout for national elections. An appropriate clarification of the passage would be the qualification that the author's argument only applies to:

- ○ **A.** the United States.
- ○ **B.** countries with socioeconomic gaps.
- ○ **C.** democratic countries.
- ○ **D.** local elections.

Question 60

Suppose that a voter's identification was rejected at the polls. What advice would the author most likely give?

- ○ **A.** Wait to vote in the next election.
- ○ **B.** Contact local news outlets to publicize this unequal treatment.
- ○ **C.** Reach out to family and friends for help in obtaining valid identification.
- ○ **D.** Move to an area where voter identification laws are not as strict.

Question 61

Based on information provided in the passage, it is reasonable to conclude that:

- ○ **A.** voter identification laws decrease levels of fraud.
- ○ **B.** electoral participation is usually expensive.
- ○ **C.** voter identification laws always decrease voter turnout.
- ○ **D.** the voter identification controversy is relatively new.

Question 62

Which of the following findings would most strengthen the author's argument about voter ID laws and disadvantaged populations?

- ○ **A.** A recent state election reported a record high turnout of minority voters in the last five years.
- ○ **B.** Most elected politicians come from advantaged backgrounds and are members of the majority party.
- ○ **C.** Voting fraud levels have remained steady after the implementation of voter ID laws.
- ○ **D.** Most Americans do not view voting fraud as a major concern.

Question 63

Which of the following qualities would the author most likely value in the election process?

- ○ **A.** Honesty
- ○ **B.** Inclusivity
- ○ **C.** Compassion
- ○ **D.** Forethought

STOP. IF YOU FINISH BEFORE TIME IS CALLED, CHECK YOUR WORK. YOU MAY GO BACK TO ANY QUESTION IN THIS TEST BOOKLET.

30-MINUTE IN-CLASS EXAM FOR LECTURE 3

Passage I (Questions 64-70)

In Western cultures, gender identity is presumed to be a corollary of assigned sex, with sex assignment determined primarily by visual inspection of the genitalia. People for whom this assumption is incorrect may desire hormone therapies or surgeries aimed at modifying their bodies so that they more closely align with their preferred gender identity. At present, accessing such treatments requires a diagnosis of gender dysphoria as specified in the DSM-5 [the official handbook of psychiatric disorders], which emphasizes the "distress that may accompany the incongruence between one's experienced or expressed gender and one's assigned gender." The fact that gender dysphoria exists in the DSM is an admission on the part of psychologists that our society has clearly defined gender roles that contribute to what is generally considered "normal."

A recent case history of gender dysphoria described "Chris," a female-assigned-at-birth patient who identified more closely with the male gender and stated a wish to be addressed by male pronouns. It is important to stress that, when looking for causal factors for Chris's disorder, Chris was in no way confused about his identity and was described as a well-adjusted individual. Basic defects in personality can be ruled out as causes of his uneasiness with his assigned sex. One must then ponder the age-old question of society as the cause.

The notion of gender identity is so heavily dependent on societal norms that, in this case, many psychologists may believe society is the culprit. The mere labeling of some behaviors as "masculine" and others as "feminine" may have created the criteria for Chris's experience to be labeled as deviant or abnormal. In another culture, where the labeling is different, would Chris have even felt the need to identify as distinctly male? Along the same lines of thinking, would the incongruity even be considered a "disorder" in another culture?

Evidence varies regarding the two sides of the issue. Upbringing and/or some biochemical processes may account for the etiology of the disorder, indicating that it is not simply due to societal labels. Indeed, it may seem convincing to argue that Chris strongly identified with males very early in his life, and that this was reflected in his interest in "male" activities. Yet one could also argue that certain activities were labeled male, and Chris molded his interests to include them so that he would be considered "male." It is virtually impossible to unravel which came first, the labeling of his favored activities as "male" or his interest in them. Almost certainly, there is a complex interaction between the two.

Remaining, however, is the question of treatment for Chris. He expresses a desire for hormone treatment to lessen his experience of gender dysphoria. One might ask if this is really necessary since he is already well adjusted. Part of what we strive for as psychologically healthy individuals is an acceptance of ourselves in a "natural" state. It is sometimes the case that, through psychotherapy, one learns that one may not necessarily have to change oneself as much as one's perception of self. The effect of hormone treatment on Chris' happiness cannot be foretold with complete certainty.

In conclusion, it is interesting to note that Chris' desire to have the physical characteristics of a man is considered part of a "disorder," while a small-breasted woman's desire for breast implants would usually be construed as a desire to increase her femininity and not be labeled as such. Perhaps Chris is somewhere on a male-female continuum and is pushing himself toward the end of the spectrum in our neatly constructed gender binary that is closest to his identity.

This passage was adapted from "Healthcare Experiences of Gender Diverse Australians: A Mixed-methods, Self-report Survey." Riggs DW, Coleman K, Due C. *BMC Public Health.* 2014. 14(230) doi:10.1186/1471-2458-14-230 for use under the terms of the Creative Commons Attribution License 4.0 (http://creativecommons.org/licenses/by/4.0/legalcode).

Question 64

The passage suggests that its author would probably disagree with which of the following statements regarding Chris's gender identity and expression?

○ **A.** It is possible that Chris participated in "male" activities in order to be considered male.

○ **B.** It is possible that Chris naturally participated in "male" activities.

○ **C.** Chris was not confused about his gender identity.

○ **D.** Chris's discomfort resulted from the fact that every culture has defined gender roles.

Question 65

The passage claims regarding hormonal treatment for Chris rely on the implicit assumption(s) that:

    I. one should be happy in one's "natural" state.

    II. one can be well-adjusted, yet unhappy with one's "natural" state.

    III. one's perception of self is most important.

○ **A.** I only

○ **B.** II only

○ **C.** III only

○ **D.** I and III only

Question 66

The author of the passage would be most likely to agree with which of the following conclusions regarding psychological phenomena and the DSM-5?

○ **A.** A DSM-5 'disorder' may not actually be a disorder at all.

○ **B.** The DSM-5 is a poor descriptor of abnormal behavior and desires, since it is easily influenced by societal norms.

○ **C.** Some DSM-5 'disorders' are simply an attempt to characterize socially abnormal behavior and desires.

○ **D.** Behavior and desires must fall within the parameters of the DSM-5 to be considered normal by society.

Question 67

The author hints that the fact that Chris is well-adjusted indicates that his "uneasiness with his assigned sex" (paragraph 2):

- ○ **A.** is a problem which should be overcome through psychiatry.
- ○ **B.** is influenced by the culture he lives in.
- ○ **C.** can be overcome through surgery.
- ○ **D.** is a basic personality defect.

Question 68

Suppose it were discovered that antidepressant prescription medication allows Chris to become somewhat more comfortable with his "natural" state. Would this discovery support the author's argument about the causes of gender dysphoria?

- ○ **A.** Yes; it confirms it.
- ○ **B.** No; it does not affect it.
- ○ **C.** No; it weakens it.
- ○ **D.** No; it disproves it.

Question 69

Which of the following is a passage argument that supports the idea that other cultures might not view Chris's experience as "disordered"?

- ○ **A.** Other cultures do not strictly assign gender according to the inspection of genitalia at birth.
- ○ **B.** Societally determined labeling can determine what is viewed as abnormal behavior.
- ○ **C.** Socially constructed gender roles have precluded Chris from being as well-adjusted as he might have been in another culture.
- ○ **D.** Chris may have intentionally sought out activities that our society views as "gendered."

Question 70

The author's attitude toward "our" societal norms is most accurately described as:

- ○ **A.** favorable.
- ○ **B.** neutral.
- ○ **C.** distrustful.
- ○ **D.** disapproving.

Passage II (Questions 71-77)

The question of human overpopulation and its relationship to human carrying capacity – the planet's limited ability to support its people – has been controversial for over two centuries. In 1798 the Reverend Thomas Malthus hypothesized that population growth would exceed the growth of resources, leading to periodic reduction of human numbers by either "positive checks," such as disease, famine, and war, or "negative checks," by which Malthus meant restrictions on marriage. This "Malthusian view" was rapidly accepted and remained popular until fairly recently.

Malthus's worst fears were not borne out in the century following his death in 1834 – food production largely kept pace with the slowly growing global population. However, soon after 1934, the global population began to rise steeply as antibiotics, vaccines, and technology increased life expectancy. By the 1960s, concerns of a mismatch between global population and global food supply peaked.

The 1970s surprised population watchers. Instead of being a period shadowed by calamitous famine, new crop strains (especially grains such as rice and wheat) caused a dramatic increase in the global production of cereals, the main energy source in the global diet. Despair turned into cautious optimism. By the end of the decade, the public health community felt sufficiently empowered to proclaim "Health for All by the Year 2000." Average life expectancy continued to zoom upward almost everywhere.

The tremendous successes of the era had a pernicious effect: this rise in life expectancy coincided with fading concern about overpopulation, reaching a nadir with the election of US President Ronald Reagan in 1980. Unlike his predecessor, Richard Nixon, Reagan considered concerns about global population size to be "vastly exaggerated." In the same year, the US surprised the world by abdicating its previous leadership in the effort to promote global family planning. This reversal has since proved disastrous in many disciplines outside of public health.

As foreign aid budgets fell, the Health for All targets began to slip from reach. Instead, international agencies promoted structural adjustment programs, health charges for patients, and the "trickle down" effect as the best ways to promote development. It is plausible that a fraction of the public who remained concerned about Third World development thought that these economic policies deserved a chance. Less charitably, the new economic policies also allowed people already financially comfortable to give up concern for Third World development because the new orthodoxy asserted that market deregulation, rather than aid, was the royal road to development.

The harvest that market deregulation and generally high birth rates have sown in many Third World countries is now clear. Health for All, if recalled at all, is now seen as absurdly optimistic. The failure of development is most obvious in many sub-Saharan countries, where life expectancy has fallen substantially. But life expectancy has also fallen in Haiti, Russia, North Korea, and a handful of other nations.

Among the multitude of causes that can be identified for declines in either total population or life expectancy, overpopulation is hardly considered, except by "dissidents" such as Maurice King. Amid the many different explanations for the horrific

1994 Rwandan genocide, the possibility of a Malthusian check is scarcely mentioned. There is even less discussion entertaining the possibility that the sub-Saharan epidemic of HIV/AIDS may also be a check. King refers to the silence on overpopulation as the "Hardinian Taboo," after the ecologist Garrett Hardin, who described the proscriptions used to avoid confronting the need for population control. Whatever the cause of the scarcity of modern academic analysis, the related issues of human carrying capacity and overpopulation deserve fresh consideration.

This passage was adapted from "Human Carrying Capacity and Human Health." Butler CD. *PLoS Med.* 2004. 1(3) doi:10.1371/journal.pmd.0010055 for use under the terms of the Creative Commons CC BY 2.0 license (http://creativecommons.org/licenses/by/2.0/legalcode).

Question 71

Which of the following ideas concerning foreign aid is most strongly implied by the information in paragraph 5?

- A. The Health for All targets were always doomed to fail.
- B. Selfishness among citizens of wealthy nations probably contributed to the global decline in foreign aid.
- C. Reagan-era development strategies were largely unpopular in Third World countries.
- D. The failure to reach the Health for All targets should be blamed on the "already financially comfortable."

Question 72

Which of the following statements, if true, would most weaken the author's arguments concerning carrying capacity and overpopulation?

- A. Vaccines contributed more to increased life expectancy in the 20th century than antibiotics.
- B. Malthus's views were widely criticized at the time of their publication.
- C. Historical population reduction is fairly uncommon.
- D. Historical population reduction is most common when resources exceed population demands.

Question 73

Which of the following passage assertions is LEAST supported by evidence within the text?

- A. There were terrible consequences for disciplines outside public health after the US pulled back from the family planning effort.
- B. High birth rates and unregulated markets have led to clear negative effects in many Third World countries.
- C. Malthus's dire predictions were not borne out in the century following his death.
- D. The successes of the 1970s were followed by decreased attention to the problem of overpopulation.

Question 74

Assume that a new strain of rice is developed that can be harvested in half as much time as traditional rice. The passage author would most likely respond that:

- A. this development should solve the problem of carrying capacity and overpopulation.
- B. the Malthusian viewpoint is no longer relevant to the analysis of global population levels.
- C. this development will simply mask the increasing risk of overpopulation until it has grown even higher.
- D. this development represents a new "positive check."

Question 75

Based on the information in the first paragraph, which of the following would the author most likely consider a modern-day "negative check"?

- A. The rise of national vaccination programs
- B. Widespread famine among sub-Saharan nations
- C. Escalating violence in the Middle East
- D. Growing rates of birth control usage

Question 76

The passage author most likely believes the Rwandan Genocide and AIDS crisis are:

- A. examples of the dangerous consequences of excessive foreign aid.
- B. less serious than population declines in Haiti, Russia, and North Korea.
- C. widely recognized "positive checks."
- D. unacknowledged consequences of overpopulation.

Question 77

The author's use of quotation marks around the word "dissidents" in paragraph 7 is most likely meant to convey which of the following?

- A. A literal military conflict
- B. An ironic reversal of fortune for a once widely accepted theory
- C. The author's disappointment with current overwhelming support of the Malthusian theory
- D. The author's disdain for Maurice King and his views

Next ▶

Passage III (Questions 78-84)

Hobbes dedicated his life to articulating and teaching men, in a clear and exact method, the material dynamics of human nature and the moral and civil rules that follow from it. He believed that a true understanding of human nature begins with the first principles of motion and body, and it is from these principles that the rules of moral and civil life are correctly established. Hobbes writes,

> "After physics, we must come to moral philosophy; in which we are to consider the motions of the mind, namely, appetite, aversion, love, benevolence, hope, fear, anger, emulation . . . And the reason why these are to be considered after physics is, that they have their causes in sense and imagination, which are the subject of physical contemplation."

Hobbes turned to materialism in order to provide a new foundation for the generation and understanding of meaning, language, and political stability. He sought to discover the material causes of human sensation, perception, thought, and action because he believed that knowledge of these processes would provide the scientific, and hence undisputable, knowledge that would end the moral and religious civil wars. However, Hobbes's account of materialism reveals a dynamic process of perceptions, imaginings, and desires that lead to a fragmentation of meaning, which in turn contributes to the chaos of the state of nature and the unlikelihood of commonwealth. Characterized by the absence of a highest good, the equal vulnerability of each to a violent death, radical diversity of perception and meaning, and the absolute freedom to pursue one's desires, Hobbes's state of nature is not just a theoretical model but rather a product of his materialist account of sensation, imagination, and desire.

Hobbes's account of materialism leads toward greater anarchy of perception, meaning, and condition, and away from agreement or commonwealth, because at each stage of the argument, and the potential for a diversity of perceptions, images, and ideas, creates deeply subjective interpretations of the physical, social, and political environment. Therefore, Hobbes's materialist account of human nature defeats the very purpose for which it is conceived. To illuminate this claim, examine Shakespeare's *Macbeth*.

Performed approximately 50 years before Hobbes's *Leviathan* appeared, *Macbeth* foreshadows Hobbes's account of the state of nature, and expresses many of the psychological and political themes that also occupied Hobbes. Macbeth is considered a tragic hero because he should have known better and acted differently. However, seen from the perspective of Hobbes's materialist account of human nature, Macbeth is not tragic at all. The subjective and fluid motion of Macbeth's senses, the images they create, his vainglorious imagination, and his boundless desire for power create the terror and political instability of *Macbeth*. *Macbeth* provides graphic examples of the problems that arise from Hobbes's materialism, and these problems illuminate the political significance of *Macbeth*. By reading *Macbeth* in light of Hobbes's materialist account of human nature, we witness the self-defeating tendencies of Hobbes's materialism as they manifest themselves in Macbeth's perception of himself and the world. Following Hobbes's materialism, it is Macbeth and his violent end – and not the rational individual who creates the commonwealth – that is the more likely result.

If Macbeth is the "natural" consequence of Hobbes's materialism, and yet we insist that the problem with Macbeth lies in his rejection, or forgetting, of moral reasoning or the natural law, we risk misunderstanding the source of our moral and political problems. Because Macbeth is this way, and because he shares the world with others, significant political ramifications follow. If Hobbes's materialism is an accurate account of our sensation, perception, imagination, and their effect on our decision making and desires, the political significance lies in the recognition that rational resolution to the diversity of imaginings and desires will be exceedingly difficult.

This passage was adapted from "Shakespeare and Hobbes: Macbeth and the Fragility of Political Order." Dungey N. *SAGE Open.* 2012. 2(2) doi: 10.1177/2158244012439557 for use under the terms of the Creative Commons CC BY 3.0 license (https://creativecommons.org/licenses/by/3.0/legalcode).

Question 78

Which of the following facts presented in the passage would support the claim that Macbeth does NOT follow the expectations of Hobbes's material logic?

○ **A.** The political turmoil that Macbeth generates

○ **B.** Macbeth's vainglorious desire for power

○ **C.** Macbeth's appreciation as a tragic hero

○ **D.** The self-defeating tendencies that Macbeth possesses

Question 79

Which of the following objections would most weaken the author's argument regarding *Macbeth*'s implications for Hobbes's materialism?

○ **A.** Shakespeare intended for the tragedy of Macbeth to illuminate the tolerance of people for insane leaders and to describe an unbalanced mind.

○ **B.** Hobbes intended for people to embrace the evidence gathered by their senses rather than to make assumptions about the unknown motives of others.

○ **C.** Shakespeare intended for the tragedy of Macbeth to resonate with the English people who were emerging from the chaos of Hobbes's era.

○ **D.** Hobbes intended for the social contract he described to be viewed as a utopian instrument of philosophical discourse, not practical advice.

Question 80

According to the passage, Hobbes believes that people who rigorously study human nature would be most likely to:

○ **A.** achieve a scientific education.

○ **B.** live peacefully and amicably.

○ **C.** make war civilly and righteously.

○ **D.** stand up to political injustice.

Question 81

Which of the following statements about Hobbes's materialism CANNOT be concluded based on the passage?

○ A. It acknowledges greed and selfishness as valid motives.

○ B. It is based on rigorous logic.

○ C. It offers a path away from moral and religious war.

○ D. It informs Hobbes's views on the state of human nature.

Question 82

Based on the information in the passage, with which of the following statements would the author most likely agree?

○ A. Macbeth is a tragic hero, but not in the traditional sense.

○ B. Macbeth's actions are justified by Hobbes's materialism.

○ C. Hobbes was influenced by *Macbeth* when writing Leviathan.

○ D. Careful analysis is required to apply Hobbes's teachings to human actions.

Question 83

Which of the following findings would most strengthen the author's point about materialism and discord?

○ A. A treatise by a contemporary of Hobbes that further illustrates the causal link between materialism and commonwealth

○ B. An excerpt from Hobbes's private journal showing that he intended a strictly theoretical interpretation of his State of Nature

○ C. An annotation attributed to Hobbes contemplating the role of dynamic processes in establishing a peaceful commonwealth

○ D. A prominent philosopher's analysis of Hobbes's materialism in the actions that led to a civil war

Question 84

Which of the following best describes an assumption made by the author in the discussion of Macbeth's motivations and conduct?

○ A. Macbeth's violent actions were illegal.

○ B. Macbeth should be considered a rational actor.

○ C. The motivations ascribed to Macbeth were intended to be beyond realism, as obvious farce.

○ D. Hobbes's materialism is a valuable tool in analyzing Shakespearean characters.

STOP. IF YOU FINISH BEFORE TIME IS CALLED, CHECK YOUR WORK. YOU MAY GO BACK TO ANY QUESTION IN THIS TEST BOOKLET.

STOP

30-MINUTE IN-CLASS EXAM FOR LECTURE 4

Passage I (Questions 85-91)

Helping individuals make decisions that promote their own welfare, without limiting their freedom of choice, is one of the hallmarks of "libertarian paternalism." Paternalism is often considered a serious threat to the autonomy and choice of an individual, and is associated with perceived authoritarian policies. Libertarian paternalism, however, aims to provide a framework where individuals make decisions that benefit themselves and society, whilst still maintaining a range of available options. In other words, by changing the "choice architecture" for decision making, individuals can be "nudged" into making the right choices.

The premise for this approach is based on behavioral economics, which has characterized the decision making processes and the biases that may lead to "reasoning failure." These biases can result in choices that negatively impact welfare, which is particularly relevant to medical practice where patients are often required to weigh the risks of survival, toxicity, and quality of life when making treatment decisions. Under these circumstances, patients may be influenced by an array of emotions, such as fear and grief. Studies of cancer patients have found that demands for particular treatments do not come from a neutral evaluation of risks and benefits but rather from a perception of hope even when faced with a high likelihood of major toxicity and low benefit. Further inconsistencies in decision making may arise from previous experiences, particularly if these have been unpleasant.

Informed decision making requires the provision of comprehensive and objective information. This can be problematic because patients may struggle with probabilities, over-estimating their level of risk of disease and the potential benefits of treatment. It has been argued that too many options can have negative consequences by resulting in individuals using heuristics (rules of thumb) to counter the numerous choices on offer, leading to suboptimal decisions. Individuals may suffer from "myopia" where they are not able to imagine decisions that will impact them in the future, specifically not anticipating how their preferences may change over time.

Critics of nudge policies suggest that they do not unbias individuals' decision making, but rather utilize these biases to trick them into certain decisions. They contend that the use of such mechanisms impacts individuals' autonomy as they are not fully in control of their actions, and that there should be greater transparency. Freedom of choice is a core tenet of the libertarian paternalism philosophy, but opponents claim that there remains incongruity between the "nominal freedom of choice" and the "effective freedom of choice." For example, auto-enrolled opt-out schemes (e.g. organ donation) result in only a small proportion of people leaving the scheme, due to exploitation of their status quo bias.

It may be that using paternalism and autonomy as the two overriding principles is overly simplistic. Some critics of medical paternalism have suggested that it is perhaps more accurate to consider nudge techniques a form of "manipulation," a term meant to evoke images of the advertising industry. While many clinicians are quick to dismiss the comparison, the similarities in technique are undeniable and raise some interesting ethical issues. Many proponents of libertarian paternalism have replied that, in medicine at least, the use of nudge policies should be transparent and publicly defensible. For example, a clinician might acknowledge to a patient that he or she was delivering the information in a specific way by saying, "I am giving you the information in this way to help you understand why I think this is the best course of action." This approach is ideal and effective: if the motivation is for the patient's benefit and the clinician is open about the way he or she delivers information, claims of manipulation can be refuted and patient autonomy maximized.

This passage was adapted from "'Nudge' in the clinical consultation - an acceptable form of medical paternalism?" Aggarwal A, Davies J, Sullivan R. *BMC Medical Ethics*. 2014. 15(31) doi:10.1186/1472-6939-15-31 for use under the terms of the Creative Commons CC BY 2.0 license (http://creativecommons.org/licenses/by/2.0).

Question 85

Which of the following ideas established by the passage author is LEAST supported by evidence?

- ○ A. Patients do not always think optimally when making medical decisions.
- ○ B. Libertarian paternalism has become the unyielding dominant philosophy in modern medical ethics.
- ○ C. Medical paternalism and the advertising industry employ the same techniques.
- ○ D. Clinicians can make efforts to maintain patient autonomy.

Question 86

Why does the passage author most likely give the example of "opt-out" programs in paragraph 4?

- ○ A. To demonstrate how opt-out programs can improve medical decision making
- ○ B. To show that the appearance of autonomy does not guarantee actual autonomy
- ○ C. To give an example of patients with no freedom of choice
- ○ D. To explain the similarities in tactics between clinicians and advertisers

Question 87

Based on passage information, critics of medical paternalism would most likely respond to news that billions of dollars per year could be saved if clinicians downplayed the effectiveness of a powerful but often unnecessary new treatment by:

- ○ A. supporting this practice because the money saved is significant enough to outweigh the loss of autonomy.
- ○ B. opposing this practice because the money saved is significant enough to outweigh the loss of autonomy.
- ○ C. supporting this practice because it utilizes patients' biases.
- ○ D. opposing this practice because it utilizes patients' biases.

Next ▶

Question 88

Which of the following best describes the relationship between "nudge policies" and libertarian paternalism described in the passage?

- ○ **A.** Nudge policies are techniques used to fight libertarian paternalism.
- ○ **B.** Nudge policies are techniques that fall within the philosophy of libertarian paternalism.
- ○ **C.** Nudge policies are unrelated to libertarian paternalism.
- ○ **D.** Nudge policies can maintain patient autonomy when clinicians explain why they present information in a certain way.

Question 89

Suppose a new chemotherapy drug is developed that has the potential to extend one out of every ten thousand cancer patients' lives by up to four months. The drug costs $125,000 per year, and has horrific side effects that can lead to prolonged hospitalization. The passage author would most likely respond to this news by arguing that clinicians should:

- ○ **A.** focus on informing patients of the side effects and costs of the treatment.
- ○ **B.** prescribe the treatment in all cancer cases.
- ○ **C.** provide patients with all known information on the drug so they can decide their treatment options.
- ○ **D.** refuse to prescribe the drug to any patient under any circumstances.

Question 90

It is likely that the critics of nudge policies object to their "[utilization of] ...biases" (paragraph 4) for all of the following reasons EXCEPT:

- ○ **A.** They are overly manipulative.
- ○ **B.** They exploit a symptom of the problem rather than unbiasing the patient.
- ○ **C.** They are ineffective.
- ○ **D.** They rob the patients of their freedom of choice.

Question 91

Which assumption, if proven false, would most weaken the case for medical paternalism?

- ○ **A.** Clinicians are generally better informed of the optimal medical decision than patients.
- ○ **B.** Patients are generally better informed of the optimal medical decision than clinicians.
- ○ **C.** All patients are poor medical decision makers.
- ○ **D.** Nudge techniques are ineffective at changing behavior.

Passage II (Questions 92-98)

There is considerable research explaining how Australian Aboriginal symbols hold semantic meaning, but there is little acknowledgement of how they achieve a psychological response. From an Aboriginal standpoint, the purposeful use of repetitive visual form acts as a sensation and connects individuals to the self and their environment. A common symbol used is the circle, which offers an opportunity to discuss correct and improper interpretation.

Circular impressions left on rock surfaces are expressions of a cultural connection between mind, body, and emotions. Such evidence can be seen in the many circular images engraved on rock surfaces within Dharug Country in northern Sydney, which include concentric circular forms that acknowledge the harmony between external and internal worlds. These symbols contain a deep central engraved hole with three emitting circles built out from the central core, which contain up to twenty radiating lines. The first circle represents individual internal roots, such as intuition with the ancestral world. A second, larger circle represents relationships to place and space. The third, outermost circle relates to close primary cultural connections such as totems, spiritual affiliations, and the extended earthly environment. Radiating lines relate all the relationships to personal place and create a sense of timelessness.

Western misinterpretations of these circular engravings are common, and include the assumption that these depictions represent the moon, or some other cosmic image. Perhaps such notions of mere representation are due to prejudgment, with many non-Indigenous people observing symbols as simple forms of communication based on notions of primitiveness. Indeed, such classification of these symbols within a Western interpretation of "art" devalues thousands of years of generational knowledge systems, where visual information has been respected, appreciated, and valued. The creative form within such a cultural framework illustrates knowledge, and therefore has little relevance to aesthetic pleasure in viewing, or acquirement within a sense of ownership, but reflects vital information based on living.

More recent studies have focused on contemporary Aboriginal dot work, but little attention has been paid to the origins of such processes. Historically, the Aboriginal contemporary art movement of the early 1970s in Central Australia has been categorized as one that discredits traditional creative practices. Art teacher Geoffrey Bardon's observations while witnessing ground designs performed during ceremonial proceedings was one of the first comprehensive Western studies ever conducted. Bardon presented the idea of reproducing these non-permanent designs in a public arena on wall surfaces. Such public exposure of pure sacredness created offense within many Aboriginal Nations. Publicly expressed traditional reproductions of visual spiritual images are believed to cause harm to those not initiated.

In response, attempts were made to cover sacredness by manipulating creative form. Recent scholarship has argued that the use of dotting was implemented as a safe alternative to cover up forms of sacredness. From an Aboriginal standpoint, multi-layering techniques such as dotting are an intentional act of concealing knowledge, whereby only the initiated are able to comprehend scared information. Yet dotting techniques have also been used within ancient ceremonial healing practices, in which images are sculpted by the hands, with fingers used to make indentations on the surface of the ground. These fingerprints within the earth's surface are the original process of dot making, and functioned as one of the original methods of multi-layering in many Aboriginal Nations.

This passage was adapted from "Is It Art or Knowledge? Deconstructing Australian Aboriginal Creative Making." Cameron E. *Arts*. 2014. doi:10.3390/arts4020068 for use under the terms of the Creative Commons CC BY 4.0 license (http://creativecommons.org/licenses/by/4.0/legalcode).

Question 92

If the information presented in the passage is true, a member of an Aboriginal Nation would be upset to find a sacred work in a museum primarily because:

○ **A.** the artwork could pose a threat to museum patrons.

○ **B.** presentation in a museum would be a disgrace to Aboriginal cultural traditions.

○ **C.** Aboriginal art is always impermanent, and the piece could not be dismantled at the appropriate time.

○ **D.** Aboriginal Nations tend to dislike Western conceptions of art.

Question 93

If a scholar claimed that he had discovered evidence of Aboriginal art that recorded the yearly movement of the stars, the author of the passage would probably:

○ **A.** agree, because the scholar has the ability to view Aboriginal art as a member of the initiated.

○ **B.** agree, because astronomy is central to Aboriginal mythology.

○ **C.** disagree, because the scholar's interpretation emphasizes aesthetic pleasure in viewing.

○ **D.** disagree, because the scholar's interpretation makes no connection between the self and the environment.

Question 94

As a part of therapy, psychologist Carl Jung encouraged his patients to create artwork of concentric circles, concluding that "to paint what we see before us is a different art from painting what we see within." The author would probably see Jung's view of art as:

○ **A.** unlike the Aboriginal view, because Jung could only approach art from a Western perspective.

○ **B.** unlike the Aboriginal view, because psychotherapy is distant from Aboriginal cultural practices.

○ **C.** similar to the Aboriginal view, because Jung allows for an art that transcends representation.

○ **D.** similar to the Aboriginal view, because Jung was familiar with Aboriginal artistic symbols.

Question 95

Based on the information in the passage, "dotting" can be best described as:

○ **A.** an Aboriginal rhythmic visual form.

○ **B.** a way of imparting special significance to a work of art for those initiated into Aboriginal culture.

○ **C.** one of several multi-layering techniques.

○ **D.** a common practice in contemporary ceremonial healing rituals.

Question 96

The author implies that Geoffrey Bardon's understanding of Aboriginal symbols is most limited by Bardon's:

○ **A.** ignorance of the importance of context in Aboriginal art.

○ **B.** confusion about aboriginal compositional techniques.

○ **C.** Western view of art as a permanent object.

○ **D.** lack of familiarity with the methods of professional scholarship.

Question 97

If an equilateral triangle were found etched into a rock surface in Dharug Country, the author would most likely agree with which of the following interpretations?

○ **A.** The triangle is the symbolic representation of a Dharug deity.

○ **B.** The apices of the triangle are connected by lines to suggest the interdependence of mind, body, and feelings.

○ **C.** The triangle is a territorial marking, promising harm to the uninitiated.

○ **D.** The unavoidable imperfections in the triangle serve to remind the viewer of a higher order of geometric purity.

Question 98

Given the passage information, one would most reasonably conclude that a member of an Aboriginal Nation would find the ownership of art:

○ **A.** possible only if the piece were subjected to a multi-layering technique.

○ **B.** threatening to basic Aboriginal values.

○ **C.** difficult to understand from an Aboriginal cultural context.

○ **D.** reasonable as long as the artwork brought aesthetic pleasure.

Passage III (Questions 99-105)

The end of the colonial era saw the birth or rebirth of many nations, especially in Africa and Asia. Not only did these events transform the face of the globe, they also had an immediate impact on archaeology. Nations wishing both to legitimize their own existence and to foster feelings of national pride began to define their own past and paid tribute to the achievements of their ancestors. Such feelings were especially strong in those countries where the colonial rulers had consistently subordinated the history of local peoples to that of the conquerors. In Rhodesia, as it was then called, the British were unable to accept the hypothesis that the magnificent structures at Great Zimbabwe were built by "mere natives" and it was not until several generations of archaeologists brought accumulated evidence to bear on the subject that Great Zimbabwe became known to the world as a uniquely African development.

Hunger on the part of these people to establish their cultural ancestry, and to right the historical balance, led to the expenditure of large sums of money on the creation of national antiquities services and on the training of local archaeologists. In some cases archaeological artifacts appeared on postage stamps or in souvenir shops, while the sites themselves became rallying places and even national shrines. The new state of Israel used the imposing fortress of Masada as the location where new recruits were sworn in to the army, for it was there that the Jewish Zealots had held out with great bravery against the occupying Roman armies.

Many states poor in natural resources have come to realize that their archaeological heritage is also an important financial asset, providing them with attractions for tourists. The past becomes an invisible export and a powerful tool for public relations. Here archaeology is well and truly out of the ivory tower and stands amidst many attendant temptations – both ideological and financial. If the past is not quite as glorious as might be wished, perhaps it would be a good idea to manipulate the facts; if, on the contrary, other carefully selected "facts" prove useful in the battle for hearts and minds, they can be embellished; if the monuments are not quite picturesque enough, perhaps they should be improved.

The misuse of the past for political ends is also widely recognized as a problem. The political importance of the past is immense. Archaeology and history are not purely scholarly pursuits – knowledge for knowledge's sake – but are intrinsically powerful weapons in ideological discourse and indoctrination. The perversions of archaeology and history for propaganda are worth studying in their own right, once their true nature has been recognized, because they give us important insights into how people and nations wish to be seen and, in some cases, what their ideals and objectives are.

We may never know exactly how the past was, but it is relatively easy to show how the past was not. Hypotheses can be shown to have a better, or worse, fit to data. Debates over interpretations will continue; this is how research proceeds. But when we leave the even playing field of the observational sciences, and begin to make strident connections between the past and present, we are on our way down the slippery slope of ideology and self-interest. This is not to say that it is inappropriate that peoples take pride in their past, but simply that we should not labor to glorify our ancestors in the face of evidence to the contrary.

This passage was adapted from "Prehistory as Propaganda." MacDonald KC, Hung FYC, Crawford H. *Papers from the Institute of Archaeology*. 1995. 6 (1995) for use under the terms of the Creative Commons CC BY 3.0 license (http://creativecommons.org/licenses/by/3.0/legalcode).

Question 99

In the second paragraph, the author's reference to "these people" refers to:

○ **A.** British colonial powers.

○ **B.** builders of the Great Zimbabwe in Rhodesia.

○ **C.** nations wishing to legitimize their own existence.

○ **D.** Israeli army recruits.

Question 100

Which of the following assertions in the passage is LEAST supported with explanation or examples?

○ **A.** Historic sites become rallying places and national shrines.

○ **B.** Archaeology is a tool for nations wishing to legitimize their own existence.

○ **C.** The misuse of the past for political ends is a widely recognized problem.

○ **D.** The past can be an invisible export and a powerful tool for public relations.

Question 101

Which of the following conclusions is most strongly implied by the passage?

○ **A.** Political gain is often the motivating force behind developing historical sites for tourism.

○ **B.** Manipulating knowledge about archaeology is more important among oppressed people than among their oppressors.

○ **C.** Academic archaeology more accurately represents prehistory than popular archaeology.

○ **D.** Objectivity in archaeology is threatened by a variety of motivations.

Question 102

For which archaeological practice would the author of the passage be LEAST likely to advocate?

○ **A.** DNA analysis to determine genetic identity of prehistorical peoples

○ **B.** Speculation on the uses of various objects unearthed through archaeological digging

○ **C.** Identifying the geographic origin of objects through chemical analysis

○ **D.** Independent dating of archaeological objects

Question 103

Which of the following is most likely to represent the author's opinion about archaeological artifacts appearing on postage stamps and in souvenir shops?

- ○ **A.** Such practices cheapen the field of archaeology.
- ○ **B.** Archaeology is a more effective tool of propaganda when used by a culture on itself rather than as a tool for the conquerors against the conquered.
- ○ **C.** It shows that archaeological artifacts can become potent symbols of national pride and unity.
- ○ **D.** These items are beneficial because they provide a way for archaeology to get out of the ivory tower.

Question 104

Which practice relating to newspaper journalism is LEAST analogous to the attendant temptations described in paragraph 3 of the passage?

- ○ **A.** Embellishing a story to make it more interesting to the reader
- ○ **B.** Re-publishing an old story to remember the past
- ○ **C.** Publishing sensationalized stories to sell more newspapers
- ○ **D.** Omitting sections from an interview to change the meaning of the quotations

Question 105

Suppose that a country chosen to host the Olympics decides to beautify several national historic sites to be even more extravagant than their original conditions before the games begin. Based on the information in the passage, which is the most likely logic behind the restoration project?

- ○ **A.** Historical artifacts can be leveraged for gains in finances and public relations.
- ○ **B.** Restoration emphasizes national pride and unity.
- ○ **C.** The selected changes provide insight into how the nation wants to be seen by the world.
- ○ **D.** Archaeologists cannot know exactly how the past was.

STOP. IF YOU FINISH BEFORE TIME IS CALLED, CHECK YOUR WORK. YOU MAY GO BACK TO ANY QUESTION IN THIS TEST BOOKLET.

STOP

ANSWERS & EXPLANATIONS

FOR

30-MINUTE IN-CLASS EXAMINATIONS

ANSWERS FOR THE 30-MINUTE IN-CLASS EXAMS

Lecture ii	Lecture 1	Lecture 2	Lecture 3	Lecture 4
1. B	22. C	43. D	64. D	85. C
2. A	23. B	44. C	65. B	86. B
3. B	24. B	45. D	66. C	87. D
4. C	25. D	46. B	67. B	88. B
5. D	26. D	47. D	68. C	89. A
6. A	27. A	48. C	69. B	90. C
7. B	28. B	49. D	70. D	91. A
8. C	29. A	50. B	71. B	92. A
9. A	30. B	51. D	72. D	93. D
10. B	31. C	52. A	73. A	94. C
11. C	32. A	53. C	74. C	95. C
12. A	33. C	54. C	75. D	96. A
13. C	34. A	55. D	76. D	97. B
14. A	35. C	56. C	77. B	98. C
15. B	36. C	57. B	78. C	99. C
16. D	37. D	58. A	79. A	100. C
17. C	38. A	59. B	80. B	101. D
18. C	39. B	60. C	81. C	102. B
19. D	40. D	61. D	82. D	103. C
20. A	41. B	62. C	83. D	104. B
21. C	42. A	63. B	84. B	105. A

SCORING

Any attempt we could make at score correlation to the MCAT® would mislead. Unlike the AAMC MCAT®, which includes easy questions, Examkrackers deliberately asks questions only of medium and high difficulty in order to optimize your practice time and maximize the increase to your MCAT® score. To accurately predict your MCAT® score, use an official AAMC MCAT® practice test.

Your goal is to see your raw score improve with each Examkrackers In-Class Exam and full-length EK-Test® you take. Look closely at each question you get wrong to find areas for review and to notice the habits that don't work. As you approach each new In-Class Exam or practice test, make commitments to replace what doesn't work with the approach you need to get questions right. Focus on the questions you get wrong to learn to think like the MCAT® and increase your score.

Toward your success!

EXPLANATIONS FOR 30-MINUTE IN-CLASS EXAM ii

Passage I (Questions 1–4)

1. **B is the best answer.** Both experiments show that NLP provides no benefit over pure guessing in assessing whether someone is lying. There is no stated comparison between trained and untrained practitioners, so choice A is not the best answer. It is possible that trained practitioners would be able to effectively use NLP, but this cannot be shown by the experiments described in the passage. Both studies showed that NLP had no effect, so there was no inconsistency, making choice C a weak answer. Choice D is also a weak answer based on the results shown in Table 1. Confidence was almost exactly the same in both groups, and the given p-value is very large. The p-value cutoff for statistical significance can vary between experiments, but $p = 0.67$ would never be considered significant ($p = 0.67$ means that there is a 67% probability that the difference between groups is due to chance)!

2. **A is the best answer.** This modification to the experiment constitutes systematic error by biasing outcomes in one direction. Participants who were informed of NLP techniques would be likely to modify their behavior to mask potentially revealing eye movements. Note that it is not really necessary to understand exactly how the modification would change participants' behavior to realize that systematic error, rather than random error, would result. By definition, random error is random and could not be induced by a particular experimental modification (outside of the factors that normally cause random error, such as the use of faulty equipment). Choices B and D can be eliminated. Systematic error is associated with accuracy, not precision, making choice A a stronger answer than choice C.

3. **B is the best answer.** The hypothesis is phrased in such a way that it would be impossible to prove wrong, or falsify. Imagine that NLP is never effective. This would make falsifying the hypothesis presented an impossible task: it would require testing the efficacy of NLP in every situation imaginable (of which there are an infinite number of possibilities!) in order to show that it is NOT effective in any situation. Rather than simply requiring a large number of experiments, no number of experiments would make it possible to falsify the hypothesis, so choice B is a stronger answer than choice A. Since the hypothesis cannot be disproven, the findings of the passage experiments cannot possibly disprove it; choice C is not a strong answer. There is no indication that deception would be required to test the hypothesis, making choice D weaker than choice B.

4. **C is the best answer.** Independent variables are those that are manipulated by experimenters. In the first experiment, participants were told whether to lie or not to lie. For that reason, lying vs. not lying was the independent variable, while pattern of eye movement was the dependent variable. For that reason, option III is true, eliminating answer choices A and B. In the second experiment, NLP training was the independent variable: the experimenters assigned participants to training and non-training groups. Number of correct judgments about and rated confidence were the variables measured by the experimenters and were thought to possibly vary according to the independent variable. In other words, they were the dependent variables. Option I is false while option II is true, making choice C the best answer.

Passage II (Questions 5-9)

5. **D is the best answer.** This question tests for understanding of what a p-value represents; the specific time points in Figure 1 are not important. Recall from the lecture that a p-value indicates the likelihood that a difference between data sets was obtained by random chance alone. This is also known as the null hypothesis. A p-value of 0.01 means there is a one percent chance ($0.01 = \frac{1}{100} = 1\%$) that this null hypothesis is true, meaning the best answer must be choice C or D. Remember that no matter how small the p-value, there is always *some* possibility that the result is due to random chance, even if it is incredibly small. There is no statistical test that can tell with total certainty that the null hypothesis must be incorrect. For this reason, choice C can be eliminated and choice D is the best answer.

6. **A is the best answer.** This question stem contains some helpful clues. It states that the experimenters are testing some new independent variable to try and mimic the effects of prazosin. This implies that the effects of prazosin are already known. The independent variable in this scenario is the antioxidant treatment, and the dependent variable is the level of liver toxicity. Neither of these refers to the prazosin group, so choices C and D can be eliminated. Variables refer to aspects of each group that are being manipulated or studied, not the groups themselves. Both choices A and B refer to types of control groups. Recall from the lecture that a negative control is a group in which no effect is expected. This is most similar to the untreated mice, described in the passage – no treatment effect is expected if there is no treatment. This makes choice B a weak answer. The prazosin group is a positive control since the researchers already know what effect should be expected from prazosin treatment. Choice A is the strongest answer.

7. **B is the best answer.** The caption for Figure 1 states that each bar represents the mean for the values collected at that particular time point. Recall that the mean describes the central tendency of a data set. Option I is true. Note that because choices A, B, C, and D all contain option I, it has to be true. The most common value in any data set is known as the mode. Figure 1 does not indicate the frequency of any values, so option II is untrue, eliminating choices A and D. The error bars in Figure 1 represent standard deviation. Standard deviation is a descriptive statistic used to indicate the spread of a data set, making option III true and choice B the best answer.

8. **C is the best answer.** Random assignment is a powerful tool that researchers use to ensure that all groups are equivalent so that experimental observations can be attributed only to manipulations of the independent variable. Ideally, this process removes a subjective element (assigning subjects to groups) from experimental design, so choice B can be eliminated. Since random assignment ensures that significant effects do not come from biased experimental groups, it should not guarantee that significant differences are found – this depends only on the phenomenon being studied and the experimental procedure – so choice A is also not a strong answer. Although random assignment should eliminate bias, it does not do so by forcing results to be continuous. Continuous data is data that can take any value in a range, like a wavelength of visible light. The second half of choice D is unconnected to the elimination of bias. Random assignment attempts to control for within-group variability by distributing that variability randomly across all groups. For this reason, choice C is the best answer.

9. **A is the best answer.** Note that the question stem only tells you that a relationship was found between two variables; it says nothing about the specifics of that relationship. For this reason, it is possible that either high or low body fat could be correlated with lower risk of liver damage. This means that either choice B or C could be true, so both answer choices can be eliminated. This is a somewhat uncommon example of two answers that appear to contradict each other both being true or false. It is also possible that a chi-square test could reveal a break from the expected liver damage levels at extreme body fat percentages, so choice D can be eliminated. One of the limitations of correlation tests is that they cannot describe the causality of a statistical relationship. This means that a correlation can never prove that one variable depends on another, making choice A untrue and the best answer.

Passage III (Questions 10-14)

10. **B is the best answer.** The figure indicates that the optimal E/S ratio is somewhere between 5 and 15, as the battery with an E/S ratio of 10 is more efficient than either of the end points. Recall that the goal of the experiment was to find an optimal E/S ratio. The researchers can expect that batteries with E/S ratios of 4, 16, or 25 would similarly be inferior to the E/S ratio of 10, so researchers would not want to test either of these values. Choices A, C, and D can be eliminated on that basis. It is possible that another value between 5 and 10 or between 10 and 15 would be even more efficient. Choice B provides an E/S ratio falling in one of these ranges and is the best answer.

11. **C is the best answer.** As described in the passage, the electrolyte solvent serves as a medium for ion movement. If the solvent were polar, it could react with either the lithium ions or lithium polysulfides that were being released into it, interfering with the reactions that are of interest in the experiment. No passage information indicates that molar mass, density, or volume could affect the experimental conditions. These properties, after all, are physical properties that will not alter the chemical properties of the product. For that reason, choices A, B, and D are weaker than choice C.

12. **A is the best answer.** The scenario described in the question stem provides an example of systematic error: all of the readings will be about 10mV higher than the true value. As a result, accuracy is compromised. However, all readings of a repeated measure should still agree with each other as well as they would if the equipment were not flawed, so precision is not affected. Choices B and C can be eliminated, and choice A is a strong answer. Choice D is a nonsense error because the type of measurement scale would not be affected by measurement error.

13. **C is the best answer.** This question could be restated as: "Which E/S ratio has the lowest capacity when all the cycles have been completed?" The E/S = 15 cell appears to maintain capacity retention well at first, but as time progresses it short circuits while the other two cells continue to recharge and discharge to some degree. Because an E/S ratio of 15 has no capacity at the highest cycle indicated in Figure 1, choice C is stronger than choices A and B. While E/S ratios of 5 and 15 both lose capacity beyond 80 cycles, Figure 1 indicates that the E/S ratio of has more capacity and better long-term cycling efficiency. With this reasoning, choice D can be eliminated.

14. **A is the best answer.** A confounding variable is a variable that is correlated with the independent variable (in this case, E/S ratio) and has a causal effect on the dependent variable (capacity retention). This is exactly the situation being described in the question stem, limiting the possible answer choices to choices A and B. (C and D are distractors; "biased variable" is not a required term for the MCAT®). Internal validity refers to whether a causal relationship between the independent and dependent variable can be justifiably concluded from an experiment. It can be greatly affected by confounding variables, which may give the appearance of a causal relationship where none actually exists. External validity refers to the generalizability of results from a sample to a wider population, and is determined by factors like whether or not the characteristics of the sample are representative of those of the population. The presence of a confounding variable would impair the researchers' ability to demonstrate causality, so internal validity is compromised in this question stem. Choice A is the best answer.

Passage IV (Questions 15-18)

15. **B is the best answer.** Option I would show the researchers whether the mutant half of the Aqp2 proteins were retained in the endoplasmic reticulum while the wild type half were in their normal location. Option II would allow the researchers to see if the Aqp2 protein ended up in the endoplasmic reticulum in the recessive phenotype. Option III would allow the researchers to look at the wild type and use it as a control for where the protein is supposed to be located. Choosing option I, II and III would allow a comparison of where the Aqp2 protein localized in each of the mice groups. Choices A and D are not the best choice because they exclude the control group. Choice C is not the best answer because it excludes the heterozygote. A heterozygote is needed because it allows the researchers to see if the tissue showed a hybrid of the two localizations as further support for the hypothesis. This makes choice B the best answer.

16. **D is the best answer.** According to information contained in the passage, a valine is substituted for a phenylalanine in the aquaporin channel and this mutated channel is used to model NDI. A heterozygous advantage occurs when the phenotype of the heterozygote is more fit than that of either homozygote. Figure 2 provides the best information to answer this question. Comparing the Wild Type (WT) and Aqp2$^{F204V/wt}$ mice, there is no difference in the urine osmolarity. If the Aqp2 F204V mutation conferred a heterozygous advantage, a significant difference would be expected between WT and heterozygous mice. Because no difference is seen, choice A can be eliminated. Figure 2 also provides the best information for considering choice B. The heterozygote contains one functional wild type copy of Aqp2 and one mutated copy, with a valine substituted for a phenylalanine. Notice that there is no difference in the urine osmolarity between the wild type and heterozygote, meaning that one functional copy appears to be enough to regulate osmolarity control. Choice B is unlikely to be the best answer. Sense mutations are those nucleotide substitutions that do not change the primary amino acid sequence. The Apq2 F204V mutation is a missense mutation because the phenylalanine changes to a valine upon mutation in the gene. According to information in the passage, a missense mutation, not a sense mutation, would prevent regulation of water reabsorption via the aquaporin channel, eliminating choice C. Nonconservative mutations are a subtype of missense mutations. Conservative mutations change the amino acid identity but do not change the type of amino acid. In this instance, the change in amino acid identity is from a phenylalanine to a valine. Phenylalanine is a nonpolar amino acid, as is valine. The mutation changes the identity of the amino acid but not the type, making it a conservative mutation. Phenylalanine contains an aromatic R-group that does not structurally resemble the isopropyl side chain of valine. It is reasonable to assume that removing the phenylalanine and substituting a valine could result in a change in the structure of the aquaporin channel, rendering it non- or less functional. This assumption may be confirmed by looking at the urine osmolarity of the homozygous recessive mouse in Figure 2 and noting that it can no longer concentrate urine via the aquaporin channel. Choice D is the best answer choice.

17. **C is the best answer.** Looking at Figure 2, Aqp2$^{F204V/F204V}$ mice had increased urine osmolality in response to dDAVP. This is somewhat confusing because NDI is characterized by the inability to concentrate urine in response to AVP and dDAVP is an AVP analog. Choice A and choice D are weak choices because the passage states that the researchers controlled for water and food intake. Choice B is not the best answer because ligand-receptor matching normally has very high specificity. Choice C is the best answer because it supports the principle that mutations can result in variable expressivity or phenotypical outcomes.

18. **C is the best answer.** This answer is best determined by examining the Western blot in Figure 3. A Western blot shows how much of a specific protein is prevalent in a tissue sample by first using gel electrophoresis to separate proteins by size and then using labeled probes to highlight the target protein. Figure 3 shows the prevalence of each of the Aqp2 forms in each of the mice groups. The darker the smear, the more prevalent the Aqp2 form is. The 31kDa form is more prevalent in the Aqp2$^{F204V/F204V}$ mice and not uniquely prevalent in the Aqp2$^{F204V/wt}$ mice, so choice A is not the best answer. Similarly, the 31kDa form is not uniquely prevalent in the Aqp2$^{F204V/wt}$ mice, so choice B is not the best choice. Figure 3 indicates that the 31 kDa form is expressed in the Aqp2$^{F204V/F204V}$ mice, a mix of the three forms are expressed in the Aqp2$^{F204V/wt}$ mice, and the 35-45kDa form is expressed in the wild type mice. Choice C reflects this pattern of expression and is a strong choice. Since choice C accurately describes the pattern of expression, choice D can be eliminated.

Stand-alones (Questions 19-21)

19. **D is the best answer**. This table describes the enthalpy of hydration of ions going down the first column of the periodic table. The enthalpy of hydration is a thermodynamic quantity which describes the energy liberated when an ion is surrounded by water molecules. A more negative enthalpy of hydration reflects a greater attraction between the ion and the water molecules surrounding it. Besides enthalpy of hydration, atomic radius also changes when going down a column in the periodic table. However, it changes in the opposite direction, increasing down a column. Based on the data, it seems that these parameters show an inverse relationship, with greater enthalpies of hydration being associated with smaller atomic radii. Choice A implies the opposite and should be eliminated. At first glance, choice B seems to be a valid possibility. Sulfuric acid will release protons (H$^+$ ions) into solution, and H$^+$ ions are associated with a very exothermic $H_{hydration}$. Nonetheless, since this table does not address the effect of hydrating the bisulfate anion, which comes after deprotonation of sulfuric acid, it is unknown what will really happen. Perhaps hydrating this anion is so endothermic that it actually decreases the temperature of the solution. Continue looking at choices before selecting choice B. Choice C is contradicted by evidence in the table. H$^+$ does not have filled p orbitals and yet it has the most exothermic $H_{hydration}$. Such a great $H_{hydration}$ implies the most favorable solute-solvent interactions. Choice D restates the inverse relationship of $H_{hydration}$ and ionic radius. This choice is better supported by the data in the table than choice B and is the best answer.

20. **A is the best answer.** The question describes a classical conditioning paradigm where the boy learns to associate a tone with ice cream. As a result, he starts salivating when he hears the tone in anticipation of this ice cream reward. However, one day there is no reward presented after the tone sounds. This question is testing the concept of spontaneous recovery, which is what occurs following a period of lessened response. Spontaneous recovery states that the learned behavior will not simply disappear, but that it will be reinstated if the stimulus is given again in the time before extinction occurs. Because the boy has been participating in this paradigm for 14 days at the time that the lessened response trial occurs, it is unlikely that one evening would be enough time for the learned association to become completely extinct. It would be expected that the boy would still anticipate the reward and start salivating when he hears the tone on day 16 of the trial. Choice B states that he would not experience increased salivation, which is inconsistent with the principle of spontaneous recovery, so this answer can be eliminated. Choice C states that he would no longer associate the tone with ice cream. This would suggest that complete extinction has occurred, which is not the best answer based on the time frame in the question stem, so choice C can be eliminated. Choice D states that the boy would continue to wait for the tone to sound again. There is no indication in the question stem that the tone would be sounded repeatedly to signal the presence of the reward, so while this could be true, it is not the best answer. The above logic leaves choice A as the best answer.

21. **C is the best answer.** Distillation is the process of separating compounds that have a significant difference in boiling point, usually requiring that two compounds have at least a 20°C difference in boiling point in order to be separated. Because drug A and B only have a 5°C difference, it is likely that scientists would not be able to separate the two drugs, making choice C a strong answer choice. The difference in molecular weights would allow size-exclusion chromatography, eliminating choice A. The difference in molecular charge would allow ion-exchange chromatography to be used, eliminating choice B. Because distillation would be unable to separate the two compounds, choice D is less likely than choice C to be the best answer.

EXPLANATIONS TO IN-CLASS EXAM FOR LECTURE 1

Passage I (Questions 22-28)

22. **C is the best answer.** This answer is best arrived at through process of elimination. Choice A draws from the first paragraph, but the author believes this is an "upside," so it does not need to be remedied. This reference is also tangential to the overall argument of the passage and is unlikely to be the strongest answer to a question that speaks directly to the author's main point. Choice A can be eliminated. The author is primarily arguing in favor of the humanities; even though he or she draws a parallel between the humanities and the (basic) sciences in acknowledging the "unprecedented attack on the idea of curiosity driven abstract research," there is nothing to suggest that increasing science funding would help the humanities. Choice B can be eliminated. Choice C aligns with the general argument that the author is making about the importance of the humanities and the fact that it should not be discarded in favor of applied research. Choice C is a strong answer. The "primacy of applied knowledge" is exactly what the author is opposed to, as this comes at the expense of the humanities, so choice D can be eliminated. Though nothing in the passage directly suggests that choice C is the best answer, it is consistent with the main idea, while choices A, B, and D can be eliminated because they contradict passage information.

23. **B is the best answer.** Choice A is supported by the first paragraph and is a major point of the passage, so it can be eliminated. While gaining well-rounded knowledge is commonly used as an argument in support of the humanities, this argument is not brought up in the passage. This is an example of a statement meant to appeal to test-takers who try to apply outside knowledge rather than relying on the passage. Choice B is a strong answer choice. The third paragraph provides extensive support for choice C, so it can be eliminated. While budgetary constraints are not directly indicated as a reason that the humanities are "besieged," there are numerous allusions to a shift in research priorities, which can reasonably be inferred as affecting research funding. Choice D is not the best answer. Out of the choices given, choice B is least supported by the passage and is the best answer.

24. **B is the best answer.** Thomas Peacock's remarks indicate that he fails to recognize the merits of any endeavor that does not produce a tangible benefit to society (and that Peacock is exactly the sort of person the author finds him or herself at odds with when making a case for the humanities). Because the study of this ion pump in amoebas has no stated objective aside from increasing understanding (it would be categorized as basic science, rather than applied science), Peacock would fail to recognize how it is a worthy use of time and resources, making choice A a weak answer. Choice B reflects Peacock's criticism of basic science research, so it is a strong answer choice. As the humanities have no tangible benefit, and especially considering Thomas Peacock's abhorrence of poetry, he would not advocate study of the humanities, making choice C not a very strong answer. While choice D could be a reasonable answer, there is no way of knowing whether Thomas Peacock would consider studying business "useful knowledge." The use of the word "business" in choice D is different than that in the passage. Peacock intends "the real business of life" to refer broadly to the study of the tangible and salient issues of the day. Choice B is a stronger answer because its meaning hews closer to that of the passage, so choice D can be eliminated.

25. **D is the best answer.** McDougall is arguing against the author's position and in favor of research that "has commercial value," a value that he says the humanities lack. The author does not recognize the concerns about non-commercially directed research as a valid concern, making choice A a weak answer. The passage implies that McDougall has the opposite viewpoint of the leading scientists who protested budget cuts, rather than supporting their cause, so choice B is not supported in the passage and can be eliminated. The author never directly challenges the commercial viability of different kinds of research. Rather than discussing what types of research are commercially valuable, the passage argues that this consideration should not be the primary concern. In addition, no information is given about the criteria that McDougall uses to judge the commercial value of research. Choice C can be eliminated. Choice D is consistent with the author's argument for challenging an emphasis on "the primacy of applied knowledge," so it is the best answer.

26. **D is the best answer.** While the author does draw a comparison with scientists within and outside of universities in paragraph four— i.e., people who are involved in academia outside the humanities— he never passes judgment on these scientists beyond acknowledging that they find themselves in a similar situation as academics within the humanities. Likewise, despite threats that focus on applied research as encroaching on the turf of the humanities, the author never passes judgment on those performing the applied research. Choice A runs counter to the overall point of the passage, which defends the value of the humanities, and cannot be an expression of the author's views; choice A can be eliminated. Paragraph four indicates that scientists who pursue basic research receive less funding than those who carry out applied research, but this is a difference in funding between different areas of academia outside of the humanities; no comparison is made with funding for the humanities. This makes choice B not a strong choice. Choice C could seem consistent with the author's opinions, but it is a distortion of the passage argument. The author argues for the value of the humanities but does not devalue other areas of study. This leaves choice D as the best answer. This answer may not "feel good" because the author does refer to academia outside the humanities in the passage, but it is a better answer than any of the other choices.

27. **A is the best answer.** The author's major argument is that the humanities are under attack by those who value applied research more highly and direct funds toward that type of study, rather than the humanities and other non-applied academic areas. The assertion in choice A is the exact opposite of this argument; if the humanities were better funded now than ever, it would be difficult to believe that they are under attack. Choice A is a strong answer. The author starts the passage by discussing the digital revolution and indicating that it has impacted the perceived value of the humanities. However, the digital revolution is not directly relevant to the author's central argument, which specifically refers to funding of the humanities. For that reason, choice B is not as strong of an answer as choice A. Choice C refers to the *basic* sciences, not the applied sciences. The author implies that the basic sciences are in the same position as the humanities, so he or she would not expect them to be in competition with the humanities. Choice C can be eliminated. Choice D refers to the comparison drawn in paragraph three to a similar historical attack on the humanities. However, even if this proved not to be an analogous situation, this would not challenge the author's thesis, which is concerned with the *current* state of the humanities. Choice D can be eliminated, and choice A is the strongest answer.

28. **B is the best answer.** Answering this question requires an understanding of the fundamental opposing concepts discussed in the passage: study that does not have a specific application, particularly the humanities, versus applied study. If necessary, look back at paragraph five to review the meaning of "serious" knowledge. The phrase refers to applied study like that valued by Peacock, so the best answer will be an example of applied study. "Entrenched assumptions" refers to assumptions about humanities that changed as a result of the digital revolution. This is a distractor choice that cannot easily be defined as "serious" or non-serious knowledge, so choice A can be eliminated. Choice B describes the type of practical research that Peacock supports, so it is a strong answer. The humanities are exactly the opposite of Peacock's "serious" forms of knowledge, making choice C a weak answer. Choice D is likewise an example of a course of study that would not be considered to be "serious." It is the type of research that has been losing funding due to the increased value placed on "serious" knowledge like the type described in choice B. Choice D can be eliminated. Notice that choices B and D directly conflict with each other, so they could not both be "serious" forms of knowledge and one is likely to be the best answer.

Passage II (Questions 29-35)

29. **A is the best answer.** The passage dissects the distinct pattern of seating locations by individuals in a religious setting. The author introduces this concept by proposing that individuals arrange themselves into patterns when in social gatherings. Religious events, like sermons, are considered social events then, since the individuals sit in particular spots. Choice A is a strong answer. While the author suggests that popular culture pokes fun at the idea of certain people sitting near the back of the church, the author does not suggest that it accurately depicts entire religious practices. Choice B is too general of a claim and misstates the author's meaning. It can be eliminated. While the author suggests that certain religions or denominations involve more individual practices than others, he stresses the different worship practices that can occur in one congregation, depending on where the pew is located. Because worship practices vary within a religion, it is likely not the primary determinant of the practices, so choice C can be eliminated. At the end of the passage, the author suggests that these patterns can be analyzed to alter church services to best address the individuals and their likely religiosity based on where they are sitting. Choice D is an implication of the author's ideas for future practice, so it is not an assumption in the passage. Choice A is a stronger answer than choice D.

30. **B is the best answer.** The passage presents a spectrum of the importance of seating arrangement in religious practices. The author believes that even though worshipping can be an individual experience, people tend to sit in certain areas of the church depending on their religiosity. The author argues that this pattern does not occur purposefully because he introduces the decision of where to sit as an "unreflective" one. Choice A can be eliminated because it includes the word "purposefully." The author believes that this pattern occurs almost universally, and would expect a certain individual to sit in the same region regardless of which church he/she is in. Choice B is a strong answer. The passage does not address how seating arrangement can affect an individual's enjoyment of the services. He simply describes a pattern, and does not suggest that individuals sit in certain spots to have a more positive experience. Choice C cannot be assumed true. While the author proposes that individuals sitting in the back of a church perform less and act more as spectators, there is no reason to assume a new churchgoer would feel pressured to sit there. The individual might be more likely to sit in the back, but there is no passage evidence to support the claim that the individual would feel pressured by other individuals. According to the passage, church seating is a function of religiosity, not seniority or social stratification. Choice D is a weak answer. Choice B is the best answer.

31. **C is the best answer.** The spectrum in the passage debates the existence of seating patterns in social settings that may seem to be more individually-focused, like religious events. The author argues that individuals sit in certain arrangements in religious settings because the congregation is set up almost like a stage, with the attention directed towards the front. The author does not suggest that height or stature affect seating arrangement, so choice A can be eliminated. The author believes that individuals who sit near the front are more prepared to "perform" in front of others, but the main idea of the passage is that those who sit closer to the front want more direct engagement with religious exercises. Choice of seating reflects internal considerations more than external ones. Choice B is not particularly strong. The author proposes that individuals near the front cannot see as many other people and are less likely to be distracted. Choice C is stronger than choice B because the entire answer choice is supported by passage information. The author does not address relationships with church members or leaders affecting seating arrangement, so choice D cannot be assumed true. Choice C is the strongest answer choice.

32. **A is the best answer.** The main idea of the passage is that the physical arrangement of worshipers in a church has more to do with an individual's own religious zeal rather than a need to prove one's fervor to others. The question stem presents a situation in which those in the front give more money – though the reason is unclear. It is possible that this behavior is tied to greater religious zeal or perhaps to a need to give conspicuously before others. If the latter were true, the findings would weaken the author's claim that physical arrangement is motivated primarily by internal considerations. Choice A is a possible answer. These findings do not speak to the nature of those in the back nor how they are regarded, so choice B is not a strong answer. Choice C, like choice A, puts forth group considerations as a possible explanation for behavior. The author does indeed advance the claim that the back rows are the audience of those in the front but goes on to dismiss conspicuousness to others as the primary factor in the arrangement of worshippers. This finding would *strengthen* the claim in choice C, so that answer can be eliminated. While the degree of surveillance may influence the giving of those in the front, this finding does not directly explain the behavior of those in the back. Notice that choice D would not be undermined by this finding but potentially reiterated. Choice A is the strongest answer.

33. **C is the best answer.** The author argues that individuals likely sit in certain areas of a church depending on their religiosity. In this situation, the audience at a theatrical performance is similar to a congregation, as they both sit in rows facing the front. An avid fan sitting in the back of a performance is not similar to any scenarios discussed in the passage since the author only describes very religious individuals sitting near the front. Choice A is not particularly strong. Because the star of a show is onstage during a performance, that individual is most similar to a preacher. The author does not directly discuss how preachers feel about attention, so choice B cannot be assumed true. If an audience member near the front influences the reactions of other audience members further back, then that individual is being watched by others. The author describes this situation occurring in religious settings, even if that is not the primary explanation he ultimately advances. Choice C is a promising answer. Crew members would be most comparable to church members or leaders who set up the stage or technical aspects of a sermon, which is outside the scope of this passage. Choice D is a weaker answer than choice C. Notice that none of the answer choices are perfectly analogous to the passage, but choice C is closest to one of the theories presented within it.

34. **A is the best answer.** The author argues that individuals follow a pattern with seating arrangements in religious settings. He mentions that popular culture tends to depict the back of the church as less religious but does not cite any specific examples to support this claim. Choice A is a strong answer. The author specifically addresses the intentionality of worship potentially affecting the presence of patterns in seating arrangements. Choice B is supported by passage evidence and can be eliminated. The author's primary argument supports the claim that Christian congregations are susceptible to structurating forces, as he describes the characteristics of a church that resemble a stage or auditorium. Choice C is a weak answer. Similarly, the author describes at length the differences between worshippers sitting in the front of the church versus the back. Choice D can be eliminated and choice A is the best answer.

35. **C is the best answer.** The author argues that there are distinct seating patterns in religious settings, and that these findings can be used by church leaders and developers. The author does not believe that individuals should have to sit in the back for a particular reason—he simply discusses what kind of worshippers usually sit in the back. Choice A is not suggested by the passage. While the author believes that church developers can utilize this information, he does not go so far as to suggest that worshippers should be separated depending on their practices. Choice B is not particularly strong. The author does argue in the last paragraph that sermons or homilies placements can be altered depending on the congregation and the individuals' seating pattern. Choice C is stronger than Choice B because it is directly suggested by the author near the end of the passage. The author does not believe that individuals should have to sit near the front of the church for any reason. Choice D contains an extreme measure that is more authoritarian than the ideas in the passage, and it can be eliminated. Choice C is the best answer.

Passage III (Questions 36-42)

36. **C is the best answer.** The best answer will both strengthen the claim referred to in the question stem and will be a fact presented in the passage. The fact that the Congressional Record and Coast Guard Report were inconsistent with observations from the scene does not necessarily support the claim that the Coast Guard's efforts were unsuccessful. Other details about the situation could have been reported inaccurately, so choice A can be eliminated. While Alaskans might have been disappointed in the Coast Guard after the epidemic, that is not explicitly stated in the passage. Choice B is not a fact presented in the passage, so it can be eliminated. In the last paragraph, the author points out that only a small fraction of the population was left after the epidemic, indicating that the Coast Guard's efforts did not save many lives. For this reason, choice C is a strong answer. The report of the Bureau of Fisheries of the Department of Commerce about the misguided Coast Guard effort is not enough support to claim that the rescue effort was unsuccessful. Their report also could have been biased and may not have been the most accurate source of information. Choice D is not as strong as choice C, which is the best answer.

37. **D is the best answer.** Throughout the passage, the author describes how the Coast Guard attempted to alleviate the situation in Bristol Bay but did not know the best way to help and did not accurately report the situation. The best answer choice will likely be relevant to this main idea of the passage. The author specifically discusses the spread of the pandemic to Bristol Bay because it has not garnered enough attention over the years, so choice A can be eliminated. Throughout the passage, the author indicates that the Coast Guard had an opportunity to help the community—they just did not properly take advantage of it. The author does not suggest that external assistance could never help in a medical emergency, just that it did not in Bristol Bay. For this reason, choice B is too extreme and can be eliminated. Similarly, the author does not suggest that the spread of pandemics is unavoidable since the Spanish influenza was prevented from reaching this Alaskan community until it communicated with the outside world. Choice C is not a strong answer. The passage describes how much money was spent on the Coast Guard's mission to Alaska that summer and how ineffective the efforts were. The author would likely believe that the Coast Guard did not investigate the situation beforehand to distribute resources accordingly during the medical emergency, and that such research is necessary for effective assistance. Choice D is also a stronger answer than choice C because the author's main idea relates to the allocation of resources, not the spread of pandemics.

38. **A is the best answer.** Throughout the passage, the author suggests that if accurate reports had been written about the Coast Guard's mission, it might have been possible to readjust their plan and help the Alaskan population more. The passage stresses that many individuals were harmed due to inaccurate reporting about the success of the mission. Choice A reflects the major point of the passage by discussing a lack of appropriate documentation. More individuals may be endangered without the availability of written records, so the situation would strengthen the author's argument. For this reason, choice A is a potential answer. Even if countries without written records are not discussed in schools, that does not necessarily put them in danger because world leaders may still know about their circumstances and be able to provide aid. Choice B is not a strong answer. If countries write biased reports about their past civil wars, that is not likely to directly harm any individuals or jeopardize foreign aid. Choice C is not as strong as choice A. Choice D does not necessarily put a society in danger, so it does not provide the greatest support. Choice A is better answer than the other choices, even though it is somewhat ambiguous.

39. **B is the best answer.** Since the passage uses this quote to describe the unsuccessful Coast Guard mission, consider this context in order to interpret the phrase. Although repudiation can mean "rejection," that definition does not apply to this passage, since the Alaskans did not reject the efforts of the Coast Guard. Choice A can be eliminated. The mission was planned with the best intentions, but when it was unsuccessful, the Coast Guard refused to acknowledge their failure or adjust their approach. A mother providing financial support to her struggling son is a kind act, but if the money is spent on unnecessary items and the mother still keeps paying, the situation is similar to the mission described by the phrase in the question stem. Choice B is a strong answer. A movie star donating to charity only demonstrates benevolent intentions. Because the outcome of the donation is unknown, there is no repudiation or refusal to acknowledge the truth, so choice C can be eliminated. If a high school student begins tutoring simply to add it to her resume, then she does not have benevolent, or compassionate, intentions. For this reason, choice D is not a strong answer. Choice B is the best answer.

40. **D is the best answer.** The author establishes the importance of a particular event in history and emphasizes the consequences of ineffective medical assistance, focusing on the deadliness of the influenza pandemic. The author could potentially want to shock readers by referencing the Holocaust, although he probably does not want to distract them from the serious nature of the passage. Choice A is a possible answer. The author is not likely to use a reference to the Holocaust to offend the readers, since he wants them to keep reading in order to gain important information. Choice B can be eliminated. The author does not compare the influenza to the Holocaust at any other point in the passage and instead redirects his argument to documentation and communication during the outbreak. This indicates that the central thesis of the passage does not involve the Holocaust, so choice C is not the best answer. The author describes the influenza pandemic as a medical Holocaust as an introduction to the discussion of how grave the situation was and how important it is to learn about it. For this reason, choice D is a stronger answer than choice A. Note that even for those unfamiliar with details of the Holocaust, this question can be answered based on the rest of the sentence and the author's main point in the first paragraph.

41. **B is the best answer.** The main idea of the passage relates to the importance of proper medical assistance and accurate reporting on its success during an emergency, so the best answer will likely draw a similar conclusion. The author mentions the amount of money that Congress allocated to this mission and does not suggest that it should have been more, but rather that it could have been used more effectively. Choice A is not a strong answer. He suggests that Congress blindly accepted the Coast Guard report describing their efforts as heroic and effective. If Congress had checked in with Bristol Bay after this report was turned in, they might have realized how much danger the population was still in and provided proper medical assistance. For this reason, choice B is a strong answer. The author does not delve into how different populations are affected by the same disease, nor does he stress the role that the dogs played in transmitting influenza. While choices C and D might be true statements, they are not emphasized in the passage and can be eliminated. For these reasons, choice B is the best answer.

42. **A is the best answer.** Throughout the passage, the author argues that if the Coast Guard had been more honest about their failures, they could have adapted and provided more support in the long run. Choice A is consistent with the main idea of the passage, so it is a strong answer. While selflessness may be an admirable quality, the author does not stress its importance in this situation, and the Coast Guard could have been selfless but still unhelpful. Choice B can be eliminated. Similarly, confidence and intelligence can be advantageous traits to have in life, but the author does not suggest that the failure of medical assistance described in the passage was caused by a lack of these particular traits. Because confidence and intelligence are not discussed in the passage, choices C and D can be eliminated, and choice A is the best answer.

EXPLANATIONS TO IN-CLASS EXAM FOR LECTURE 2

Passage I (Questions 43-49)

43. **D is the best answer.** The main idea of the passage is that race and ethnicity have inappropriately been used as a shortcut to predicting different health outcomes, despite shifts in racial categories and the fact that only a detailed history can be used to accurately assess health. The passage emphasizes changes in racial categories over time, including in the 20th century, so choice A can be eliminated. The passage argues that a variety of health-related fields, such as epidemiology, have "always" been interested in racial categories. In addition, the first paragraph describes a recommendation of the United States Food and Drug Administration based on race. Choice B can be eliminated. The third paragraph discusses misconceptions about cardiovascular deaths in African-Americans, and never states the likelihood of dying from syphilis in that population, so choice C is a weak answer. Although the author does not approve of using racial categories, the passage describes how self-identified racial categories have become entrenched as a common proxy for genetic homogeneity in research and clinical practice, so choice D is the best answer.

44. **C is the best answer.** This question is asking about what information the author thinks can help clinicians make the best patient evaluations. At the end of the passage, the author discusses the importance of recognizing the biological and cultural history of specific populations. In his opinion, knowing the patient's population of origin allows the physician to provide better care. The author does not believe that racial categorizations provide sufficient or reliable information when they are used as proxies for biological aspects such as genetics. Instead, they are a shortcut used by time-pressured physicians. Choice A can be eliminated. The passage does not focus on patients' professions, so choice B is out of the scope of the passage and can be eliminated. Choice C is related to the author's conclusion about knowing patients' populations of origin and their characteristics, so it is a strong answer. Choice D might be appealing on the basis of common knowledge, but the passage does not address individual medical histories. Remember not to use outside information when answering CARS questions. Choice D can be eliminated, and choice C is the best answer.

45. **D is the best answer.** The author argues in the last paragraph that even if physicians have limited time, they should not resort to simple racial categorizations, so choice A is unlikely to be true. The example on House is a lead-in to the passage argument about the use of race in actual medical care. The fact that the scenario introduces the passage, as well as the author's overall focus on racial categorizations, makes choice B contradictory to the main idea. Choice B can be eliminated. The author would not describe race-based prescribing in positive terms. Furthermore, the impact on the pharmaceutical industry is out of the scope of the passage. For these reasons, choice C is not a strong answer. The author chooses to put the phrase "self-identified" in quotations because in the scenario described, the doctor wants to prescribe a drug for an African-American man based on race against his own wishes. This suggests that the doctors identified him as African-American and he did not necessarily identify himself that way or believe that his race should be used to determine his health care. Choice D accurately describes the author's opinion and is the best answer.

46. **B is the best answer.** The new findings must be applied to the author's feelings about the subject. The author feels passionately that racial categorizations are not adequate for guiding patient care, and would not likely give up this point on the basis of a single study. Keep this in mind when reviewing the answer choices. The author thinks that patient outcomes are important, but not that they are the only significant factors. Recall that the passage begins by describing an African-American patient's unhappiness with being classified by race. The author cares about the patient's satisfaction with care, not just the health outcome. Also, extreme words like "only" are not usually found in strong answer choices. For these reasons, choice A can be eliminated. Choice B reflects the author's opinion about the importance of factors other than health outcomes and aligns with the fact that the author would probably not change his opinion when faced with this study, so it is a strong answer. The author certainly would not concede that racial categorizations should be "standard," so choice C can be eliminated. Choice D takes the author's argument too far because the author is unlikely to completely ignore the study. Choice B is less extreme than choice D and is a better answer.

47. **D is the best answer.** The passage emphasizes that racial categorizations are common and ingrained in the medical profession. Although the author argues against simplistic racial categorizations, passage evidence suggests that the medical community is not currently trying to eradicate the use of these racial categories as a tool in clinical practice and research. Choice A can be eliminated. The author does not discuss the prevalence of cultural competency education in medical schools, so choice B is not the best answer. The passage indicates the importance of examining biological and cultural factors that are unique to each patient population, but does not suggest that cultural competency is helpful only for certain populations. The author would likely argue that all populations would benefit from a more complex view of biological and cultural factors. Choice C is not a strong answer. The passage description of cultural competency training focuses on the importance of historical factors such as the cultural and biological backgrounds of each patient population. The emphasis on social history is consistent with this passage emphasis, making choice D the best answer.

48. **C is the best answer.** This question asks how the first paragraph contributes to the argument of the entire passage. The episode is most likely described to help develop the author's main point, which is that racial categorizations are simplistic and can negatively affect patients. At this point in the passage cultural competency has not been addressed, and the TV episode is not related to the definition of cultural competency laid out in the passage. Choice A is simply using a phrase from the passage in order to act as a distractor. It can be eliminated. Choice B is contrary to the tone of the passage, which is not at all lighthearted. The author believes strongly that racial categorizations are inappropriate and that this is a serious topic within healthcare and multiple health-related disciplines. Choice B can be eliminated. By describing the patient interaction in detail, the author explicitly shows the reader how offensive racial categorizations can be to a particular patient, so choice C is a strong answer. The author never mentions the frequency of negative patient-physician interactions due to racial categorizations, so choice D is not supported by passage evidence and can be eliminated. Choice C is the strongest answer.

49. **D is the best answer.** The statement referenced in the question stem is used to open the passage argument that simple racial categorizations are often not helpful in clinical practice and research. The best answer will support the author's negative opinion on quickly assigning patients to racial categories. It is true that "eyeball" is a slang term in this context, so choice A is a possible answer, although it does not support the passage argument. The author does not quote characters from a television show until later in the paragraph, so choice B can be eliminated. In some passages, quotation marks may be used to introduce important terminology. In this case, the author does not use the term again, indicating that incorporating a new phrase was not the goal. Choice C is not a strong answer. The rest of the passage after the opening sentence consists of the argument that racial categorizations are convenient oversimplifications. The author does not believe that physician can or should "eyeball" a person's race. Choice D is consistent with the author's argument, so it is a stronger answer than choice A.

Passage II (Questions 50-56)

50. **B is the best answer.** The author presents a range of viewpoints about abortion. On one end of the spectrum exists the conservatives, who put the sanctity of life above all other possible arguments. On the other end of the spectrum are the liberalists, who are pro-choice and believe that there are many valid reasons to have an abortion, especially since personhood begins well after conception. The author leans toward the conservative side of the spectrum but admits that some types of abortion are unavoidable. This question asks how someone who opposes the author's opinion would respond to religious arguments condemning abortion. Choice A talks about the death of a human being, but it is not a strong answer because it does not allude to the liberalist idea that fetuses are unconscious and not yet alive. Choice A can be eliminated. Choice B accurately describes the liberalists' fundamental belief and directly negates the Qur'an's statement about killing human beings, so it is a strong answer. Choice C ignores the liberalists' fundamental belief about when life begins. It is also not as strong because the quality of the *child's* life outside of the womb is a distractor beyond the scope of the passage. It is important to notice that choice C refers to the child rather than the fetus, and is not referring to the type of abortion that is performed by removing the fetus from the womb. Choice C can be eliminated. Choice D does not speak to the liberalists' beliefs and is beyond the scope of the information provided in the passage. For these reasons, choice D can be eliminated and choice B is the best answer.

51. **D is the best answer.** Although the question refers to a specific quote, it requires an understanding of the author's position on a spectrum that ranges from extreme conservatives to extreme liberalists based on the passage as a whole. The passage provides several hints through language choice and tone that the author is opposed to abortion. The author ultimately calls abortion an odious social issue that needs to be rectified. The author would not agree that calling an abortion a funeral service is ridiculous, and would not include a quote with the goal of criticizing the argument against abortion. Choice A is a contrary distractor and can be eliminated. Choice B may be correct from a technical standpoint. However, it neglects the author's tone in the sentence, which seems mournful rather than calculated to make a rhetorical point. Choice B can be eliminated. Choice C is consistent with the author's argument, and is a possible answer, although the passage has already repeatedly characterized abortion as the ending of life. Compared to choice C, choice D is a more forceful statement reflecting the author's strongly negative views towards abortion, so it is the strongest answer.

52. **A is the best answer.** This question asks the reader to understand the author's preferred definition of abortion and apply it to a new scenario. The author provides two definitions of abortion, but then describes the "most accurate" definition as the unnatural removal of a non-viable fetus. "Non-viable" in this context means the inability to live by itself outside of the mother's womb. The answer that most closely matches the definition of abortion will include an unnatural intervention to remove an undeveloped organism from the environment that is allowing it to survive. In choice A, human intervention (the pipette) is moving the organism from a nurturing environment (culture) to a place it is likely to perish (the plastic slide). This is a strong answer. Since the petunia in choice B is being moved somewhere that is equivalent to its original environment (a different flower bed), it is likely to survive. Choice B can be eliminated. Because the kitten in choice C could survive in the outside environment, this answer is not as strong as choice A. The "organism" (DNA) in choice D is not being removed from its environment, so choice D can be eliminated and choice A is the best answer.

53. **C is the best answer.** The passage presents both pro- and anti-abortion perspectives, but the author's viewpoint is revealed in the underlying tone and use of negative, emotionally charged language. The author's opinion lies with the conservative anti-abortionists. The presentation of religious condemnation of abortion without the use of contrary philosophical arguments, the use of charged words like "crime" and "abominable," and the call for urgent social change all point toward the author's main idea about how abortion negatively impacts individuals and society. Since the passage specifically discusses pregnancy from incest as a scenario in which abortion frequently occurs, negative outcomes for children of incest would bolster the argument for allowing abortion. Choice A can be eliminated. The author also notes that having an unwanted child can have a negative financial impact, another consideration that might lead a woman to procure an abortion. Choice B supports the argument for abortion by providing evidence for this point, so it can be eliminated. Choices C and D both support the author's opinion because they provide reasons not to have an abortion. Choice C focuses on the potential life of the fetus, which is at the heart of the passage. The author often references the needs of the child over the needs of the mother. Choice C also provides a justification for the impoverishment that can result from being denied an abortion, rebutting one of the potential arguments against abortion. For these reasons, choice C is a strong answer. Choice D references only the needs of the mother and does not directly address any passage arguments against abortion. Choice C is a stronger answer.

54. **C is the best answer.** Recall that the passage differentiates spontaneous and self-induced abortions. Self-induced abortion is said to have moral implications because it is the intentional taking of life. According to the passage, conservatives believe that, beginning at conception, all life is sacred and has the right to live. However, the main idea of the passage is that forced abortion, not natural abortion, is the killing of an innocent life. The author does not condemn the loss of life that is not caused by an intentional abortion. Since the fetus was not killed by a human, but by some pathology within the human, choice A can be eliminated. The passage specifically notes that spontaneous abortion is out of the mother's control. For this reason, choice B can be eliminated. Choice C is consistent with the author's view that spontaneous abortion is not an intentional act. Since the author would probably not see a naturally occurring abortion as a murder, choice C is a strong answer. The fate of the child after death is beyond the scope of the passage, so choice D can be eliminated and choice C is the best answer.

55. **D is the best answer.** This question asks about the beliefs of the conservatives and the liberalists provided in the passage. Liberalists believe that fetuses do not yet have consciousness and are not yet alive, while conservatives believe that life begins at conception. The best answer to this question will describe liberalist and/or conservative views accurately, and will accurately describe how one or both of these groups would respond. Choice A inaccurately describes the conservatives' beliefs, since they argue that life begins at conception. Choice A is not a strong answer. The liberalists believe that life begins with consciousness, so choice B seems to be a possible answer. However, the question stem and passage do not provide enough information to determine when consciousness starts to develop. Choice B is a distractor beyond the scope of the passage and can be eliminated. The passage also does not discuss a 12 week cutoff for proponents of abortion, and the CARS section will not require this type of outside knowledge. Choice C can be eliminated. Choice D includes a discussion of consciousness and accurately indicates that the information in the question stem does not affect the central arguments of the conservatives or liberalists. Choice D is the strongest answer.

56. **C is the best answer.** This question asks the reader to identify where the author lies on the spectrum from extreme conservatives to extreme liberalists. The passage indicates that the author is anti-abortion, and the main idea of the passage is that self-induced abortions are a moral disgrace to society. The author repeatedly values the life of the fetus over the well-being of the mother or the repercussions that the mother may experience after being denied an abortion. Although the author presents reasons that it may be in the mother's best interest to have an abortion, this discussion is immediately followed by the assertion that abortion is unacceptable under any circumstances. Choice A is not consistent with the main idea and can be eliminated. Similarly, choice B is not supported by the tone and argument of the passage, so it is not a strong answer. Choice C reflects the author's belief that abortions should not occur for any reason, so it is a strong answer. The relationship between maternal and fetal health is not discussed, so choice D is beyond the scope of the passage. Choice C is the best answer.

Passage III (Questions 57-63)

57. **B is the best answer.** The author indicates that strict voter identification laws might put some populations at a disadvantage and challenge the foundation of equality in America. The author does not believe that voter ID should be the decisive factor in voting eligibility, so choice A can be eliminated. In the second paragraph, the author states that the voter identification laws can have an impact on whether all citizens can vote. The passage implies that even if individuals do not possess the proper identification, they should not be turned away from voting polls if they are American citizens. For this reason, choice B is a strong answer. The author does not suggest that past electoral participation should affect current electoral participation, so choice C can be eliminated. As discussed in relation to choice A, the author does not believe that the ability to obtain photo identification such as a driver's license should dictate the ability to vote. Choice D can be eliminated. Even if choice B does not feel like an obvious answer, it is the strongest compared to the other answer choices.

58. **A is the best answer.** The author argues that voter identification laws might create barriers for minorities and disadvantaged populations. In the second paragraph, the passage states that a valid driver's license or other form of identification is required to vote under voter identification laws, so the best answer will likely involve an individual who does not have valid identification. If an 18-year-old man has never driven a car, he probably does not have a license to use as identification. For this reason, option I is true and choices B and D can be eliminated. If an elderly woman was upset at the results of the last election, then her desire to vote might be affected, but not her ability to vote. There is not enough information in the answer choice to determine that she does not have proper identification or would have difficulty obtaining it. Option II is not true, and choice C can be eliminated. The mom in option III likely drives for her carpool duty, so she probably possesses a driver's license. Although she is a busy person, the enactment of voter identification laws would not affect the difficulty she faces finding time to vote. For these reasons, option III is not true and choice A is the best answer.

59. **B is the best answer.** The author argues that voter identification laws might create barriers to voting for disadvantaged groups. The end of the passage draws attention to the seminal economic theory which proposes that voting costs and electoral participation are inversely related. Although the author focuses on American politics, he does not suggest that this is solely an American problem. He does not mention practices that other countries use, so choice A is not a strong answer. The author suggests that voter identification laws can negatively affect voter turnout in populations where some individuals are disadvantaged—they might not have the time or money required to obtain proper identification. Another country with citizens that are all members of a similar socioeconomic group might not experience the same effect, so choice B is a strong answer. The question of voter identification and turnout would be irrelevant in non-democratic/non-voting countries, so choice C would not clarify the finding described in the question stem and can be eliminated. The author does not suggest that the size of the election affects voter turnout or the impact of voter ID laws, so choice D can be eliminated. Choice B is the strongest answer.

60. **C is the best answer.** The passage focuses on voter identification laws because the author recognizes the importance of voter turnout. He does not want voter ID laws to prevent any citizens from voting because he believes that all Americans should be allowed to voice their opinions. For this reason, it is unlikely that the author would advise a citizen to wait for the next election when they could potentially be eligible to vote in the current one. Choice A can be eliminated. While news reports of the inequality might be a benefit of the situation, the author is more likely to make a suggestion directly related to voting. He would want the citizen to be able to participate in the election, so choice B is a possible answer but not particularly strong. The author mentions that disadvantaged individuals might struggle to get proper identification, so if they reach out to family and friends to help accomplish the task, they are more likely to receive identification in time to vote in the election. For this reason, choice C is a better answer than choice B. The author is unlikely to advise the extreme action of moving from an individual's home on the basis of voting laws, so choice D is not as strong an answer as choice C.

61. **D is the best answer.** Throughout the passage, the author's argument pertains to how voter identification laws affect politicians and voters. He does not discuss the actual voter identification laws or how well they decrease levels of fraud. Choice A is not a strong answer. Though the author proposes that electoral participation and voting costs usually display an inverse relationship, he does not suggest that participating in elections is usually expensive. He discusses how voter identification laws could increase costs, but does not cast judgment on how expensive electoral participation is in general. Choice B can be eliminated. The author seems to believe that voter identification laws can lead to a decrease in voter turnout, but the evidence does not clearly support his theory. He presents conflicting evidence that does not reach an agreement, so the word "always" makes this answer choice unsupported by the passage. Choice C can be eliminated. The author focuses on how new voter ID laws will affect voter turnout in the future, since there is not enough data to analyze yet. He also describes this controversy as the latest problem of United States politics. This makes choice D the best answer.

62. **C is the best answer.** The author believes that voter identification laws may create inequality among the American population, and that this risk is not worth the benefits of preventing voter fraud. Choice A does not involve the implementation of voter identification laws, so it does not directly relate to the author's argument. For this reason, choice A can be eliminated. Even if elected politicians come from privileged backgrounds, they might have received votes cast by minority and disadvantaged populations. This finding does not directly strengthen the author's argument that the laws can affect voter turnout, so choice B can be eliminated. If voting fraud levels have not decreased after voter identification laws have been put into effect, the laws may be failing to achieve their stated purpose while also affecting voter turnout. Choice C supports the author's belief that voter identification laws are not beneficial to the voting process, so it is a strong answer. The author's argument relates to the inequalities that can be created by voter identification laws, not how concerned Americans are with voting fraud. Choice D is not related to the main idea of the passage, so it does not strengthen the author's argument and can be eliminated. Choice C is the strongest answer.

63. **B is the best answer.** The author believes that all eligible citizens should be allowed to cast their vote, because they all deserve a voice in political matters. The author does not suggest that politicians or government officials' honesty affects voter turnout. This answer choice might be selected by a test-taker who interprets honesty as relating to voter fraud, but voter fraud is not the author's main interest or concern. Choice A does not relate to the main idea of the passage and can be eliminated. If politicians and government employees want to include the opinions and votes of all citizens (inclusivity), they are not likely to implement unfair voter identification laws. Choice B aligns with the main idea of the passage and is a strong answer. The fact that politicians or employees are compassionate does not mean that they will necessarily value or consider opposing opinions and encourage every individual to vote. The concept of inclusivity is more related to the main idea of the passage than compassion, so choice C is not as strong as choice B. The author does not mention any individual's forethought, or ability to plan ahead, in the passage or how that might affect voter turnout. Forethought could be related to people thinking ahead by obtaining voter identification, but the author would not think that individuals should be punished for not having the forethought to get identification before the election. Choice D can be eliminated, and choice B is the best answer.

EXPLANATIONS TO IN-CLASS EXAM FOR LECTURE 3

Passage I (Questions 64-70)

64. **D is the best answer.** Choices A and B correspond to the "two sides of the issue" discussed in paragraph four. The author concludes that both probably contribute to the formation of a gender identity that is incongruent with one's assignment at birth. Both are statements that the author would agree with, so these answers can be eliminated. Notice that the phrase "it is possible" is what enables the author to agree with both statements even though they are opposites. The author states that "Chris was in no way confused about his identity." Even without remembering this exact quote, it can be intuited that the author would agree that Chris is not confused. The author is supportive of Chris's preferred pronouns and gender identity and seems interested in exploring Chris's experience rather than questioning it. Choice C can be eliminated. The author would disagree with the statement that every culture has defined gender roles. The word "every" is what makes this a bad answer choice. The author would agree that "some" or even "many" cultures have defined gender roles. In the first sentence of the paragraph, the author states that "Western cultures" assign gender based on genitalia. This leaves open the possibility that many non-Western cultures do not have such rigid gender roles. The author also alludes to *other* cultures where Chris might not have felt the need "to identify himself as distinctly male." The culture/society wherein Chris lives is clearly defined as "our" culture/society, implying that there are others. For these reasons, choice D is the best answer.

65. **B is the best answer.** As in the previous question, the wording here is important. The author does not imply that one *should* be happy in a "natural" state. The author states that psychotherapy may sometimes allow people to be happy in their natural state, but there is no value-judgment-type "should" or "should not" implication that would justify option I. Furthermore, the author seems to have no problem with the idea that Chris would want hormone treatment to alter his "natural" state. Option I is a weak answer and choices A and D can be eliminated. Option II provides an accurate description of the author's overall view about Chris, who is well-adjusted but wants to change his "natural" state. It can be inferred that Chris wants to change his natural state because he is unhappy with it, particularly since the passage also indicates in paragraph 5 that hormone treatment may affect Chris's "happiness." Option II is a strong answer, and choice B must be the answer. Although it is not necessary to address option III to narrow the answer choices down to choice B, it can also be determined that option III is not the best answer. That one's perception of self is most important is not implied. This assumption is defined by the quote from the passage that "through psychotherapy, one learns that one may not necessarily have to change oneself as much as *one's perception of self*" (paragraph 5). There is no indication or implication in the passage that this is "most important," or more important than changing the "natural state" to fit our perception of self, ruling out option III for similar reasons that option I is eliminated. Notice the tentative wording of the quote ("may not necessarily") in contrast to the strong connotation of "most."

66. **C is the best answer.** Choice A seems like a possible answer, considering the author's views on the DSM-5. Choice B clearly takes the author's choice a step too far. Though it seems that the DSM is influenced by societal norms, there is no indication that it is "easily" influenced, or that overall it is a "poor descriptor" of abnormal behavior. It may actually be a very accurate descriptor of behavior that society has deemed abnormal. Choice B can be eliminated. Choice C is similar to choice A. Choice A is vague and simplistic compared to choice C, so it is not as well supported by the passage. The author does argue that in another culture, Chris's disorder *might* not even be a disorder. However, the author still seems to consider Chris's experience to be disordered, at least within "our" society. The author tries to elucidate the "causal factors for Chris's disorder," indicating that he or she considers Chris to have a disorder. Choice C is a better answer because it restricts itself to "*some* disorders" and because it specifically refers to the social influence on DSM categorization, a major point of the passage. Choice D can be eliminated because behavior falling "*within*" the parameters of the DSM-5 is considered *abnormal*, not normal. Furthermore, the author believes that societal norms have determined the DSM parameters, not the other way around. This is another reason why choice D is a weak answer. Choice C is the strongest answer.

67. **B is the best answer.** There is no value-type "should" judgment in the discussion of psychiatry as a possible treatment for Chris, so choice A can be eliminated. The notion that Chris's "uneasiness with his assigned sex" is influenced by the culture he lives in is definitely hinted at by the author. The entirety of paragraph three strongly argues this answer, beginning with the statement that "in this case, many psychologists may believe society is the culprit." Choice B is a strong answer. The author never discusses surgical treatment in relation to Chris. Although the author states at the beginning of the passage that some people "may desire hormone therapies or surgeries aimed at modifying their bodies so that they more closely align with their preferred gender identity," there is no "hint" by the author that surgery would be a useful treatment for Chris. The author instead discusses Chris's desire for hormone treatment, which is not a surgical procedure (as indicated by the quote referenced above, which refers to "hormone therapies" and "surgeries" as separate treatments). By this reasoning, choice C can be eliminated. Far from hinting that Chris's experience is due to a "personality defect," the author explicitly states that "basic defects in personality" are *not* involved. Choice D can be eliminated, and choice B is the best answer.

68. **C is the best answer.** Consider the author's argument. This passage is *not* a completely objective representation of a psychological case study. The author's main argument is that "society is the culprit." Although the passage does not completely rule out "biochemical processes" as a possible cause, there is a strong emphasis on the involvement of societal and cultural factors. The hypothetical scenario of the effectiveness of antidepressant treatment, which alters biological functioning while leaving cultural gender norms intact, could indicate that biological factors play a larger role than is indicated by the author's argument. Since the new discovery is opposed to the author's argument, it does not confirm the argument and does affect it; choices A and B can be eliminated. The author's argument may be weakened by the scenario described in the question stem, but it is not disproved. For one thing, Chris only becomes "'*somewhat* more comfortable." The fact that antidepressant treatment has an effect does not necessarily mean that Chris's discomfort was initially *caused* by biological factors. Social factors could still be the more significant cause. For that reason, choice D can be eliminated, and choice C is the best answer.

69. **B is the best answer.** Note that the strongest answer must both be a passage "argument" and support the idea that "other cultures might not view Chris's experiences as 'disordered.'" Any answer choice that fails to meet one of these requirements can be eliminated. Choice A could be tempting, but it does not describe a passage argument. Although the author implies that other cultures do not carry out this practice by saying that "many Western cultures" do so, this is a passage *implication*, not a passage argument. Choice A can be eliminated. The author argues that labeling influences perceptions of "abnormal" (i.e., disordered) behavior and suggests that differences in labeling between cultures could influence how Chris's experience is perceived. Choice B is a strong answer. The author argues that Chris is already well-adjusted; there is no reason to think that he would have been *more* well-adjusted in another culture. For this reason, choice C can be eliminated. Unlike choice C, choice D is a passage argument, but it does not relate to the question that is being asked; in other words, it does not provide any insight into the views of other cultures. Choice D can be eliminated, and choice B is the best answer.

70. **D is the best answer.** This passage is not simply a descriptive case study. The author presents a particular viewpoint towards "our" society and its gender norms, presenting an unfavorable comparison to other cultures that may not be so restrictive. Since the author's view is clearly negative in some way, the answer choices can be narrowed down to choices C and D. "Distrustful" does not convey the strength of the author's negative attitude towards what he or she sarcastically terms as "our neatly constructed gender binary." Furthermore, "distrustful" simply is not as good a fit for the author's tone. Who or what exactly would the author be said to "distrust"? Choice D is the better answer.

Passage II (Questions 71-77)

71. **B is the best answer.** The strongest answer to this question must satisfy two criteria: 1) It pertains to the information in paragraph four, and 2) It is *implied* by the information in that paragraph. Saying that "the Health for All targets were always doomed to fail," although relevant to paragraph four, goes far beyond the implications of the paragraph (and the passage in general), so choice A can be eliminated. Remember, a strong MCAT® answer usually does not use extreme words like "always." Similarly, there is no mention in the passage of the popularity of Reagan's development policies in other countries. Although it seems likely that cutting foreign aid would be unpopular among the former recipients of that aid, this assumption requires outside knowledge, making this a classic beyond distractor. Choice C is a weak answer. Choices B and D are similar answers. Note, however, that choice D is an absolute statement, whereas choice B contains softeners like "probably." For this reason, choice B is the better answer choice. The idea that selfishness could have contributed to declining aid is a major implication of the author's description of domestic support for Reagan's economic policies, making choice B the best answer.

72. **D is the best answer.** This question requires an understanding of the main idea of the passage. The author's argument is that Malthus's theories about overpopulation leading to negative population health outcomes, which were once widely accepted, have now become taboo – even though they could explain many recent global developments. The idea that vaccines have been more beneficial than antibiotics does not affect the main idea. The author lists both of these as factors allowing large populations, but makes no distinction between them. This makes answer choice A not a strong choice. Although the scenario described by answer choice B would conflict with the author's statement that Malthus's ideas were initially widely accepted, the major arguments of the passage, which involve *later* views of Malthus's theories, would be unaffected. Choice B can also be eliminated. The author would probably respond to choice C by arguing that the population has yet to exceed the Earth's carrying capacity. Although this answer choice is relevant to the main idea, it does not challenge or weaken it and is a weak answer. Evidence that population reduction is most likely to occur when population does *not* exceed resource capacity, however, would directly challenge the author's assertion that Malthusian "checks" are likely responsible for modern population reduction. This makes choice D the best answer.

73. **A is the best answer.** A good way to approach a question like this is to look for answers that can be eliminated because they deal with the main idea of the passage, which is typically well supported with examples. The best answer to this type of question will be a claim that the author states but then does not follow up with examples or evidence. Although much support is provided for the claim that increased birth rates have been damaging to modern population health, there is none for the assertion that they have been disastrous for "many disciplines outside of public health." Choice A is a strong answer. Choice B is similar to a statement was the first sentence of a paragraph that then goes on to discuss several examples of countries in which life expectancy has fallen. Choice B can be eliminated. Choice C is slightly less relevant to the main idea, but looking back at paragraph 2 reveals the supporting example that "food production largely kept pace with the slowly growing global population" during the century after Malthus's death. For this reason, choice C can be eliminated. The author argues that huge advances in life expectancy in the 1970s undermined wariness about overpopulation. Choice D is well supported by examples and can be eliminated. Choice A is the best answer.

74. **C is the best answer.** Recall that rice was mentioned in the passage as one of the "new crop strains" of the 1970s. The author states that the success of these crop strains previously contributed to baseless optimism about the issue of overpopulation, rather than solving the problem. The author would not view these crop strains as some panacea that allows for indefinite population expansion. For this reason, choice A can be eliminated. Note that choice A is also an absolute statement – a common characteristic of CARS distractors. There is no reason to believe that the author would abandon his or her main idea because of this one new piece of evidence, so choice B can be eliminated. Choice C is a non-extreme nuanced statement that fits with the author's description of population growth in the 1970s, so it is a strong answer. Choice D describes the development of more prolific rice as a "positive check." Recall from the passage that positive checks are events that limit the population by causing deaths, such as war and famine. This is the opposite effect of that expected from the new rice strains, so choice D can be eliminated. Choice C is the best answer.

75. **D is the best answer.** This is one of the less common types of CARS questions in that it tests a specific piece of passage information. If necessary, look back at the passage to remind yourself of what a "negative check" is. In the first paragraph, the author calls restrictions on marriage an example of a negative check. Given this information and the description of distinct "positive checks" as factors that limit the population by causing higher rates of death, it can be inferred that negative checks limit the population by lowering rates of birth. Of the answer choices, only growing birth control usage would decrease the population in this way, making choice D the best answer. Violence and famine are both examples of positive checks, meaning that choices B and C do not answer the question and can be eliminated. A higher vaccination rate is not a Malthusian check at all since it would allow for increased population growth, which makes choice A not a strong answer. Even if the definition of a negative check had been forgotten, it is still possible to deduce the best answer. Choices B and C are similar enough that neither can be the strongest answer. The main idea is that "checks," both negative and positive, decrease the population. Between the answer choices that remain after eliminating choices B and C, only choice D will cause population decline.

76. **D is the best answer.** This is another question testing knowledge of the main idea. Remember that the author's "point" is that Malthusian views on overpopulation are valuable but underused in today's global health theory. The idea that current population threats are the result of *excessive* foreign aid goes completely against the author's assertions concerning the policies of the Reagan administration, so choice A can be eliminated. Note that strong answers rarely contradict the author's viewpoint unless the question specifically asks for such an answer. The passage never makes any claims about the seriousness of population declines in other countries relative to each other, so choice B is beyond the scope of the passage and can be eliminated. While it is true that the author probably considers the Rwandan genocide and the AIDS crisis to be positive checks, his or her main point is that there is not enough acknowledgment of them as such, making choice C only half true. This is an example of a simpleton, "feel-good" distractor. Since Malthusian checks are consequences of overpopulation and are generally unacknowledged, according to the author, choice D is a stronger answer.

77. **B is the best answer.** A dissident is someone who opposes official policy, often of an authoritarian state. The author is using the term here to allude to the overwhelming current lack of support for the "Malthusian view" discussed in the first paragraph. For this reason, choice C is a weak answer – there is almost no current support for this important theory, according to the author. While many political dissidents are involved in military conflicts, there is no indication of one involving Maurice King, who is likely an academic, so choice A can be eliminated. All of the information given indicates that the author agrees with King and is advocating for more consideration of his views, so choice D can also be eliminated. Quotation marks here are used to indicate irony: what was once an overwhelmingly accepted viewpoint (and one that the author claims is still valid) is now embraced by so few academics that they can be likened to dissidents fighting against an oppressive state.

Notice that although familiarity with the word "dissidents" is useful in answering this question, it is not required to find the best answer. Looking back at the passage shows that the word "dissidents" is used to refer to people who consider overpopulation as a possible cause of population or life expectancy decline. There is no indication in the passage that such people would be involved in "military conflict," so choice A can be eliminated. Choice B immediately looks like a good choice because it is in line with the major argument of the passage. Choices C and D can both be eliminated because they are not consistent with passage information or the author's beliefs. There is NOT overwhelming support of Malthusian theory, and if there were, the author would not disapprove. Choice C is inconsistent with information presented in the passage. Similarly, the author agrees with people like King who urge a reconsideration of Malthusian theory, so choice D can be eliminated.

Passage III (Questions 78-84)

78. **C is the best answer.** When answering this question, remember that the author *does* believe that Macbeth's actions are in line with Hobbesian logic. This question is asking about a potential counterpoint to the author's argument, as implied by the word "would" in the question stem. Choice A is in line with the author's assertion that materialism would in fact cause conflict, so this answer can be eliminated. Macbeth's desire for power is a valid materialist motivation, so choice B can be eliminated. According to the author, Macbeth is not a tragic hero. He does not choose to leave behind his morality, but rather acts in accordance with the expectations of materialism. However, the consensus among other commenters is that Macbeth is a tragic hero. This implies that they do not believe he was motivated by materialism. Choice C is a strong answer. Choice D refers to the author's conclusion that materialism inevitably brings conflict and destroys the commonwealth Hobbes aimed to create. Like choices A and B, choice D aligns with the outcomes that the author argues inevitable follow from Hobbes's materialism. Choice D can be eliminated. All of the answers other than choice C are specifically mentioned in the passage as support for the author's argument that Macbeth *does* adhere to the expectations of Hobbes's materialism, so choice C is the best answer.

79. **A is the best answer.** In questions where the reader must go beyond the text, it is helpful to determine how each scenario would impact the main idea of the passage and the structure of the author's argument. If Shakespeare was examining the tolerance of individuals for irrational behavior on the part of their leaders, Macbeth can no longer be viewed as an example for how materialism taken to its logical conclusion would undermine the establishment of a peaceful state. He would instead be a case study of an insane person whose actions would not reflect the behavior of people in general. Choice A is a strong answer. Choice B would not significantly disrupt the author's logic, since Macbeth is examined by observing the character's actions, not just making assumptions about his motives. Choice B can be eliminated. Choice C directly contradicts passage information: the passage states that Macbeth appeared half a century before Hobbes's writings were published. This answer is also a roundabout distractor. Even if it were true, it would not necessarily contradict the author's argument. Choice C can be eliminated. Choice D can be thought of as an unintelligible distractor, since the passage does not focus on "instruments of philosophical discourse" or "utopia." It does not relate directly to the author's argument, unlike choice A. Choice D can be eliminated, and choice A is the best answer.

80. **B is the best answer.** Choice A distorts Hobbes's ideal of pursuing philosophical enlightenment only after physical and scientific study. He believed that people who were educated in these pursuits would be in the best position to discover the truth about humanity, not that those who study humanity would achieve scientific education. Choice A is a simpleton distractor and can be eliminated. As discussed in the beginning of the passage, Hobbes's goal was to codify the principles by which people should live. He advocated for the establishment of a moral and civil code that would ultimately lead to peace. Choice B is consistent with Hobbes's argument, so it is a strong answer. Hobbes does not advocate war or describe how his citizens would fight it in the passage. Those more familiar with Hobbes might be tempted by choice C due to Hobbes's famous quote, "The state of nature is a state of war." This is out of scope of the passage. Remember not to bring in outside information when answering CARS questions. Choice C can be eliminated. Similarly, choice D is not addressed in the passage and can be eliminated. Choice B is the best answer.

81. **C is the best answer.** To answer this type of question, the reader should look for ideas that have strong support in the passage but are not explicitly stated. In this case, the best answer will either lack passage support or be contradictory to the argument in the passage, due to the 'NOT' in the question stem. The discussion of *Macbeth* indicates that the author views Macbeth's motivations, which can be described as greedy and selfish, as materialist motives. If they were not materialist, the author would not view them as a case study of Hobbes's materialism in action. Choice A is supported by the passage and can be eliminated. The scientific approach that Hobbes recommends to moral philosophy can be characterized as a form of "vigorous logic," so choice B is a reasonable conclusion from the passage and can be eliminated. The author devotes several sentences to stressing that Hobbes's materialism would in fact result in discord as it "leads toward greater anarchy of perception, meaning, and condition, and away from agreement or commonwealth." Since materialism leads toward conflict and fragmentation, as seen in the example of Macbeth, choice C is not supported by the passage and is a strong answer. The author describes Hobbes's materialism as arising directly from his study of human nature, so choice D is supported by the passage and can be eliminated. Choice C is the best answer.

82. **D is the best answer.** The author's main idea is most evident in the last paragraph. The author claims that Macbeth's actions make sense, and that to understand individuals, all motivations that they hold as valid have to be considered. Choice A softens the description of Macbeth as a tragic hero by adding a caveat. This makes the answer more attractive, but it does not align with the author's consistent and absolute rejection of that descriptor throughout the passage. Choice A contradicts the main idea and can be eliminated. Choice B implies a moral judgement about Macbeth. The author contends that Macbeth's actions can be explained by Hobbes's theories, not that those theories justify the actions Macbeth takes. Choice B can be eliminated. Choice C may be tempting for two reasons. It brings together both subjects of the passage, and it seems possible that Hobbes as a literate man writing well after Shakespeare's death would have read his plays and been familiar with their content. However, there is no support for this assumption in the passage, and nothing to suggest that the author would advocate this conclusion. Choice C can be eliminated. To the author, the problem with the standard interpretation of Macbeth as deluded is that the reader's biases and presuppositions about what motivations can be defined as valid interfere with an accurate analysis. In fact, the author claims, Macbeth acts quite rationally throughout, and in a fashion consistent with Hobbes's materialism. This implies that the author would likely agree with a statement acknowledging the difficulty in applying Hobbes analysis to people due to the wide spectrum of motivations they exhibit. For this reason, choice D is the best answer.

83. **D is the best answer.** The author argues that Hobbes's materialism, taken to its logical conclusion, ultimately leads to discord as people act according to impulses that are rational but selfish. The author points out that materialism ensures that the cooperation required for a commonwealth is impractical. Choice A would oppose the author's argument, rather than supporting it, and can be eliminated. The author's argument does not rely on the assumption that Hobbes intended for his ideas to be taken literally. Regardless of Hobbes's intentions, the author can still use his ideas to analyze human behavior. Choice B would not significantly affect the author's argument and can be eliminated. Choice C acts as a distractor by using a particular phrase from the passage, "dynamic process." However, the phrase was actually used in the context of the argument that Hobbes's materialism cannot actually lead to the formation of a commonwealth. Similarly to choice A, choice C contradicts the author's argument and can be eliminated. Choice D describes a philosopher who analyzes Hobbes's materialism from the same perspective as that of the author. It is consistent with the author's argument that materialism leads to discord. For this reason, choice D is the best answer.

84. **B is the best answer.** The author describes Macbeth's actions as violent and greedy, but does not comment on their legality. Choice A is a beyond distractor and can be eliminated. The author's use of the fictional character Macbeth to illustrate his point about Hobbes's materialism relies on the assumption that we can attribute to Macbeth not only the qualities of a real individual, but those of a cognizant and self-aware one. If Macbeth was simply insane, out of control of his own actions thanks to the role of fate, he would no longer be a viable tool for explaining Hobbes's ideas. For this reason, choice B describes a necessary assumption for the author's argument and is a strong answer. Choice C, if true, would directly undermine the author's argument. It is also out of the scope of the passage, since farce and realism were not discussed. Choice C can be eliminated. Choice D presents a misunderstanding of the purpose of the passage. The author is using Macbeth to support an argument about Hobbes's materialism. The suitableness of materialism for analyzing Shakespeare is irrelevant, so it is not a necessary assumption. Choice D can be eliminated, and choice B is the best answer.

EXPLANATIONS TO IN-CLASS EXAM FOR LECTURE 4

Passage I (Questions 85-91)

85. **C is the best answer.** The quickest way to answer questions like these is to first eliminate any answer choices that are supported by evidence without going back to the passage. This approach will often result in the best answer. The passage author gives an example of cancer patients to illustrate that it can be challenging for patients to make optimal decisions, so choice A is not a strong answer. The last paragraph gives an example of how a physician might talk to a patient to preserve their autonomy while still "nudging" them toward the best decision. This is evidence of choice D, which can also be eliminated. Choice B is not supported by any passage evidence, but it is also not an idea advanced by the passage author. For this reason, it does not answer the question and is a weak answer. It is important to read each question carefully. Although the author claims that advertising and medicine use "undeniably similar" techniques to coerce consumers to make certain choices, no evidence supporting this statement is provided, making choice C a strong answer.

86. **B is the best answer.** The author describes opt-out programs in support of the idea that "nominal freedom of choice" does not necessarily equal "effective freedom of choice." In other words, although people in an opt-out program appear to have the choice of whether or not to participate, the small percentage opting out indicates that they are not truly empowered to choose in practice. This explanation is summarized by choice B, which is the best answer. Choice C is similar to choice B, but the wording is too extreme for a strong MCAT® answer. The author did not give an example of people with *no* freedom of choice, as indicated by the fact that some small percentage do opt out. They simply have *reduced* freedom of choice, and choice C is not a strong answer. Choice A is weak for a different reason: rather than improving medical decision making, the author indicates that opt-out programs *restrict* decision making. This does not necessarily mean that the quality of decision making suffers, but there certainly is no indication that it improves. Choice D is also not a strong answer. The author's point about the link between advertising and medicine comes later in the passage and is not relevant to this example. Choice B is the best answer.

87. **D is the best answer.** Note that each answer choice has two parts, meaning the best answer must satisfy two requirements: 1) it must answer the question accurately, and 2) both parts of the answer choice must agree. The question stem gives an example of a potential application of medical paternalism that could save a large amount of money. Critics of medical paternalism would likely not support such a measure, and there is not enough information in the passage to indicate that any amount of monetary savings would be sufficient to justify medical paternalism. Based on passage information, the only thing that can be known for certain is that paternalism's critics oppose the philosophy because it hurts autonomy. Choices A and C can be eliminated. Choice B can be eliminated because the two parts of the answer do not logically agree: if the money saved is significant enough to outweigh the cost of lost autonomy, there is no reason to oppose the measure. Process of elimination leaves choice D as the best answer. The passage states that critics of paternalism oppose its exploitation of existing biases, but it was not necessary to remember that to answer the question.

88. **B is the best answer.** The passage establishes libertarian paternalism as a school of philosophical thought before describing the nudge techniques used by practitioners of this philosophy. In other words, nudge policies are one tool in the larger toolset of paternalism, making choice B the strongest answer. Nudge policies are not used to fight libertarian paternalism according to the author, so answer choice A can be eliminated. There is a definite passage relationship between the two, so choice C is also weak. Choice D is a good example of a round-about distractor: it uses information from the passage to make a true statement but does not answer the question. Note that there is no mention of libertarian paternalism in choice D, so this answer choice cannot conceivably describe the relationship between nudge policies and libertarian paternalism.

89. **A is the best answer.** This question tests your knowledge of the author's stance on the passage topic. In the last sentence of the passage, the author proclaims that the "ideal" approach involves using nudge factors while promoting patient awareness. This indicates that the author is a proponent, at least to some degree, of medical paternalism. Based on the author's lack of a strongly opinionated tone, it is highly unlikely that he or she would argue for anything as extreme as refusing to write any prescriptions for the new drug or, conversely, prescribing it for every patient. Remember that answer choices using extreme wording like *all* or *under any circumstances* are usually not particularly strong. This eliminates B and D. According to the author, giving patients access to all available information and letting them decide on their own leads to the problems that clinicians try to correct through tactics like nudge policies, so the author is unlikely to support this argument, and choice C is not a strong answer. Based on the author's stance on paternalism, he or she is likely to recommend that the clinician use a nudge technique to ensure that patients who do not need this new drug do not insist on it due to the variety of biases and other factors that unduly influence difficult medical decision making. This makes choice A the best answer.

90. **C is the best answer.** This question tests how well you understand the viewpoint of the opposition to nudge policies, which is a major idea of the passage. The critics explicitly refer to nudge policies as "manipulation," so choice A is a likely reason for their objection and can be eliminated. Although the language of a "symptom of the problem" is not found in the passage, answer choice B lines up with the assertion that nudge policies exploit (utilize) biases rather than eliminating them. Choice B is a weak answer. There is no mention of paternalism's critics questioning its effectiveness in the passage, and in fact the author mentions that it is effective. Presumably, if nudge policies were ineffective, critics would not be particularly concerned about them. For this reason, choice C is a strong choice. The passage author also refers specifically to critics decrying the limitations on freedom of choice that nudge policies impose, so choice D is not a strong choice. Choice C is the best answer.

91. **A is the best answer.** This question stem requires careful reading. Look for the assumption that would most weaken the argument for paternalism if proven *false*. Disproving choice D would show that nudge techniques are effective at changing behavior, which strengthens the argument for paternalism. Choice D can be eliminated. Similarly, proving that patients are not better decision makers than clinicians would only support the idea that clinicians need to steer patients toward the right decisions. Choice B is not a strong answer. If, on the other hand, it was proven that clinicians are *not* better decision makers than patients, there would be no justification for giving clinicians the authority to "nudge" patients toward any decision. This would greatly weaken the argument for paternalism, making choice A a strong answer. Disproving that *all* patients are poor medical decision makers would not necessarily weaken the case for paternalism. After all, it could still be the case that *almost all* or *most* patients are poor medical decision makers and could benefit from medical paternalism. Choice A is a stronger answer than choice C.

Passage II (Questions 92-98)

92. **A is the best answer.** The passage sets up a spectrum between Aboriginal and Western artistic viewing practices. The author favors the side of Aboriginal viewing practice, and defends Aboriginal art against misinterpretations formed by Western expectations. The main idea is that the purpose of Aboriginal art is to connect individuals initiated into Aboriginal culture with their environment, in contrast to the Western emphasis on aesthetic pleasure and ownership. The conflict with Western artistic values forms the occasion for many of the examples offered within the passage. The various forms of cultural misinterpretation demonstrated by other scholars are there to help set apart the author's true position. While the author is discussing Geoffrey Bardon's observations, it is revealed that members of an Aboriginal Nation were upset by the notion of displaying a sacred work in a public place because such images "are believed to cause harm to those not initiated." Choice A is promising. While it is tempting to assume that relocation of those images would be cause for cultural offense, this view is not supported anywhere in the passage, so choice B can be eliminated. Choice C addresses the question of Aboriginal artistic permanence. While an example of a deliberately impermanent artwork is given in the context of Bardon's research, it cannot be concluded that all Aboriginal art is intended to be impermanent. Choice C is an overstatement and can be eliminated. Choice D is tempting with the use of the softener "tend," but the passage does not suggest that Aboriginal Nations have a conception of Western art. For that reason, the reader cannot draw any conclusions about how it is viewed. Choice A is the best answer.

93. **D is the best answer.** In the middle of the passage, the author argues against interpretations of Aboriginal art that rely on an understanding of the culture as "primitive." Instead, the author contends that Aboriginal art expresses a complicated set of relationships between an individual and his or her environment. It cannot be assumed that the scholar was initiated into Aboriginal culture. Even if that were the case, the author cannot be expected to allow that scholar's interpretation any automatic legitimacy. Choice A can be eliminated. Because the passage does not discuss astronomy or Aboriginal mythology, choice B is also not a good candidate. In fact, the author specifically rejects the interpretation of concentric circles in Dharug Country as "cosmic images." While the author discounts aesthetic pleasure in viewing as an inappropriate way to approach Aboriginal art, it cannot be said that the scholar mentioned in the question stem has made that particular mistake. Recall that distractors often use language from the passage in order to make an answer more tempting. Choice C can be eliminated. Choice D makes the clearest reference to the main idea of the passage—that the purpose of Aboriginal art is to connect individuals initiated into Aboriginal culture with their environment, which is in contrast with Western artistic expectations—and so best captures the author's opinion.

94. **C is the best answer.** To answer the question, information must be extrapolated from the text, so it is important to distinguish the author's position from the other views in the passage. The main idea is that Aboriginal art involves the self and its important relationships, which distinguishes it from Western ideas of art that focus on aesthetic pleasure or ownership. The author's position must be separated from the range of views provided in the passage and apply that position to a new situation. It is not certain that Jung is incapable of approaching art from a non-Western perspective. The author seems to have a good understanding of both Western and Aboriginal ideas of art, and there is no reason to conclude that Jung should not have the same. Choice A is weak. The passage does not comment on psychotherapy, so its relationship to Aboriginal cultural practices cannot be determined, and choice B can be eliminated. The author criticizes those who would see Aboriginal art as "mere representation." For Jung, the creation of art is a project that involves the self and its relationships ("what we see within") and not just depictions of the world ("what we see before us"), a message that is consistent with the passage's main idea. Choice C is very promising. It is tempting to assume that Jung was familiar with Aboriginal art, given its similarities to his therapeutic practice, but neither the passage nor the question stem gives the reader any reason to be sure. Choice D can be eliminated. The best answer is choice C.

95. **C is the best answer.** The main idea of the passage is that the purpose of Aboriginal art is to connect individuals initiated into Aboriginal culture with their environment, which is in contrast with the emphasis on aesthetic pleasure and ownership found in Western art. The end of the passage describes the challenges of preparing sacred artworks for view by the uninitiated. The author of the passage disputes the claim (proposed by other scholars) that the technique known as "dotting" was invented for this purpose. Instead, the author contends that it originated in traditional healing practices, and was later adapted to its current use. Choice A borrows a quotation from the beginning of the passage, but "rhythmic visual form" is used to describe all Aboriginal art, not specifically the dotting technique. Choice B misrepresents dotting and its aims. Dotting is not used to increase appreciation for the initiated. It is to prevent the uninitiated from coming to harm, as the author notes toward the end of the passage. Choice B can be eliminated. At the very end of the passage, the reader learns that dotting is but one of several multi-layering techniques, and the author's discussion implies that it is multi-layering more generally that is incorporated into artistic practice for the goal of protecting uninitiated viewers. Choice C is promising. While the passage does say that dotting is a common practice in ancient healing rituals, it does not comment on whether the technique is used in contemporary healing rituals—only that it is used in contemporary artistic practice. Choice D is not well supported. Choice C is the best answer.

96. **A is the best answer.** Near the middle of the passage, the reader learns that the members of the Aboriginal Nation object to having their sacred art objects placed in public view. The main idea of the passage is that the purpose of Aboriginal art is to connect initiated individuals with their environment, and this view is altogether different from Western attitudes towards art, which emphasize aesthetic pleasure and ownership. Bardon's intention to transfer ceremonial ground designs onto public walls—and the negative response of the Aboriginal Nations—reveals the important role that context plays in the Aboriginal experience of art. Choice A is consistent with the main idea of the passage and is a strong answer. While it is plausible that the transfer of ceremonial designs onto walls would require changes in compositional techniques, the passage gives no evidence that Bardon was ignorant of these techniques, or that those techniques had anything to do with the objections raised against the project. Choice B is for these reasons unlikely. The intentional impermanence of the ground designs are mentioned, but the passage establishes no connection between the question of permanence and the Western view of art, which choice C implies, so it is not optimal. Bardon's scholarship is not criticized, but is commended as "one of the first comprehensive Western studies ever conducted," so Choice D describes the opposite of the author's view. Answer choices that contradict the author are rarely the best answer unless the question stem has words like "least likely" or "except." Choice D can be eliminated, and choice A is the best answer.

97. **B is the best answer.** The main idea of the passage is that the purpose of Aboriginal art is to connect individuals in Aboriginal culture with their environment. The spectrum of the passage contrasts this view of art with a Western emphasis on aesthetic pleasure and ownership. Teasing out this position from the other views mentioned in the passage will simplify this question. Though the word "symbolic" is tempting from its importance at the start of the passage, nowhere does the author mention a deity, so Choice A is unlikely. Choice B matches the main idea, and even hews rather closely to the description of symbols near the beginning of the passage as "expressions of cultural connection between mind, body, and emotions." Choice B is promising. Choice C relies on language taken out of context. While the answer borrows words from the part where the author describes how members of Aboriginal Nations believe the uninitiated can be harmed by sacred images, it does not match this question. The passage does not address ideas of perfection or imperfection in geometric shapes, so choice D can be eliminated. Choice B is the best answer.

98. **C is the best answer.** This question asks the test-taker to imagine how Western artistic practices, specifically ownership, would be viewed from the perspective of someone within an Aboriginal cultural context. The reader is told near the end of the passage that multi-layering techniques are used to prepare sacred work for view by the non-initiated, but there is no indication that this relates in any way to ownership. Choice A can be eliminated. Though it might be tempting to infer that art ownership would threaten Aboriginal values, the only time the passage mentions unrest among Aboriginal peoples is in the context of Bardon's scholarship, where they agitate for the protection of the uninitiated viewer—not the protection of their own culture. Choice B also uses the extreme word "threatening," which is not supported by the passage, so choice B is a weak answer. Make sure to carefully separate the author's position from others mentioned in the passage by distinguishing between Aboriginal and Western viewing practices. Recall that the author sets up a spectrum of Aboriginal art, which serves to connect an individual with his or her environment, and Western art, which provides the rewards of aesthetic pleasure and ownership. The other views mentioned in the passage are examples of Western misinterpretations of Aboriginal artistic work. Because cultural barriers serve to limit the understanding of different viewing practices, it is reasonable to conclude that cultural limitations to understanding could also affect Aboriginal viewers. Choice C the most promising answer. Choice D brings together the idea of ownership with the idea of aesthetic pleasure, but the author would not expect this set of attitudes from an Aboriginal viewer. Aesthetic pleasure is associated with Western viewing practices, as can be demonstrated by organizing viewing practices along a spectrum of Aboriginal and Western art. Choice D can be eliminated, and choice C remains the best answer.

Passage III (Questions 99-105)

99. **C is the best answer.** "These people" used in this context refers back to the discussion of local peoples that had been subordinated to the historical narratives of their conquerors. The first paragraph states that this population had especially strong feelings about promoting national pride and legitimizing their situation through the ability to define their own past. This idea is continued in paragraph two with the discussion of their hunger to establish their own cultural ancestry and culture-affirming archaeological practices. Choice A is a weak choice because, in this case, the British were the conquerors, not the conquered. The Israelis described in choice D were not described as oppressed, but rather discussed in the context of an example of historical sites taking on new national importance. The Rhodesians in choice B do represent one group of formerly oppressed peoples who are described as hungering for new national identity. However, strictly speaking, the builders of the Great Zimbabwe were not oppressed by the British, but were rather the ancestors of the oppressed. Furthermore, the implications of "these people" as it was used in the passage implies more general applicability to formerly oppressed people building new senses of national identities rather than being confined to a specific group. This makes choice C the best answer.

100. **C is the best answer.** Choice A is supported by the example of the Israeli army recruits. Choice B is supported by the example of the importance of recognizing the Great Zimbabwe as an African achievement. Choice D is explained in detail through the descriptions of how manipulation of archaeological interpretation can create a more valuable commodity for tourism. Choice C is mentioned in the passage, but the following information is more of a restatement than an explanation and no example is provided.

101. **D is the best answer.** Choice A is not a strong answer because the passage actually seems to imply that financial gain (not political gain) is the main motivating force behind developing historical sites for tourism. The passage does discuss the importance of manipulating archaeology among formerly oppressed people to develop a sense of native identity, but there is no reason to assume that manipulation of archaeology is not equally important to supporting the hegemony of the oppressors. On the contrary, the rejection of the 'natives' by the British as possible builders of the Great Zimbabwe suggests that selective interpretation of archaeology was a force in supporting their oppression, making choice B a weak answer. Choice C is not discussed in the passage and is a beyond distractor. Choice D encompasses one of the main ideas of the passage and is supported with many specific examples that threaten objectivity (financial gain, political gain, creating national unity, etc.) making choice D the best answer.

102. **B is the best answer.** The tone of the passage is one of criticism toward biases and taking liberties when interpreting the past. The final paragraph of the passage strongly implies that archaeological research should be conducted in as an objective and scientific manner as possible. Choices A, C, and D all result in factual data, while choice B is based on subjective interpretation, which the author is more likely to discourage. Even without reading the article, it might be possible to identify choice B as the best answer from the language of the answer choices. The three weaker answer choices are very concrete in their language and goals whereas the term "speculation" in choice B implies a subjectivity that is unlike the others.

103. C is the best answer. In the passage, the appearance of archaeological artifacts on postage stamps and in souvenir shops is discussed in the context of peoples' hunger to establish their cultural heritage as legitimate. That reasoning provides a hint that choice C might be the best answer. The relevant paragraph goes on to discuss the lengths societies are willing to go in using archaeology as propaganda to legitimize their existence in their current form including investing money, training local professionals and creation of archaeological infrastructure. All of these factors, along with the example of how the Israeli historical site becomes a national rallying place provides a sense of the pride and unity that can be inspired by archaeology. The other three example choices, which sometimes use vocabulary from the passage, are not explicitly discussed by the author. Choice C is the best answer.

104. B is the best answer. The attendant temptations described in this section of the passage involve behaviors that use misrepresentation of archaeological knowledge to accomplish specific ideological and financial goals. Embellishing a story is analogous to unjustly glorifying the past or over-restoration of historical monuments, while publishing sensationalized stories is akin to "selling" a sensationalized version of history to affect beliefs and world views. Omitting sections from an interview is very like the passage's description of choosing only the "facts" that best support the chosen story. Only choice B seems out of step with the description of the temptations described in the passage, by not aiming to manipulate the story to suit the purposes of the author or publisher. Choice B is the best answer.

105. A is the best answer. This question can be a tricky one because all four answer choices are mentioned in the passage and represent opinions of the author. The key to selecting the best answer choice is to consider the context in which they were discussed. Choice B was discussed in the context of rebuilding national identity after a period of oppression; this does not seem particularly relevant to the hypothetical example of improvements before hosting the Olympics. Choice D is discussed toward the end of the passage as a transition into emphasizing the importance of relative objectivity (rather than subjective interpretation) in archaeology and does not relate to the question stem. Choice C is plausible in that the plans for beautification MIGHT demonstrate how the nation wants to be seen by the world, now that the spotlight of the Olympics is upon them. However, this point in the passage is brought up within the context of a discussion on the misuse of archaeology as propaganda, which is only tangentially related to the question. The description in the question stem of the over-development of historic sites most closely echoes discussion of exploiting archaeology for ideological and financial gain in the third paragraph of the passage. The likely influx of tourism that accompanies the Olympic Games would fit nicely with this context and supports answer choice A as the best available answer to the question.

Photo Credits

Covers

Front cover, Open book: © no_limit_pictures/ iStockphoto.com

Lecture i

Pg. 1, Herd of sheep scattered near mountain summit: © Horia Varlan/Flickr, adapted for use under the terms of the Creative Commons CC BY 2.0 license (http://creativecommons.org/licenses/by/2.0/legalcode)

Pg. 9, Teacher and students in math class: © Slobodan Vasic/iStockphoto.com

Pg. 11, Calculator: © Dana Kelley

Pg. 15, Abacus: © Michelle Gibson/iStockphoto.com

Pg. 15, Dice: © porcorex/iStockphoto.com

Pg. 16, Close-up of student solving a sum on the blackboard: © Jacob Wackerhausen/iStockphoto.com

Lecture ii

Pg. 32, Sir Isaac Newton Drawn by Wm. Derby and engraved (with permission) by W.J. Fry: Images from the History of Medicine (NLM)

Lecture 1

Pg. 62, Professor reading book: © Grigory Bibikov/iStockphoto.com

Pg. 66, Clock: © deepblue4youi/Stockphoto.com

Pg. 71, Students in study group: © Nikada/iStockphoto.com

Lecture 2

Pg. 73, Keys to lock: © Thomas Vogel/iStockphoto.com

Pg. 74, Hiker on summit: © Danny Warren/iStockphoto.com

Lecture 3

Pg. 89, Hammer on wood: © Dzmitri Mikhaltsow/iStockphoto.com

Pg. 90, Hourglass: © Alexander Shirokov/iStockphoto.com

Pg. 103, Thinking young woman: © DRBimages/iStockphoto.com

About the Author

Jonathan Orsay is uniquely qualified to write an MCAT® preparation book. He graduated on the Dean's list with a B.A. in History from Columbia University. While considering medical school, he sat for the real MCAT® three times from 1989 to 1996. He scored above the 95th percentile on all sections before becoming an MCAT® instructor. He has lectured in MCAT® test preparation for thousands of hours and across the country. He has taught premeds from such prestigious universities as Harvard and Columbia. He has written and published the following books and audio products in MCAT® preparation: "Examkrackers MCAT® Physics", "Examkrackers MCAT® Chemistry", "Examkrackers MCAT® Organic Chemistry", "Examkrackers MCAT® Biology", "Examkrackers MCAT® Verbal Reasoning & Math", "Examkrackers 1001 questions in MCAT® Physics", "Examkrackers MCAT® Audio Osmosis with Jordan and Jon", all of which have evolved when the MCAT® has changed, and which continue to be the number one bestselling MCAT® materials available.

A Student Review of This Book

The following review of this book was written by Teri from New York.

"The Examkrackers MCAT® books are the best MCAT® prep materials I've seen-and I looked at many before deciding. The worst part about studying for the MCAT® is figuring out what you need to cover and getting the material organized. These books do all that for you so that you can spend your time learning. The books are well and carefully written, with great diagrams and really useful mnemonic tricks, so you don't waste time trying to figure out what the book is saying. They are concise enough that you can get through all of the subjects without cramming unnecessary details, and they really give you a strategy for the exam. The study questions in each section cover all the important concepts, and let you check your learning after each section. Alternating between reading and answering questions in MCAT® format really helps make the material stick, and means there are no surprises on the day of the exam-the exam format seems really familiar and this helps enormously with the anxiety. Basically, these books make it clear what you need to do to be completely prepared for the MCAT® and deliver it to you in a straightforward and easy-to-follow form. The mass of material you could study is overwhelming, so I decided to trust these books—I used nothing but the Examkrackers books in all subjects and scored in the 99th percentile in all sections. Thanks to Jonathan Orsay and Examkrackers, I was admitted to all of my top-choice schools (Columbia, Cornell, Stanford, and UCSF). I will always be grateful. I could not recommend the Examkrackers books more strongly. Please contact me if you have any questions."